Mr. Marshall

The Rural Economy of the Midland Counties

Including the Management of Live Stock in Leicestershire and its Environs together

with Minutes on Agriculture and Planting in the District of the Midland Station

Mr. Marshall

The Rural Economy of the Midland Counties
Including the Management of Live Stock in Leicestershire and its Environs together with Minutes on Agriculture and Planting in the District of the Midland Station

ISBN/EAN: 9783741183812

Manufactured in Europe, USA, Canada, Australia, Japa

Cover: Foto ©knipser5 / pixelio.de

Manufactured and distributed by brebook publishing software
(www.brebook.com)

Mr. Marshall

The Rural Economy of the Midland Counties

THE
RURAL ECONOMY

OF THE

MIDLAND COUNTIES;

INCLUDING

THE MANAGEMENT OF

LIVESTOCK

IN

LEICESTERSHIRE AND ITS ENVIRONS:

TOGETHER WITH

MINUTES

ON

AGRICULTURE AND PLANTING

IN THE DISTRICT OF THE

MIDLAND STATION.

By Mr. MARSHALL.

IN TWO VOLUMES.

VOL. I.

LONDON:

PRINTED FOR G. NICOL, BOOKSELLER TO
HIS MAJESTY, PALL MALL.

M,DCC,XC.

TO HIS

ROYAL HIGHNESS

THE

PRINCE OF WALES.

S I R,

IF Your Highness's virtues were not publicly known, I fhould think it my duty, and it would be my higheſt gratification, to declare them in this addrefs. But on a fub-ject fo well underſtood, and fo fully illuſtrated in Your Royal Highnefs's conduct, the tribute of my pen could not avail.

Therefore, without *attempting* to praife, and without *daring* to flat-ter, I prefume to inform Your Highness that I am purfuing a Plan,

Vol. I.   A   which,

DEDICATION.

which, in its principles, is calculated
to prolong the PROSPERITY of the
ENGLISH NATION; and that nothing
could alleviate so much the labour of
the pursuit, as the APPROBATION of
YOUR ROYAL HIGHNESS; nor anything
add so much to the celebrity of the
undertaking, as the PATRONAGE of
THE PRINCE OF WALES.

Permit me, then, in YOUR HIGH-
NESS's known goodness of disposition,
to commit these Volumes, as a part
of the General Work, to YOUR ROYAL
PATRONAGE; and to declare myself
with becoming respect, and with the
most perfect attachment to YOUR
HIGHNESS's CHARACTER,

YOUR ROYAL HIGHNESS'S

MOST OBEDIENT AND

MOST HUMBLE SERVANT,

WILLIAM MARSHALL.

LONDON, JULY 1, 1790.

ADVERTISEMENT

TO THE

FIRST VOLUME.

THE MATERIALS of this Volume were collected, chiefly, some years ago, during a residence in the MIDLAND COUNTIES of somewhat more than two years*.

But, with a view to the fulness and accuracy of the register, I have since thought it expedient to make a second survey of LEICESTERSHIRE and its ENVIRONS, where I spent three months of the last summer (1789); my principal object, in this second view, being that of making myself more fully acquainted with the subject of LIVE-STOCK.

A 2   THUS

---

* At STATFOLD, near the junction of the the four counties of LEICESTER, WARWICK, STAFFORD, and DERBY, where I chiefly resided, from March 1784 to April 1786.

ADVERTISEMENT.

THUS THE PUBLIC are furnished with a detail of the progress of this undertaking, from the first proposal of it, in 1780, to the present time: a period of somewhat more than ten years.

The practice of NORFOLK was collected in the years 1780, 1781, and 1782, and published in 1787.

That of YORKSHIRE, in 1782 and 1787, and published in 1788.

That of GLOCESTERSHIRE, in 1782 and 1788, and published in 1789.

That of the MIDLAND COUNTIES, in 1784, 1785, 1786, 1789, and is now under publication.

It may be proper to add, that the PUBLIC are now likewise furnished with the whole of the information I have hitherto collected on the subject of RURAL ECONOMY ; excepting that which I necessarily obtained of the established practice of the SOUTHERN COUNTIES during five years residence in them *; also excepting a variety of detached

* See MINUTES OF AGRICULTURE, &c. IN SURREY.

ADVERTISEMENT.

tached ideas, which, being deemed in themfelves not fufficiently important, or not
yet fufficiently authenticated, to admit of
being publifhed in their prefent ftate,
ftill remain fcattered in the original papers
belonging to the feveral Diftricts I have
refided in; and excepting fuch other de-
fultory ideas as I have collected in paffing
between Diftrict and Diftrict. No part of
either of thefe, however, are intended for
feparate publication; and the practice of
the SOUTHERN COUNTIES requires a fecond
and deliberate furvey, before a detail of it
can be entitled to the reception of the
PUBLIC.

ERRORS OF THE PRESS.

Vol. I. page 65, line 4, from the bottom, for *utter*, read *entire*.

——— page 73, line 9, for *effort*, read *effect*.

C O N T E N T S

FIRST VOLUME.

CONTENTS.

THE

RURAL ECONOMY

OF THE

MIDLAND COUNTIES.

THE ISLAND, if its furface could
be brought within a fingle point of
view, would appear ftrongly featured by an
affociation of mountain, upland, and vale, interfperfed with irregular tracts of middleland country, partaking of the nature of vale,
but, having no regular chain of highlands
on their margins, are not difinguifhable by
that name.

The northern and the weftern provinces
abound with mountains and bold highlands;

Vol. I.   B   while

while the eaftern, the fouthern, and the midland counties, though they fometimes rife
to chalky heights, with fome few heathy
barren fwells, are feldom diftinguifhable into
highland and vale.

As objects of RURAL ECONOMY, how-
ever, thefe middle-land tracts are, generally,
very fimilar to vale diftricts; the foil and
produce of each being fimilar: with, however, fome exceptions; as Eaft Norfolk,
for inftance, which, though it lies flat and
fomewhat low, is moft of it covered with a
light fandy foil; and a few other inftances might be produced: but, in general, the
foil of this defcription of country is of a
ftronger, more clayey nature.

The diftrict, which forms the fubject of
the prefent volumes, bears the laft defcription; being the largeft tract of the kind in
the ifland; including the principal parts of
the counties of LEICESTER, RUTLAND,
and WARWICK, with the northern margin
of NORTHAMPTONSHIRE, the eaftern point
of STAFFORDSHIRE, and the fouthern extremities of DERBYSHIRE and NOTTING-
HAMSHIRE, the town of LEICESTER being
fituated near its center.

This

This fertile tract of country, which I shall distinguish by the MIDLAND DISTRICT, measures, in some directions, not less than fifty miles across, in none, I believe, less than forty; consequently, contains at least fifteen hundred square miles of surface; with no other drawback from its fertility, than the Charnwood hills, which do not contain fifty miles of infertile soil *.

. This district I have traversed in almost every direction, and have, I believe, made myself sufficiently acquainted with its rural affairs, to give me an adequate idea of its GENERAL MANAGEMENT; especially as it relates to LIVESTOCK.

B 2 But

---

* LEICESTERSHIRE, however, contains two other plots of surface, less fertile than the rest of the district. One on the northern margin; distinguished by the name of the WOLDS: a swell of considerable height, covered with a singularly cold, dark-coloured, clayey soil. The other in the southwestern quarter; likewise high land, with a cold retentive subsoil; but with a lighter more sandy soil. But, the rocky points of the forest hills apart, the county contains no *barren* surface: it has not, perhaps, an acre worth less than five shillings; and but few acres worth, on lease, less than ten shillings an acre. The entire county is not, at the present rental value of lands, worth much less, on a par, than fifteen to twenty shillings an acre: an estimate which, I believe, no other county will bear; RUTLANDSHIRE, perhaps, excepted.

But the part, of this extensive tract, which has engaged a more particular share of attention, is bounded by the TRENT on the north, the TAME on the west, the SOAR on the east, and the ANKER and its banks on the south: a district which, for the fertility of its soil, and a spiritedness of management, especially in BREEDING, cannot certainly be equalled in these kingdoms.

The ARABLE MANAGEMENT of the Midland District is confined within still narrower limits. The district, at large, is a grassland country. Breeding, grazing, and the dairy, prevail in different parts of it. But, in the richest finest plot it contains, the four branches of husbandry are united, and carried on by men of property and abilities.

This district is situated between the Charnwood hills and the western banks of the Trent, the Tame, and the Anker; including the four points of the counties of LEICESTER, WARWICK, STAFFORD, and DERBY; being seated everyway near the centre of the kingdom.

A more interesting subject of study, for the purpose of the plan I am executing,
could

could not well be conceived; being not more interefting on account of the nature of its fituation, foil and produce, and the repute of its occupiers; than on that of its general management, being peculiar and regular.

This being, *fortunately*, the DISTRICT of the STATION, and that of whofe ARABLE MANAGEMENT I fhall principally fpeak, it will require an accurate defcription.

The OUTLINE is irregular. The EXTENT may be eftimated at one hundred and fifty fquare miles; or about a hundred thoufand acres.

The CLIMATURE is *below* the latitude It lies in (about 52° 45′.); its feafons are near a fortnight before thofe of Eaft Norfolk, which is fituated in a fimilar latitude; and many days earlier than thofe of Gloucefterfhire, which enjoys a more fouthern fituation. On the weftern fide of the diftrict, harveft is generally as forward as in Surrey : in 1785, fome oats were cut, and much wheat and barley ripe, the 28th July. What is very obfervable, the feafons on the Tamworth fide of the diftrict are a full week

B 3   forwarder

forwarder than they are on the Foreſt ſide, only ten or twelve miles diſtant. But this, perhaps, may be accounted. for by the coldneſs of the baſe of the Foreſt hills *.

. The SURFACE of this charming plot of country is various. Its general elevation is much greater than that of moſt middle-ſoiled diſtricts. Some of its ſwells might, in regard to elevation, be deemed upland; yet, in fertility, it is throughout equal to moſt vale diſtricts.

The SOIL, in general, is a rich middle loam; interſperſed, however, with a few leſs fertile patches. Toward the foot of the Charnwood hills, much of it is of a more ſandy nature; but of a ſingularly free and fertile quality. Taking the diſtrict of the ſtation, throughout, it ranks, in utility, with the firſt diſtricts of the iſland. The ſwells, though high, are generally fertile to the ſummit; and the dips between, though wide and flat, are found, and eaſily freed from

* It is obſervable, that in October 1789, while the beans and much barley remained out, in Berkſhire and the ſurrounding counties, the Midland Diſtrict, though it lie near a hundred miles farther towards the north, had done harveſt a month or ſix weeks.

from furface water, The entire diftrict, except a few narrow bottoms, and the immediate margins of the rivers, is equally productive of corn and grafs.

The foil of the north of Warwickfhire, away from the banks of the Anker, is of a colder lefs productive quality; weft of the Tame a light fandy foil prevails; and Derbyfhire, except the fouthern extremity, and the immediate bank of the Trent, is ftill more of an upland or mountainous nature.

The DISTRICT of the STATION therefore, confidered with regard to foil, might be termed a bay of the MIDLAND DISTRICT, into which it opens on the fouth-weft; its management being traceable as far as the banks of the Soar above Leicefter; gradually affimilating with the more grazing parts of Leicefterfhire.

The SUBSOIL prevalent in this diftrict is a *red clay* (provincially " marl"), refembling the red foils of Herefordfhire and Nottinghamfhire. In fome places a concrete *fand*, increafing in hardnefs with the depth to a foft gridftone, occurs in different parts; and a *fandy loam*, or brick earth, mixed

B 4   with

with veins of fand and gravel, is a pretty common fubfoil.

The ROADS, through the nature of the foil and fubftrata, are neceffarily bad. But of thefe hereafter.

INCLOSURE. Thirty years ago, much of this diftrict was in an open ftate; and fome townfhips ftill remain open: there are others, however, which appear to have been long in a ftate of inclofure; and in which, no doubt, the prefent fyftem of management originated.

The PRODUCE of this diftrict, as has been intimated, is chiefly *corn* and *grafs*; little, very little *woodland* within it. It is, however, furrounded on almoft every fide with well wooded tracts.

In the light of ORNAMENT, the MIDLAND DISTRICT, viewed generally, and in its prefent ftate, is much inferior to the northern and weftern quarters of the ifland. The views. are frequently pleafing, through the variety of furface and richnefs of foil, but are feldom picturefque, unlefs when the Charnwood hills enter within them. The diftrict, in a general point of view, difcovers

a tame-

a tamenefs; a kind of ftill life; which, however, clothed as it is, in the verdure and
richnefs of herbage, renders this diftrict defirable as a place of refidence; though, at
prefent, it is not ftriking to the mere traveller. Neverthelefs, were the billowy fwells
of Northamptonfhire and fouth Leicefterfhire as well wooded as thofe of Herefordfhire and Kent, they would, in beauty, be inferior to neither of thofe counties. The
furface of Northamptonfhire is broken in a
manner, which renders it fingularly fufcep-
tible of ornament: and, at prefent, the
BANKS of the TRENT, efpecially about NOT-
TINGHAM (fingularly fine fituation!) are as
beautiful as ground wood and water can
make them.

The DISTRICT of the STATION has ftill
greater natural advantages: it is in a manner
furrounded with what the landfcape painter
would call good diftances. The Charnwood
hills, the Derbyfhire mountains, Needwood
Foreft, the Beaudefert hills, and other hills of
Staffordfhire; and, in fome fituations, the
Lickey, the Clent hills, and the more prominent hills of Shropfhire, may be caught.

Nor

Nor is it, at prefent, deftitute of internal beauty. The BANKS of the TAME afford fome beautiful fubjects of landfcape; and a lovely plot round HINTS, weftward of the Tame, is in the beft ftyle of Kent or Herefordfhire. The fituation of TAMWORTH *, for the richnefs and beauty of the country round it, is one of the fineft in the kingdom.

The CHARNWOOD HILLS are too ftriking a feature of the Midland Diftrict to be paffed without efpecial notice. Like the Malvern hills, their ftyle is fingular; but the ftyle of one is very different from that of the other. The Malvern hills, feen from a diftance, bear a moft ftriking refemblance to the Atlantic Iflands; towering up high and ragged; and, on a near view, appear as one large mountain fragment. The Charnwood hills, on the contrary, feen obfcurely, appear as an extenfive range of mountains; much larger, and of courfe much more diftant, than they really are. When approached, the mountain ftyle is ftill preferved; the prominencies are diftinct, fharp, and moft of them

* Formerly the refidence of the Mercian kings.

them pointed with naked ragged rock. One of these prominencies, BARDON HILL, rises above the reft; and, though far from an elevated fituation, comparatively with the more northern mountains, commands, in much probability, a greater extent of furface, than any other point of view in the ifland.

It is entirely infulated, ftanding every way at a confiderable diftance from lands equally high. The horizon appears to rife almoft equally on every fide: it is quite an ocean view, from a fhip out of fight of land; at leaft more fo, than any other land view I have feen.

The Midland Diftrict is almoft every acre of it feen lying at its feet. Lincoln cathedral, at the diftance of near fixty miles, makes a prominent object from it. With a good glafs, the Dunftable hills, at little lefs than eighty miles, may, it is faid, be diftinctly feen. The Malvern hills, Mayhill, and the Sugar Loaf in South Wales, are diftinctly in view. Enville, the Wrekin, and other mountains of Shropfhire and North Wales, are equally diftinguifhable. And the Derbyfhire hills, to the higheft peak, appear at hand.

hand. An outline, deſcribed from the extremities of the views, would include near one-fourth of England and Wales. It may be deemed, without riſque, I apprehend, one of the moſt extraordinary points of view in Nature.

ESTATES,

I.

E S T A T E S.

ESTATES, here, are fmall. Fertile diftricts were early cultivated; and, at the
Conqueft, the lordfhips probably were
dealt out feparately. Nor does there appear
to have been, fince their diftribution, any ac-
cumulation of landed property in the diftrict
immediately under furvey. It has few principal refidences *; nor any off eftates, I believe,

* Gopsal, built and laid out, at the expence of a
hundred thoufand pounds, by the late Mr. Jennings,
famous for his friendfhips to Handel and the Pretender;
and Bosworth, the feat of Sir Wolstan Dixie;
are the only refidences *within* the diftrict. Fisherwick, the princely refidence of the Earl of Donne-
gal, and a *creation* of Mr. Brown, at the expence, probably, of much more than a hundred thoufand pounds, is fituated on its northweftern margin; and
Kirkby, the feat of Lord Wentworth, on the oppofite extremity.

lieve, of more than two or three thoufand a-
year *.

, In YEOMANRY, of the higher clafs, the diftrict of the ftation abounds, in a fuperior
manner. Men cultivating their own eftates
of two, three, four, or five hundreds ayear,
are thickly fcattered over almoft every part
of the diftrict. There is an inftance of a
man whofe lands, in their prefent high ftate
of cultivation, are not worth lefs than two
thoufands ayear, cultivating them, *as a yeo-
man!*

What a fuperior character! How much
more refpectable, thus, than clinging, as a
minor gentleman, to men of fortune and
fafhion! A German prince is probably lefs
refpected, in the environs of his refidence,
than Mr. PRINCEP is, in the neighbourhood
of CROXALL.

The TENURE of this diftrict is moftly *fee-
fimple*; with fome little *copyhold*; but, I underftand, little or no *leafehold*.

THE

* Lord STAMFORD's eftate round GROBY, on the
fouthern fkirts of the Foreft hills, is more; but little if
any of it reaches, properly, within the diftrict of the
ftation.

2.

THE

GENERAL MANAGEMENT

OF

ESTATES.

THERE ARE few diſtricts in which leſs is to be learnt on the ſubject of managing eſtates, than in this. The eſtates are ſmall ; and the management little more than that of receiving the rents. It will, neverthelefs, be right to take a view of its practice.

MANOR COURTS are pretty generally held ; even where the copyhold tenure is ex-tinct ; and their utility experienced.

PURCHASE OF LANDS. Some years back, the ſame ſpecies of frenzy,—*Terramania,*— ſhowed itſelf, here, as it did in other diſ-tricts *. Forty years purchaſe was, then, not unfrequently given. Now (1785) thirty

years

* See YORK. ECON.

years purchafe, on a fair rental value, is
efteemed a good price: There are fome re-
cent inftances of lands being fold at twenty
years purchafe. But this may be accounted
for. At the time thefe purchafes took place,
the intereft of the funds was extraordinarily
high. By navy and victualling bills, new
loans, &c. five or fix percent. was made of
money. And this will ever be the cafe.
The *intereft* of the funds will always have
more or lefs influence on the price of land.
Hence, thofe who wifh to fecure lands at a
moderate price, fhould purchafe when the
funds are advantageous.

TENANCY. Farms, in general, ftill remain *at will*, and the occupiers, though
large and many of them opulent, ftill appear fatisfied with this fpecies of poffeffion :
for although eftates have been raifed, the
fpirit of over-renting cannot be faid to have
yet pervaded the diftrict. Neverthelefs,
here, as in moft other diftricts, there are
men who, through neceffity or avarice, are
ftretching their rent-rolls, and in confequence, prudently endeavouring to fecure
their rents, and their eftates—as well as they
can—

can—by *agreements* and *leafes*; either for a tenn, or from year to year. The prevailing form will be given at the clofe of this article.

For a ftriking inftance of the confidence which ftill fubfifts between landlords and tenants, fee MIN. 24.

RENT and TITHE. The rent varies, of courfe, with the foil and fituation. Near TOWNS, land lets exceedingly high. Immediately round Tamworth, a confiderable market town, the land, peculiarly rich, lets for three to four pounds an acre. This, however, is in fome meafure accounted for in the quantity of garden ground cultivated, here, for the Birmingham market.

Taking the diftrict of the ftation throughout, twenty fhillings an acre is, at prefent, the full rent, for inclofed lands. Thirty or forty years ago, the old inclofures, of the beft quality, did not let for more than twelve to fifteen fhillings: the rife, therefore, has been confiderable, but, in general, not exceffive. There are fmall parcels let for twenty-five fhillings, and fome few much

VOL. I.　　　C　　　higher;

higher; but, I believe, there is no entire
farm of any fize, let at prefent (1785) for
more than twenty fhillings an acre, round.

And even at thefe rents much of the diftrict is TITHE-FREE ; or enjoys modulfes for
grafs land ; and where the land is titheable,
the tithe is feldom taken in kind. I met
with only one inftance : " Bofworth Field"—
by Doctor Taylor.

Formerly, the tithe of fome townfhips, in
this neighbourhood, was taken in kind ;—
under a cuftom or regulation which might,
when this difgraceful bufinefs takes place,
be univerfally adopted. If the titheman fet
up his own fheaves, he took every *tenth* :
but, if the occupier undertook to fet up,—
only each *eleventh* ! Thus not only a faving
of labour; but frequently, no doubt, a faving of produce was obtained. The titheman loft nothing on the whole, and the
occupier was a gainer on a certainty.

The rent of tithes varies in this as in
other diftricts, with the value of the given
land; and the fpecies of its produce. For
arable land (little or no *fallow*), worth
twenty

twenty fhillings an acre, five fhillings may be confidered, I believe, as the medium rent of the tithe. For grafs land, about two fhillings. For an entire farm, two-and-fixpence to three fhillings an acre.

COVENANTS. By the prevailing cuftom of the country, landlord builds and does extra repairs,—tenant the ordinary repairs of buildings, and takes the fole care of fences; materials being allowed;—with, generally, the liberty of lopping hedgerow timber.

REMOVALS. To the honor of the landed intereft, the removal of tenants has been hitherto little practifed, and of courfe is little underftood. Many of the firft farms have defcended from father to fon, through a feries of generations; and fome of them, there is great reafon to hope, may long continue in the fame line of defcent.

The time of removal is Ladyday; when, according to the prevailing cuftom of the country, entire poffeffion of an inclofed

C 2   farm

farm * is given by the outgoing to the in-
coming tenant : even the barns are given
up at that time; the outgoer generally
carrying off his wheat crop; and sometimes his laſt year's manure.

RECEIVING. The cuſtomary times of
receiving are Michaelmas and Ladyday:
the tenaht being allowed ſix months
credit.

Formerly, an extraordinary cuſtom has
been in uſe, in this quarter of the kingdom; and, by ſome old *leaſes*, ſtill remains
in force, in the interior parts of Staffordſhire. Inſtead of the landlord giving the
tenant ſix months credit, the tenant, by
this cuſtom, agrees to be ſix months in
advance; covenanting to pay what is called a " FOREHAND RENT;" that is, to
pay down the rent prior to the occuſ-
pancy. In practice, however, the rent
is ſeldom paid until four or ſix months
after

* In the open field townſhip, the outgoing tenant
has what is called " the waygoing crops :"—that is, the
wheat and ſpring corn ſown previous to the quitting.

after the commencement of the occupation ; namely, when it is due or nearly fo. This cuftom was, no doubt, founded on the fecurity of the landlord: and fome extraordinary circumftances, probably, led to its eftablifhment.

FORM OF LEASE. The leafe, from which the following heads are digefted, is the only modern leafe I have met with in the diftrict. It is, at prefent (1786), the moft prevailing form in ufe. It contains fome good claufes; but wants many alterations, and feveral additions, to render it a complete form.

LANDLORD AGREES to let, &c. &c. from year to year *.

LANDLORD

---

* An admirable claufe, fuggefted by a man whofe extenfive and accurate knowledge of rural affairs in all its branches, is fuperior to moft men's, has lately been introduced into fome articles of agreement, from year to year, in this diftrict.

The great ufe of leafes, *for a term of years,* is that of encouraging improvements, and the great objection to letting *from year to year* is their difcouragement. But if, in the latter cafe, the landlord covenant, as he does in the claufe under notice, to reimburfe the tenant, when he quits, for fuch *real improvements* as he fhall make, or

LANDLORD RESERVES mines, quarries, &c. &c.

TENANT AGREES to take, &c. and to pay the ſtipulated rent, "within forty days, without any deduction for taxes;" and double rent ſo long as he continues to hold after notice given.

ALSO to repair buildings; accidents by fire excepted.

ALSO to repair gates and fences.

ALSO, when required, to "cut and plaſh the hedges, and make the ditches, three foot by two foot, or pay or cauſe to be paid to the landlord, &c. one ſhilling per rood for ſuch as ſhall not be done after three months notice has been given in writing."

ALSO

the *remainder* of ſuch improvements, at the time of quitting, the objection is, in ſome degree at leaſt, obviated.

Some difficulty, no doubt, will lie, in aſcertaining the quantity of improvement remaining, at the time of quitting. There are, however, men, in every diſtrict, who are adequate to the taſk of eſtimating a matter of this kind, with tolerable accuracy, And it is certainly preferable to riſque the difficulty of ſettlement, than to let an eſtate ſuffer for want of due improvement.

ALSO not to lop or top timber trees; NOR to cut hedge thorns, without plashing and ditching.

ALSO not to part with the poffeffion to any perfon or perfons (the wife, child or children of the tenant excepted) without licence and confent; under forfeiture of the leafe.

ALSO not to break up certain lands fpecified in a fchedule annexed, under 20l. an acre.

ALSO not to plow, &c. more than a fpecified number of acres of the reft of the land " in any one year;" under the fame penalty.

ALSO to forfeit the fame fum " for every acre that fhall be plowed for any longer time than three crops fucceffively, without making a clean fummer fallow thereof after the third crop."

ALSO the like fum " for every acre over and above ———— acres (clover excepted) that fhall be mowed in any one year."

ALSO that at the time of laying down the arable lands to grafs, he fhall " manure them with eight quarters of lime an

acre

acre ufed in tillage, and lay the fame down in an hufbandlike manner, fown with twelve pounds weight of clover feeds, and one ftrike (or bufhel) of rye-grafs feeds upon each acre."

ALso to fpend on the premifes, in a huf-bandlike manner, all the hay, ftraw, and manure; or leave them at the end of the term, for the ufe of the landlord " or his next tenant:" the outgoing

TENANT being ALLOWED for the hay left on the premifes, " at the time of quit-ting."

ALso (provided he quit " at the requeft of the landlord (unlefs for the breaking of thefe articles) and peaceably and quietly yield and deliver up poffeffion") " for all fuch clover and rye-grafs as fhall be fown in any time in the laft year."

ALso for fuch lime as he " fhall caufe to be expended upon the premifes, within twelve months before the time he quits."

ALso " for all fallows made within that time." Thefe feveral allowances to be fettled by referees.

MUTUALLY

MUTUALLY AGREE that " without any new agreement in writing being made concerning the fame, all and every of the covenants, claufes and agreements, herein contained fhall be obligatory on each of the faid parties hereto, and their reprefentatives."

For converfation on *tenancy*, fee MIN. 24.

For a caution to extraparochial owners and occupiers, fee MIN. 33.

For a propofed claufe againft flovenlipefs, fee MIN. 76.

FARM

3.

FARM

BUILDINGS.

THE FARM BUILDINGS of this diſtrict are many of them large, ſubſtantial, and commodious; and have ſeveral particulars belonging to them, that require attention.

The MATERIALS of the diſtrict are theſe. The *walling* material almoſt wholly brick. The *timber* moſtly oak, of which the builders are ſtill laviſh. The *covering* material, formerly thatch; now, principally, in *this* diſtrict, knobbed plain tiles; but, in Leiceſterſhire, moſtly blue ſlate*. *Ground flooring,*

---

* BLUE SLATES. Theſe are raiſed near Swythland — provincially "Swidland" — on the ſouthern ſkirts of the Charnwood hills; where an immenſe excavation has, within the laſt fifty years, been made.

Superficial

flooring, moftly paving bricks. *Chamber flooring,* oak, elm, or plaifter: the two laft are now moft common in farm houfes: in this, an inland country, deal has not hitherto been much in ufe; but even here, it is now becoming the fafhionable material.

The CEMENT of this diftrict is entitled to particular notice. In *common ftucco, plaifter floors* and *water-tight walls* the midland counties excel; but in the laft moft efpecially. Water cifterns are frequently formed by a nine inch brick wall, ftanding naked above ground; yet as tight as a ftone trough!

Some-

Superficial quarries have been worked, time immemorial; but their produce was of a coarfe quality, compared with thofe which are now raifed; fome of which are nearly equal to the Weftmoreland flate.

They are raifed in blocks, blafted from an almoft feamlefs rock. The blocks are firft cleft into flabs; and the flabs afterward into flates; or, if too ftrong and coarfe for this purpofe, are thrown afide, as coarfe flags, for various ufes. Out of the larger blocks, chimney pieces and tombftones are cut.

The fame kind of blue rock is found in different parts of the Foreft hills; but none, yet, which affords flates equal in quality to the "SWIDLAND SLATES."

Something depends on management, in forming thefe walls: but much more on the nature of the LIME with which they are built. There is only one fort with which they can be rendered tight with certainty. This is the BARROW LIME, which not only fets with extraordinary hardnefs, but remains invulnerable to the elements; fetting water, drought, and froft at defiance *.

The

* BARROW LIME. Barrow, fituated on the banks of the Soar, nearly oppofite to Mountfoarhill, in Leicefterfhire, has long been celebrated for its lime.

It is an interefting fact, that the ftone, from which the Barrow lime is burnt, is, in colour, texture, and quality of component parts, the fame as the *Clayftone* of *Glocefterfhire*, from which the ftrong lime of that diftrict is burnt; and what is ftill more remarkable, it is found in fimilar fituations and depofited in thin ftrata divided by thicker feams of calcarious clay, in the very fame manner, in which the clayftone of Glocefterfhire is found. See GLO. ECON. vol. i. p. 13. 15. and 32.

One hundred grains of the *ftone* contain eightyfix grains of calcarious matter; affording fourteen grains of an impalpable tenacious filt, which feems to be poffelfed

The only preparation, of this extraordinary cement, is that of wafhing the fand, and affimilating it intimately with the lime, by beating; and the only judgement requifite in ufing it, is to hurry it into the wall as quickly as poffible from the kiln.

The FARMERIES of this diftrict, as has been intimated, are fome of them on a large fcale. That of Dunnimeer, in this neighbourhood, is the moft extravagant fuite of farm buildings I remember to have feen.

The

feffed of fome fingular properties; forming a fubject well entitled to future enquiry.

One hundred grains of the *clay* contain fortyfix grains of calcarious matter, leaving fiftyfour grains of refiduum, a fine clay.

Hence this earth, which at prefent lies an encumbrance in the quarries, is richer in calcariofity than the CLAY MARL of the Fleg hundreds of Norfolk, with which very valuable improvements are made. See NORF. ECON. vol. i. p. 22.

Since writing this article, I have obferved, in the VALE of BELVOIR, at the northernmoft point of Leicefterfhire, a fimilar ftone, fituated in a fimilar manner, and producing a fimilar kind of lime.

The only thing noticeable in the BARN
of this diftrict is an improvement, lately
introduced I believe, in the means of fup-
porting the roof. Inftead of beams and
principals, *partial partition walls* are raifed,
on either fide the floor and between the
bays, to take the purlines; leaving an opening, or large doorway, in the middle of
the building, to admit the corn.

In a capital barn, where two pair of purlines were neceffary, the cheeks of walling
are narrow; not more than five feet wide;
receiving the lower purlines only; with
fhort beams and principals, refting on the
tops of the cheeks or partial partition walls,
to fupport the upper ones.

This mode of conftruction is cheaper
than *oak* beams; takes the weight of the
roof in a great meafure off the fide
walls; and frees the body of the barn
from beams (well known nuifances in
filling a barn); yet ftiffens the building.
On each fide the floor, thefe partial
partitions are evidently eligible, on thefe
and various other accounts; without any
evident difadvantage.

BARN

BARN FLOORS. In this diftrict, a peculiar method of *laying wooden barn floors* is in practice. Inftead of the planks being nailed down to fleepers, in the ordinary way, the floor is firft laid with bricks, and the planks fpread over thefe, with no other confinement than that of being "dowled" together (that is plowed and tongued) and their ends let into fills or walls, placed in the ufual way, on each fide the floor.

By this method of putting down the planks; provided the brickwork be left truly level; vermin cannot have a hiding place beneath them; and a communication of damp air being effectually prevented, floors thus laid are found to wear better, than thofe laid upon fleepers. It is obfervable, that the planks, for this method of laying, ought to be thoroughly feafoned.

For the method of laying barn floors with bricks, fee MIN. 14.

In this diftrict, I met with a ftriking inftance of the impropriety of laying barn floors with over-grown oak. A floor
laid

laid with plank cut out of the ſtem of an *aged* tree, but which, at the time of laying, appeared to the eye perfectly *ſound*, was beaten to pieces in a few years. Barn floors require youthful, ſtout, ſtrong-grained wood.

In the STABLES of this diſtrict I have ſeen nothing remarkable; except that the manger is ſometimes of brick.

The modern COWSHED of the Midland Diſtrict, more eſpecially I believe of the Diſtrict of the Station, is built on an ex-penſive plan; being furniſhed not only with a gangway before the heads of the cattle, and mangers for dry meat, but alſo with water troughs, on a principle ſimilar to that on which the ſtill more extravagant fatting ſtalls of Gloceſterſhire are built *. But with this difference, that inſtead of each bullock having a ſeparate ſtall, di-vided from the reſt, by whole partitions reaching acroſs the ſhed, the cows, here, ſtand in pairs, with only a partial, but beautifully ſimple diviſion—provincially a "boofing"—between each pair.

* See GLO. ECON.

This

This division confifts of an upright poft, fet in the front of the manger, or between the troughs, with an arm, natural or artificial, fpringing near the ground, and rifing to the fame height as the poft; forming together the upper part of the letter K, ftiffened by flots or bars; running through the two pieces. The cattle are faftened by chains, paffing round the necks, and playing, by means of rings, upon "ftakes" fixed to the fides of the partition pofts.

By this admirable contrivance, the cattle are prevented from goring each other, as effectually as if they were divided by whole partitions; while they have the entire platform, from end to end of the fhed, as free to reft on, as if there were no guards between them *.

The

* In the fheds of a fuperior manager, however, I have feen a different method of conftructing thefe partial partitions; which, inftead of the triangular form defcribed above, are formed by two pofts placed upright, or nearly fo; the partitions being nearly the fame breadth (about eighteen inches) at top and bottom ; having found that the cows, when lying down, are liable to get their heads (frequently turned back in that

The old FARM-YARDS of this diſtrict are
principally open; with mangers round the
inſide of the fences; and with cribs in the
areas: ſometimes with hovels incloſed by
ſlabs *ſet upright*, or tall fagots cloſely woven
together. In the commonfield townſhips,
here, as in the more northern provinces,
bean ſtacks are ſtill not unfrequently placed
on theſe hovels, as temporary winter roofs.
A ſpecies of farm building, this, which I
apprehend was formerly moſt prevalent;
but which, in a few years, will probably be
forgot.

In an open yard, belonging to one of the
firſt managers of the diſtrict, I ſaw a DRINK-
ING CISTERN on an admirable plan. It is
formed by a watertight wall, raiſed high
enough above ground to prevent the cattle
from ſtepping into it, and low enough to let
                                them

poſture) beneath the common hoofings, thereby ſubject-
ing themſelves to a degree of danger; and finds that a
partition, eighteen inches deep, does not prevent them
from occupying the whole platform. Beſides, theſe
upright guards may be beneficial in preventing their
encroaching on each other's room, as they are ſometimes apt to do with the triangular guards.

them drink freely. The brickwork, which forms a ciftern about four feet fquare, is guarded by a poft at each corner, with rails paffing from poft to poft, over which rails the cattle drink. It is fed by a covered pipe (of pipe bricks) reaching to a large drinking pool, at fome diftance from the yard; fo that while this is full (which it is in winter) the ciftern is fo likewife to the brim. If it overflow (which it generally does at that feafon) a wafte-water pipe conveys the furplus out of the yard.

Cifterns of this kind, when they can be formed at an eafy expence, are much preferable to pits, in farm yards.

A long TROUGH, by the fide of a fence, and guarded by a rail, would, under thefe circumftances, be ftill better than a ciftern.

In fome few " RICK YARDS" of this diftrict, a STACKGUARD, of a peculiar kind, is noticeable. It confifts, fimply, of a circular parapet wall, of brickwork, two to three feet high; with a coping projecting on the outfide, to prevent vermin from climbing up; and with the area, or floor, on the infide, laid fecurely with brick (on a level with the

ground

ground on the outside) to prevent their undermining ; as well as to keep the bottom of the rick perfectly dry.

REFERENCES to the MINUTES on FARM BUILDINGS.

For an evidence that every *hogsty* should have a rubbing-post, see MIN. 4.

For the operation of laying *barn floors* with bricks, see MIN. 14.

For the improvement of Statfold *farmery*, see MIN. 25.

For observations on *cattle sheds*, see MIN. 28.

For the operation of *charing posts*, see MIN. 29.

For evidences that a *lobby* is requisite to a *farmery*, see MIN. 112.

ROADS.

4.

R O A D S.

IN A DEEPSOILED DISTRICT, deſtituce, in a manner, of hard materials, as this has been already repreſented, bad roads are in a degree excuſable. Yet there are few diſtricts, perhaps, in which genius and induſtry might not conſtruct tolerable roads, at a moderate expence.

The roads of *this* diſtrict had probably remained in a ſtate of almoſt total neglect, from the days of the Mercians, until ſome twenty years back ; when a ſpirit of improvement went forth. Its principal road, from Tamworth to Aſhby, lay in a ſtate almoſt impaſſable, ſeveral months in the year. Statfold Lane had long been proverbial. In winter it was unfrequented; the riding and driftways, at leaſt, being on trefpaſs, thro the adjoining incloſures. Waggons were dragged on their bellies through it : to a

D 3   coach

coach it was impaffable during the winter
months: and might ftill have lain in that
ftate, had not a material been applied to its
amendment, which is feldom ufed in that
intention: namely, SAND: a material which
had been neglefted in this cafe; though it
was lodged, in fufficient abundance, in a part
of the very road which, century after century, had lain in fo deplorable a ftate.

In this inftance, the bafe of the lane being
levelled, the fand was laid on, eighteen inches to two feet or more thick, according to
the nature of the bottom, on which it was laid.

This circumftance I mention for the ufe
of townfhips that have fand, and no better
material, in their neigbbourhoods, And,
having introduced the fubjeft, it may be
proper to make fome remarks on the method
of making SAND ROADS.

The prevailing error, which has crept
into the modern method of forming roads,
is that of raifing them too high in the middle. (See YORK ECON.) But, here, the oppofite extreme is prevalent.

The FORM of a made road, here, is that
of a trough. The fite of the road being
marked

marked out, a mound of earth, provincially
a " butment," is raifed on either fide ; and,
the bottom of the trough being levelled, the
hard materials are fpread evenly over it;
leaving the furface of the road as flat as a floor *.

The effect of forming a SAND ROAD in
this manner, efpecially where the foil is retentive as in this country, is, the trough retaining the water of heavy rains, the fand,
inftead of being hardened and rendered firm,
as in its nature it is liable to be by heavy
rains, is formed into a grout with the water; horfes wading, perhaps, halfway up to
their knees in puddle ; juft as they would do
in any other large trough filled with fand
and water. After a great fall of rain, I have
feen the dips of the road covered with large
fheets of water, which lay there as they would
in the bed of a river, until the roadman
came with his hoe and his fpade to open his
" lets ;" which in the dips of a fandy road
are prefently warped up; while the flopes

D 4   are

* A more modern method of forming a road is that
of raifing two broad banks, dipping inward, or outward,
or left with a flat furface, according to the *judgement* of the
former; leaving a trough, three or four yards wide, between them; in which trough the hard materials are
depofited.

are torn into gullies, quite down, perhaps, to the base of the road.

A sand road formed as a GRAVEL WALK, with a gentle convexity, and with an open free channel on either side, is subjected to none of these evil effects. Wet weather renders it firm; and the channels on the sides, when the descent is not too great, are rendered firm paths, for saddle horses at least, in dry weather. The SILT ROAD, across the marshlands of Norfolk, between Lynn and Wisbeach, is a proper pattern for sand road makers.

Censurable, however, as the principles of forming roads, in this country, evidently are, it would be improper to condemn them without full examination; as they have their *strenuous* advocates; and these men of the very first abilities.

ROADS incur a heavy tax on the occupiers of lands, and the principles of forming and repairing them, are as fully entitled to examination in a work on RURAL ECONOMY, as are those of FARM BUILDINGS, and FENCES. Roads are necessary to the farmer for conveying his produce to market. And, moreover,

moreover, the law obliges farmers to make and repair them for the reft of the community. They have, therefore, a twofold motive for examining carefully into the principles of making and repairing them. Yet there is fcarcely any branch of rural affairs fo little attended to, and of courfe fo little underftood, as that of roads.

In the Rural Economy of YORKSHIRE, threw together fuch practical ideas on this fubject as I had, at the time of writing, collected, in various parts of the ifland.

At that time, I was fully acquainted with the modern principles of roadmaking in the Midland Counties; but being, at the fame time, fully convinced that they were ill founded, I did not there notice them : nor fhould I, in this place, have taken up the reader's or my own time in explaining them, had I not, in going a fecond time over the diftrict, found the *theory*, inftead of being feen through and exploded, actually making its entry into common *practice*.

Roads are naturally *flat*, where the fite is level or gently floping ; and naturally wear into *hollow ways*, on the fides of hills. The

firft

firſt retain a principal part of the water which falls upon them, and are worn into inequality by rain water *ſtanding* upon them; while the latter are worn into inequalities, by the water of heavy rains *running* upon them.

To obviate theſe inconveniences, art and induſtry have been employed, during the preſent century at leaſt, in rounding the former into the *barrel* or *convex* form, that the water which falls on them may have an opportunity of eſcaping; and, of courſe, that their ſurfaces may not be injured by *ſtagnant* water: and in moulding the latter into the ſame form, that their ſurfaces may not be worn into inequalities by *currents* of water.

By adhering uniformly to this ſelfevident principle, the *ſloughs* of the former, and the *gutters* of the latter, are effectually doneaway, and, with due care, for ever prevented from returning: the entire ſurface, while this principle is adhered to, being ſmooth and even, yet free from hardneſs: of courſe, ſafe and pleaſant to the traveller.

Formerly, in the rutty roads and hollow ways of our anceſtors, it was a week or a fortnight's journey from York to London; now,

now, the road being moulded and kept up, agreeably to the foregoing principle, it may be travelled in a day.

Neverthelefs, the principle now under examination is directly oppofite to that defcribed.

By this principle round roads are reverfed, and flat ones fcooped into the *concave* or *hollow* form; the hollownefs being preferved equally on level ground, and on the face of the fteepeft hills; the entire road, from end to end, being formed into a trough, to catch the water which falls in it: not, however, with any *intention* of impeding the pace of travellers, or of reducing roads to their antient ftate, but under an idea of " *wafhing*" them.

The advantages held out, as arifing from this principle of roadmaking, are thofe of freeing the road from dirt, in wet weather, and duft, in dry; and one which is ftill more valuable, that of faving expence in the repairing of roads: thefe advantages being held out as accruing in ALL SITUATIONS: the principle being likewife extended to ALL MATERIALS.

To

To examine this principle fully, it will be neceſſary to try the effect of water on roads of every material, and in every ſituation.

The MATERIALS of roads are *ſand, looſe gravel, binding gravel, flint and chalk*, and *ſtones* of various ſorts [*], laid on looſe; and ſtones ſet regularly as a *pavement*.

The SITUATIONS of roads may be reduced to a *level* at the bottom of a hill—a gentle *ſlope*—a *hill*—and a *level* at the top of a hill : or, in other words, a *dip*, a *ſlope*, a *ſteep*, a *plain*.

To give full effect to the principle, we will ſuppoſe a poliſhed marble pavement extended acroſs a varied ſurface, including thoſe four ſites or ſituations; the ſurface of the pavement being ſo moulded that the outer margins may be nearly flat, but ſomewhat diſhing inward, with a ſhallow trough or hollow in the middle, ſome three or four yards wide : this being the required form ; if any ſettled form be really fixed ; of a " waſhway road."

Suppoſe a thunder ſhower to fall on this road ; the effect need not be explained : the

margins

* Alſo the ſcoria of metals; cinders of different kinds; burnt clay, and other factitious materials,

margins would collect the rain water and
throw it into the center, where a current would
be spread over the hollow, and carry away
with it the dust which might be lodged upon
it; and, after the shower, even the dips and
plains, *if exactly formed*, and having proper
outlets for the water, would, with a few minutes sun and wind, become perfectly dry
and clean : and, under this supposition, a
drizzling rain would have a similar effect.

Suppose this polished road, formed with
mathematical truth, to be covered with two
or three inches deep of gravel, sand, and
mud; such as all roads are more or less covered with; and to be cut irregularly into
ruts, by wheel carriages, as all carriage roads
are more or less liable to be cut.

Suppose a gentle friendly *waterspout* to
steer its course along this road, filling its cavity without deranging its base; the evident
consequence would be, the steeps and slopes
would be washed clean; the dips would
receive an addition of the best materials;
and the plains be loaded with puddle.

A *thunder shower* on such a road would
have this effect : the suillage on the steeps
and slopes being saturated, the water would
begin

begin to trickle down the ruts; as the current increased, the firſt channel, no matter
what direction it happened to take, whether
down a ſtraight rut, or a zigzag from hollow
to hollow; would be widened; every moment
drawing more and more water into it, untilthe *rut*
were augmented to a *rill*; down which the tor-
rent would pour; driving the ſand and gravel
into heaps and eddies, and carrying down
the mud, with part of the ſand and gravel,
into the neareſt receptacle; leaving the ſteeps
and ſlopes with rough irregular ſurfaces;
the dips, in this, as in the former caſe,
receiving an addition of materials; and the
plains, as before, retaining their own puddle.

A *drizzling rain* would reduce the materials on the ſteeps and ſlopes to a ſtate of
mortar; thoſe on the dips and plains to that
of puddle.

Reverſe this marble road; changing its
ſurface from the *concave* or *hollow*, to the
convex or *round* form; and cover it with
looſe materials as before.

The *waterſpout* would not leave a ſpeck
upon its ſurface; would waſh it clean from
end to end; having nearly the ſame effect
in every ſituation.

The

The *thunder shower* would be injurious on the steeps, in proportion to the degree of convexity: the rounder the form, the sooner the current would escape to the sides, and the less injury, of course, the face of the road would receive. On the slopes the effect would be similar, but in a less degree. On the dips and plains, the current being immediately from the crown to the sides, would carry off the mud, in innumerable channels, leaving the gravel and sand undisturbed on the face of the road.

The *drizzling rain* would act somewhat similarly, in this, as in the other case; with, however, this difference;—on a round surface, the sullage could never get beyond the state of mortar; which if required might be easily thrust *down* to the sides; while in a hollow it would soon take the state of puddle, which nothing but a *scoop* could *raise*.

These being the effects of rain water on roads formed with mathematical exactness, its effects on roads worn into inequalities, as all public roads, in the nature of wheel carriages, unavoidably are, may be easily conceived;

ceived; even by thofe who have not feen
the effect in practice.

In theory, a flat road with a hollow in the
middle, may be plaufible. Could the hollow be kept fmooth as with a plane, and a
fufficient body of water could be had, at will,
to cover, or fill the hollow, at once, and
could be made to run with an even current,
along a plain and down a fteep; whenever
the road might want wafhing, its effect, no
doubt, would be that of *cleaning* the hollow :
the evident effect of which would be, a binding gravel would be rendered hard, a loofe
gravel ftill loofer *, and a rough ftone road
ftill rougher.

But

* In this diftrict, I obferved a ftriking inftance of
this effect. A road up a bold afcent, being of this
material, and lying, by accident or defign, in the hollow form, had been wafhed, by a fucceffion of rains,
to a bed of clean fand and gravel; which, by a few
weeks dry weather and continued draught, had been
loofened fome inches below the furface. The confequence was, when I faw it, the horfes were drawing,
or rather fcraping, to their footlocks in loofe flippery
materials, unable without difficulty to find any firm foot-
hold; while the refiftance of fuch a bed of loofe fand
and gravel, to the wheels, requires no explanation.

But in practice, it is impossible to keep a public road in that state, nor can a body of water be had at command, to be let loose upon it in a moment*; nor, in its nature, will water run briskly along a plain, or gently down a hill. The clouds alone could give the uncertain supply; and the effect of rain-water on roads has been explained: the ruts and hollows of a level are filled with standing water; the evil effects of which, though but an inch deep, are evident; while those of a steep, by drawing the current through them, are worn still wider and deeper; sand is torn into gullies: loose gravel driven into heaps: binding gravel worn into channels; and stone roads scooped into hollows, separated by ridges of naked stone.

Where a strong current of water is collected, whether on a steep or on a more gentle slope,

---

* In some few situations, water might be pent up in reservoirs, and be let loose suddenly upon a road; but situations in general will not admit of any such expedient.

slope, and whether the material be stone or
coarse binding gravel, the road, even suppofing
the water to be fpread over it evenly, is ne-
cellarily rendered *a rough irregular pavement,
ftrewed with loofe ftones*; which, or the points
of faft ones, are the only furface left for the
travelling animals to tread on. To a ftum-
bling horfe, fuch a road is of courfe dangerous; to a thin-footed horfe, painful; and,
to an ox, it may be faid to be impaffable:
yet there are men who are at once advocates
for working oxen, and advocates for wafh-
way roads!

The unfafenefs and unpleafantnefs of
hollow roads being evident (to my mind
at leaft), the idea of their being lefs expenfive than round roads remains to be examined.

The moft perfect ftate of a road; that in
which it is the fafeft and pleafanteft to the
traveller, and in which its wear is the leaft;
confequently that in which it is the leaft
expenfive to its fupporter;—is the ftate in
which the interftices of the hard materials
are filled up level with loofe matter, as
fmall gravel, fand, &c. giving a fmooth
even

even furface; foft and elaftic to the hoof; yet firm enough to refift the wheels, without being cut into ruts, and fufficiently *covered* to prevent the hard materials from being expofed to their immediate preffure.

Suppofe a trough road to be in this defirable ftate; and fuppofe a heavy rain to fall, and a ftrong current to be fpread *theoretically*, that is evenly, over the bottom of the trough; the effect requires no explanation: the interftitial matter would of courfe be more or lefs wafhed out; and the points of the hard materials be expofed to the nail, and the hoof expofed to them; and in this unpleafant and unprofitable ftate it muft of courfe remain, until the furface of the hard materials be ground down, to fill up the interftices: which done, and the road made travellable, and fecure. from exceffive injury, another fall of rain takes place: another inch of hard materials is of courfe worn down: and thus, inch after inch, until the earthy foundation be reached. A more ingenious method of wearing away a road, could not readily be conceived: excepting that of wearing the

E 2 flopes

flopes partially with running water, and
the plains partially with ftanding water;
both of which are unavoidably effected,
and in the fulleft manner, by forming
roads on the principle now under examination.

The impropriety of *generalizing* hollow
roads being too evident to admit of farther
examination, let us endeavour to afcertain
the *particular circumftances*, under which
they can properly be rendered ufeful. It
is not probable, that men of ftrong natural
abilities, and in a found ftate of mind,
fhould attach themfelves to error, without
fome fhow of truth to lead them to it *.

The

---

* The advocates of the principle under examination
are not the only roadmakers who have been led into
error in the forming of roads. Some twenty years
ago, the road between London and Hackney (about
three miles, nearly on a dead level) was altered at an
exceffive coft, from the *barrel* to the *wave* form : under
an idea that, by throwing a number of ridges
acrofs the road, inftead of one ridge lengthway of it,
the ruts, inftead of preventing in fome degree the en-
creafe of the water, would conduct it off the road. But
experience proving, that, befides the natural length
of the road being by this form encreafed, and the draft
along

The moſt ſtriking good effect of waſh-
ways is that of covering a level road at the
foot of a high hill, with ſand and ſmall
gravel, brought down the deſcent by
heavy rains; and this moſt eſpecially when
a conſtant rill happens to ſpread over it,
and carry away the ſoil; leaving nothing
but the harder particles *.

Another good effect of running water is
on a ſhort and gentle ſlope, where the natural foundation of the road—the natural
ſubſoil—happens to be of gravel, or other
hard material. In this caſe, a current of
water, by carrying away the ſoil which is
generally mixed, in greater or leſs proportions, among ſuch a ſubſoil,—as it
riſes to the ſurface, keeps ſuch a road in
perpetual repair with little aſſiſtance of
art,

E 3 But

along it being rendered uneven, and of courſe difficult,
the dips became mere receptacles of dirt and puddle;
this road, after having had a fair trial, was, at another
exceſſive expence, re-altered to the barrel form.

* The moſt refined uſe that road water could, perhaps,
be put to, would be that of conveying it down by the
ſides of a round road, and ſpreading it over a flat at the
bottom of a ſlope.

But even thefe ufes of running water, confined as they are to a few fituations *, are ill adapted to *public* roads : the flats, during a continuance of drizzling or even moderate rains, are liable to be loaded with dirt ; a rill, not once in a thoufand inftances, being at hand to keep them free ; and the flopes are liable to be ftrewed with loofe ftones, and worn into inequalities by the *fport* of running water.

A *public* road ; more efpecially a *toll* road ; ought to be free from obftructions in all feafons :

* With refpect to the idea held out, that every foil and fituation affords " a *fomething*," of which running water will *make* a road, it is much too wild to give chace to. That foils, in general, if worn long enough, that is deep enough, would on a gentle flope afford a fomething to bear a *horfe* or other animal, may be true ; — for although a horfe path may be poached in wet weather ; yet, in dry, it is, as will be fhown, trpd level, again, to receive, with benefit, the water of heavy fhowers :—but not one foil or fituation in a hundred is capable of affording hard materials fufficient to bear the wheels of *laden carriages* ; which, as will be fhown, tending, not to fill up and level, but to deepen the holes and gutters made by running water, act in concert with it to render the road impaffable,

feafons: and may with common care be kept in that defirable ftate, except after a long continuance of moderate rain; when the levels, let them be formed as they may, unlefs they be raifed inconveniently round, and unlefs the materials be of uncommon hardnefs, will become loaded with dirt; which, as an obftruction to the traveller, and as tending, like ftanding water, to keep the road in a ftate of foftnefs, and of courfe in a ftate of extraordinary wear, ought to be removed: not, however, with fo unmanageable an inftrument as water, which *cannot* be brought to *act* in level fituations (the feet of hills excepted), but from hollow roads with *fcoops*, and from round ones with *fcrapers*; which tend, not to make the road unfafe or unpleafant, but to put it, as nearly as its general ftate of repair will admit, into the required ftate of perfection.

With refpect to *private* and *by* roads, in which carriages never travel abreaft and feldom meet each other, and on which the beafts of draft are always drawn fingle—there appears to be only one right method

E 4 of

of forming them; moft efpecially where
materials are fcarce.

The principle had long ftruck me forcibly in theory, before I faw it carried into
practice, in the Midland Diftrict.

On this principle, three lines of hard
materials conftitute the road : a middle path
for the horfes, with one on each fide for
the wheels.

In forming a road on this principle, the
middle path is fet out, by a line, or otherwife, as circumftances require, and the
fod being removed, a carriage is drawn
along, by horfes walking in this path; the
wheels of courfe marking out the middle
of the two outer paths. Three trenches
are then dug, of widths and to depths proportioned to the quantity of materials intended to be expended; leaving the paths,
on filling in the materials, an inch or two
below the adjoining furface *.

This

---

* A PRIVATE ROAD, for horfes drawing double, requires to have the entire fpace between the wheel paths
cleared from the natural foil, and filled up within a few
inches of the furface, with hard materials. In this
cafe, the collection of water may, on a long flope, be

This method of forming WAGGON PATHS, aptly fuggefts a fimple HORSE PATH, or bridle road: and the Midland Diftrict furnifhes inftances of horfe paths being formed on this principle: indeed, it appears to have been, formerly, the Leicefterfhire method of forming horfe paths by the fide of public roads:—anfwering the aukward caufeways of other diftricts.

Between Bofworth and Leicefter are ftill the remains of one of thefe paths; which, in the parts where it is tolerably perfect, is, by much, the fafeft and moft pleafant

horfe

---

too great to be fuffered to accumulate into one current, and, in fuch a fituation, a road, even of this narrow width, ought to be laid round, or to have outlets for the water, at ftated diftances, on the face of the flope. But thefe outlets require a channel and dam acrofs the road, to ftop the defcent of the current; than which nothing is more dangerous and difagreeable, efpecially to carriages: yet this is the expedient held out by the advocates of hollow public roads; on which, being wide, and the quantity of water collected great in proportion, thefe ditches and banks would require to be fo deep (to preferve the road from greater injury), that each fteep would become a ftaircafe!

horfe path by the fide of a carriage road, I have travelled upon. A lady would canter along it with the utmoft confidence*. As the lines of turf on the fides encroach upon it, they are fhaved off, and the path kept free and fufficiently wide.

Thefe paths are lefs liable to be incommoded with dirt than theory may fuggeft. The flopes are wafhed by heavy rains ; and the dips, if proper outlets be opened into the ditches, which generally run by the fides of them, may be kept fufficiently free from water.

Thus, it is more than probable, the good effect of flat horfe paths, funk a few inches below the furface, led to the idea of carriage paths, and thefe to

flat

---

* How much preferable to the high, gawky, flippery, breakneck *caufeways* of other diftriets! Thefe caufeways however, which were probably intended to accommodate foot paffengers as well as horfes, are, or rather were, ftriking evidences of the efficacy of heavy rains in wafhing convex furfaces ; for being narrow and without ruts to impede the defcent, they were in general kept perfectly clean : much too clean ; either for eafe or fafety in travelling.

flat carriage roads, with "butments" on their fides, agreeably to the practice of this diftrict.

Be this as it may, flat horfe paths are produced, in argument, as evidences in favor of flat carriage roads : a ftriking evidence, this, of the danger of generalizing ideas without due examination.

The effects of rain water, on narrow horfe paths and on wide carriage roads, are very different. The quantity collected on the former is not capable of injuring the flopes, and readily finds its way off the levels : it has but a few inches to run to the outlet ; with not a fingle lateral rut to impede its efcape : while the flopes of the latter are injured by the accumulated current, and the levels unavoidably incommoded with ftanding water, which, from the middle of a flat or hollow road, has fome yards to run, acrofs ruts and ridges, before it can find the outlet.

Befide, the effect of the feet of horfes and that of the wheels of carriages are diffimilar as light and darknefs, or right and wrong ; the one tends to level the furface

of

of a road, the other to wear it into inequalities.

The human foot, by conftant treading,
tends to render a path, free from hard
protuberances, perfectly fmooth and
level : by ftepping on the higher parts,
the wear and the preffure both tend to
lower them, and to fill up the hollows between. The foot of a horfe has a fimilar
tendency : a horfe which has the ufe of his
limbs will not, if he can avoid it, fet his
foot in a hole, but treads on its margin *;
by which means hollows, and more efpecially narrow channels, are filled up. Thus
we frequently fee, at the foot of a long
flope, a horfe path, as the middle track of a
waggon path in a by road, worn, in the
morning, by a heavy fall of rain in the
night, into a narrow channel, generally in
the

---

* I fpeak of holes which may be avoided in roads of
hard materials; not of sloughs of clayey lanes;
which, being too wide to be avoided, are of courfe
waded through, and, in proportion to the quantity of
dirt brought out by the feet and legs of the travelling
animals, are rendered deeper and wider by ufe.

the middle of the path; which, however,
in the evening, if the traffic be great, we
find entirely done away; the path being
left fmooth and level; or more ufually
fomewhat hollow; but with a regular con-
cavity; in the very form for which the advocates of hollow roads contend: and if
water were poured upon it in quantity,
it would fpread itfelf over its furface;
which being rendered firm and fmooth,
or nearly fo, by the feet of the horfes,
the water, if not too rapid, nor continued
upon it too long, would tend to render it
ftill firmer and fmoother; carrying off
the foil which lay on the furface merely;
leaving the fand and gravel in their places;
acting in the very manner held out by the
advocates for hollow roads.

To afcertain, in the fulleft manner, the
effects of wheel carriages on a road, it
will be neceffary to adjuft its furface and
roll it, until the loofe matter covering the
hard materials be fmooth and firm.

The firft effect of a carriage, paffing
along fuch a road, is that of making a longi-
tudinal impreffion or rut, of a depth proportioned

portioned to the quantity quality and ſtate
of the covering matter, to the breadth of the
wheels, and the weight of the load they bear,
raiſing up a ridge or comb of the looſe matter, and leaving it ſtanding, light and porous,
on either ſide of the rut. Another carriage
paſſing nearly, but not exactly, in the ſame
track, another rut is formed, and other ridges
of looſe matter forced up; or perhaps a line
of the covering two or three inches wide, between the ruts, looſened and raiſed up from
its firm ſmooth ſtate.

By a continuance of wear, the ſurface of
the hard materials is reached, and worn away:
not, however, evenly, as a long broad-foot-
ed ſledge paſſing along the ſurface would
wear them; but, according to the nature of
wheel carriages, in ruts and hollows: it being out of the power of art to render every
part of a road equally firm; and not at all
probable that the wheels of carriages paſſing
upon it ſhould wear every part of its ſurface exactly alike.

By the laws of gravitation and the action
of wheel carriages, holes once begun in the
ſurface of a road, no matter by what agent,

inſtead

inſtead of being made leſs, as thoſe of a path are by the feet of animals, are made deeper every time the wheel of a carriage paſſes through them. The periphery of the wheel acts as a chiſſel, which in falling into the hollow receives an impetus or acquired force, in addition to the actual preſſure it is loaded with; and, in addition to this, an undue proportion of the general load is, of courſe, by placing it out of its upright poſture, taken from the upper and thrown upon the lower wheel. See YORK. ECON.

Hence, the fact naturally ariſes, though not perhaps ſufficiently attended to by road ſurveyors, that HARD PROTUBERANCES, beſide being dangerous and diſagreeable to travellers, whether on horſeback or in carriages, are injurious to roads.

Every hard protuberance, as the point of a ſtone ſtanding above the general ſurface of the road, is, in the nature of wheel carriages and the laws of gravitation, productive of four indentures or holes: two, by throwing an additional weight on the oppoſite wheel (paſſing both ways); and two more by the impetus or additional force given by the
wheel

wheel (paffing both ways) in falling on the
common furface of the road.

And hence it becomes as indifpenfably
neceffary, to common good management,
to lower protuberances, as it is to fill up indentures: to pick out or break down with
a hammer (a work of little expence) ftones
or other obftructions; as to fill up the ruts
and holes with additional materials.

The effect of the feet of *horfes drawing in
carriages*, varies with the degree of exertion
in draft. In light carriages the effect is nearly the fame as that of faddle horfes, and of
courfe tends to remedy, in fome degree, the
ill effect of the wheels. But when much
exertion is required, the feet of draft horfes
tend to tear up, loofen, and make rough,
rather than to render firm and fmooth, the
furface of the road.

Hence upon the whole we may venture
to conclude, that the effects of water on a
horfe path and upon a carriage road, are as
widely different, as are the effects of the
wheels of carriages, and the feet of faddle
horfes. Water running down the flopes of
a carriage road worn as defcribed, is, by the

well

well known laws of running water, drawn
through the channels and hollows; acting in
concert with the wheels, in making them
wider and deeper; forming, by a continuance of wear, a rill, or perhaps two or three
rills, on the face of the road; while the rest
of its surface is loaded with loose matter, on
which the *current*, arifing from ordinary
rains, and in ordinary fituations, has no
power of action; or, where the rills approach
near each other, is left in narrow rough
ridges, most inconvenient to the traveller.

To give full fcope to the united action
of wheel carriages and running water, on
the face of a wide carriage road, we will
fuppofe it to remain in a ftate of neglect.

The effects, which would neceffarily follow, fcarcely need to be particularized.
The wheels and the water operating jointly
to render its furface more and more uneven, the breaking of horfes' knees and
men's necks, the crufhing of wheels and
axles, the overturning of utter carriages,
and, at length, the utter impaffability of
the road, would be the inevitable confequences.

Even

Even running water, without the affiftance of wheel carriages, is capable of producing the final effect; and in no great
length of time; as is proved in a thoufand
inftances, in which roads having been *turned*, and the old ónes of courfe neglected,
they have in the courfe of a few years
become, to carriages at leaft, entirely
impaffable; and this altogether through
the evil effects of running water on the
furface of carriage roads.

If in thefe examinations and conclufions
I have miffed or exceeded truth, it Has not
béen by defign. Fully convinced of the
importance of roads, as a fubject in Rural
Economy, I have long paid them great attention, and wifh to make myfelf fully
mafter of the fubject: I have even fuffered
myfelf to conceive that hollow roads might
poffibly be right; though the principle,
at fight, appears to be felf-evidently wrohg.

This fummer (1789) being unufually wet,
has afforded me a favourable opportunity
of deciding, by obfervation, on the effects
of round and hollow roads.

In

In traverſing the Diſtrict, I did not fail
to notice theſe effects ; and in riding from
Leiceſter to London, through Warwickſhire, Oxfordſhire, &c. &c. after a month
or ſix weeks continuance of rains of every
degree, I was, being more diſengaged,
ſtill more attentive to the form and ſtate
of the roads.

The road between NOTTINGHAM and
LOUGHBOROUGH is held out, by the advocates of hollow ways, as a ſpecimen of their
good effect.

This road, however, though much flatter
than modern roads in general are, is by no
means uniformly reduced to the principle
and form contended for : indeed a part,
which has been lately made, is thrown into the barrel form : a ſtrong evidence
that the trough principle, in this inſtance,
is growing into diſrepute. Taking it altogether in its preſent ſtate (rendered more
tolerable by parts which lie ſomewhat
round, or which lie ſhelving on the ſides
of hills) and conſidering the materials, a
charming gravel, and the publicneſs of the
thoroughfare to pay for the forming and repairs ;

pairs; the part I faw of it, between Trent
Bridge and the top of Bunny Hill, may,
without prejudice, be deemed one of the
worft kept roads in the kingdom. The
fteeps torn into inequalities, ftrewed with
large loofe ftones, and fet with faft ones,
in the true breakneck crufhcarriage ftyle,—
and the *levels* loaded with mud to the
footlocks. The more gentle *flopes*, though
uneven, harfh, and unpleafant to travel
upon, were certainly not indictable: a
proof that on fuch furfaces, and with fuch
materials, roads may be kept in a travelable ftate, in defiance of running water.

All that can be faid farther of this road
is, that had the materials been put into
a better form they would have afforded a
better road. In a country where good materials are fufficiently plentiful, a traveller
who pays for his road, whether on horfe-
back or in a carriage, has a right to expect
that it fhall be, not only found, but fafe
and pleafant, to himfelf and his horfes:
and a ftill greater right has the proprietor
of a loaden carriage to expect to find the
                                        furface

furface of the road, be pays for, firm, and free from obftructions.

Between Leicester and Hinkley (except about Hilton) the *material* gravel; the *form* round—(fingularly well formed;) the *ftate*, nearly perfect, notwithftanding the feafon! even, firm, and in a manner free from dirt; except in fome few places, where the middle being worn hollow, for want of being timely kept up to its form, had taken the *hollow form*, and which were, of courfe, full of water, dirt, holes, and protuberances.

Through Hilton (a confiderable length) the road is intolerably bad. The *material* large ftones: the *form* hollow—a rough irregular hollow pavement: the *ftate*, fuch as fuggefts the idea, that it is under the direction of a wheelwright, or a furgeon. No public road ought to be fuffered to remain in fuch a ftate.

Between Hinkley and Coventry, various: part of it through a coalpit country; neverthelefs, and notwithftanding the feafon, even the levels, where the form was kept up round and even, and where the dirt, which had of courfe accumulated through

the

the feafon and exceffive traffic, had been removed, were found, firm, travelable road:
altogether on the *convex* principle.; and
altogether the beft *coal* road on which I remember to have travelled.

From COVENTRY to WARWICK, the *ma-
terial* gravel, the *form* convex; the *ftate*, in
defiance of the weather, nearly perfect
throughout: ten miles of the beft gravel
road in the kingdom.

WARWICK to STRATFORD — fimilar
road; but not in fuch high prefervation.
Some of the levels worn hollow, and of
courfe dirty: fome of the flopes in the fame
predicament, and of courfe hard, fharp,
and uneven.

STRATFORD to the foot of LONG CQMP-
TON HILL, the *material* ftone, a fomewhat
foft calcarious granate: the *form*, originally,
convex; but, at prefent,—through a pre-
tended want of materials, and the exceffive
wetnefs of the feafon, but in fact through neglect,—in the true hogtrough form: the
ftate what may eafily be conceived; a difgrace to the *truft:* a canal of puddle for
miles together; and of courfe full of holes
and

and knobs; fome of them hid; others fhowing their heads above the batter. A faddle horfe could not pick out a tolerable path: even foot paffengers were wading to market, and fervants to their places, to the tops of their fhoes in dirt.

What a difgrace to the diftrict through which it paffes: what an impofition on the public, to demand toll for fuch a road: and what a lofs to the proprietors! A road let down into *fuch* a ftate, receives more injury in one day (in a wet feafon) than it would receive in a week, if properly kept up to the form, and of courfe free from ftanding water. On this road, being moftly on the level, running water has not much power of injury.

LONG COMPTON to WOODSTOCK, the country more billowy (lefs level) and the road *fomewhat* better kept.

WOODSTOCK to OXFORD,—the *material* the fame kind of foftifh ftone: the *form,* once convex; but now, like chaos of old, it is without form. The *ftate,* moft difficult to defcribe. It is barely paffable: as much worfe than the road laft defcribed, as that

F 4 is

is worſe than a fair travelable road : nevertheleſs, the toll gate is kept *locked !* and a *double*
toll exacted ! Literally highway robbery !

At preſent (October 1789) this road lies
in a ſtate of total neglect : excepting the *care*
of half a dozen men endeavouring to let off
the water ! and where this is impoſſible (the
pits in the *rock* which forms the bottom
of the *canal,* many of them lying below the
neighbouring ditches), theſe *labourers* are employed in *ſcooping* out the batter !!! mere
mockery : one ſhower of rain undoes in five
minutes their whole day's labour.

The plea held out, for its lying in its preſent ſtate of neglect is, that it is *taken,* but
not yet entered upon, by the perſon or
perſons who have taken it to repair ; it being
yet ſome weeks before their time of entrance
commences !

But why ſhall the public ſuffer through
the private quarrels or quirks of individuals ?
This is at preſent one of the principal roads
from London to Holyhead, and the main
road to a conſiderable part of England and
Wales : an avenue of Oxford ! and the
high road to Blenheim !

OXFORD

OXFORD to HENLEY various : good or bad in proportion to the roundnefs or hollownefs of the form ; and the flatnefs or elevation of the country.

HENLEY to MAIDENHEAD,—the *materials* flint and chalk ; the *form* convex ; the *flate* nearly perfect, notwithftanding the feafon. In moft places as clean and as fmooth as a gravel walk. The joint effort of the form and the materials.

Henley Hill (a great effort in roadmaking) affords, at prefent, a ftriking inftance of the evil effect of running water on a fteep. Though formed well, originally, fome ruts, through neglect, have been fuffered to catch the water ; and being fuffered, by the fame neglect, to grow deeper and deeper, they are at length worn, near the foot of the hill, into furrows a foot deep !—which, by a few minutes timely attention to the infant ruts, might have been entirely prevented.

From MAIDENHEAD to LONDON, the *material* is gravel ; the *form* convex ; and the *flate*, notwithftanding the country is a dead level, from end to end (twentyfix miles), and

and notwithstanding the unusual wetness of
the season, was altogether such as no traveller has a right to find fault with. Where the
convexity had been properly kept up, and
the rain water prevented from lodging on
the surface, it might be deemed in the state
of perfection : except near town, where the
wear is excessive; especially in places where
the reduced matter and the dung dropt
upon it, had not been timely removed, and
there it was unusually *dirty :* more especially
where it passes between rows of houses;
which, depriving it of a considerable share
of sun and wind, retards its drying in showery
weather, and prevents the soil, in dry weather, from escaping in the form of DUST.

Throughout the ride, it was observable,
that the state of the road as to *cleanness*, was,
other circumstances being similar, in proportion to its EXPOSURE.

Hence the utility of keeping down the
hedges of lanes, especially in low situations.

Hence also a disadvantage of *hollow roads*;
which not only retain MOISTURE, in wet weather, but DUST, in dry ; while that of a *round
road* is scattered over the adjoining fields.

In

In snow, their comparative advantage is still more striking: a *hollow way* is well known to be the first place drifted up: the crown of a *round road*, the last place covered. In windy snowy weather, while one is rendered dangerous or impassable, the other is left free and safe for passengers.

From the whole of this enquiry, as well as to common observation, it appears evidently, that the natural enemies of roads are *rain-water* and *snow*; and that *sun* and *wind* are their natural benefactors.

Hence, that form which lessens, prevents, or turns into a good, the evil effects of the former, and which gives the latter the greatest power of action, is evidently the most eligible: provided the *utility* of the road be not injured, or its *wear* increased, by such a form.

The perfection of a road, with respect to utility and wear, consists, as has been shown, in its *surface* being even, firm, and elastic; the interstices of the hard materials being filled, and their points sheathed, with finer matter: provided its *form* be that in which

which its utility is greateſt and its wear the
leaſt.

The ſtate of PERFECTION of a road, as to
FORM, that in which its utility is the greateſt
and its wear the leaſt, is, beyond all argument and doubt, the ſtate of perfect *flatneſs* *:
provided the SURFACE could be kept in the
ſtate of perfection, under that form.

But it being, in practice, UTTERLY IMPOS-
SIBLE, as appears demonſtrably by the foregoing examinations, to unite the *perfection of
ſurface* with *perfect flatneſs*, a more practical
form muſt be ſought.

In HOLLOWNESS we cannot hope to find
it. It has been ſhown that a hollow road,
by collecting the water which falls on the
ſteeps, is worn into inequalities; part of the
hard materials being carried off; and other
expoſed to unneceſſary wear; rendering the
ſurface unſafe, unpleaſant, and injurious to
the feet of animals; eſpecially thoſe of cattle; beſide encreaſing the reſiſtance by hollows and protuberances; and thereby doubly
encreaſing the wear of the road: while the
                                    water

water which falls on the *levels*, being unavoidably collected on the face of the road, the well known effects of standing water of courfe take place.

Thus, the great natural enemy of roads, RAIN WATER, inftead of being curbed in its mifchiefs, or converted to a friendly purpofe, is, by HOLLOWNESS of form, left with full power of injury; while the WIND, their great natural benefactor, is, by this form, deprived of a confiderable fhare of its power of relief: *dirt* and *duft*, equally, lie fafe and fecure at the bottom of the trough; which, inftead of being kept free from *fnow*, by the wind, is the firft place filled : the wind, in this cafe, being changed into an enemy.

With refpect to SNOW, the *flat* form is preferable to the *hollow* : though in moft, if not all, other refpects, as to utility of furface, flatnefs is the worft poffible form. By encreafing the hollownefs of a wide carriage road, much beyond the utility of form, the margins might no doubt be brought into a travelable ftate ; whereas, of a flat road, in a wet feafon, every part, from fide to fide, becomes equally untravelable : or, at beft, altogether

together unfit to be travelled on and paid
for.

Hence, it is sufficiently evident, that in
HOLLOWNESS nor in FLATNESS can anything
near perfection, in form and surface *jointly*,
be found. In ROUNDNESS, alone, we can,
therefore, expect to find it.

It is evident, to demonstration, that, by
rounding up a road, above the utility of
form, the evil effects of standing and running waters might be equally avoided; and
the good effect of the waters of heavy
showers, running from the crown to the
sides, carrying down with them the soil, and
leaving the sand and gravel behind, might
be obtained.

Consequently the UTILITY OF SURFACE
is obtainable, in roundness, to the required
degree of perfection.

But perfection in the UTILITY OF FORM
cannot be had in roundness; it belonging,
exclusively, to flatness: in which, however,
the requisite UTILITY OF SURFACE cannot
be preserved.

Hence we may fairly, and safely, conclude, that perfect utility of surface, and perfect

fect utility of form are UTTERLY INCOMPA-
TIBLE: the former, belonging folely to
roundnefs, the latter exclufively to flatnefs.

Therefore, all that human art and induftry
can do is to endeavour to hit the happy medium: to lower the roundnefs until a degree of flatnefs be found fufficient to render
the form, though not *perfect*, fufficiently *convenient* to anfwer, fully, the general intention: preferving a degree of roundnefs fufficient, when properly kept up, to fecure it
from the evil effects of ftanding and running
waters: a happy medium, which, though
feldom hit, is more or lefs obfervable, in
every quarter of the kingdom.

The requifite degree of roundnefs varies
with circumftances: depends on the given
fituation, the given materials, the width and
the publicnefs of the given road. The
fteeps and levels, more particularly, ought
to be kept as round as perfect conveniency
will permit: for the quicker rain water
efcapes off the former, the lefs mifchief it
occafions; and the quicker it efcapes off the
latter, the more good.

Wherever

Wherever a road is obferved to keep itfelf free from ftanding water and inequalities of furface, in a wet feafon; and this, where the form is not too round for the çonveniency of top loads, every part of its furface being travelled over, the happy medium has been hit and preferved.

Roads bearing this teft are proper fubjects of ftudy for roadmakers, rather than any theoretic rule that could be offered; except that roundnefs of form, let the mate-rial, the width, and the publicity be what they may, is requifite in all-feafons, and in all fituations.

Becaufe, under this form, heavy RAINS, inftead of being injurious, become friend-ly to them: and though more moderate fhowers will, in defpite of art and atten-tion, be caught, more or lefs, by the late-ral ruts; yet being expofed to the full ef-fect of the WIND, their mifchief is of fhort continuance; and the wind continuing, until a ftate of drynefs takes place, its ef-fect becomes fimilar to that of heavy rains; carrying off the foil; leaving the fand and
afford

gravel to guard the hard materials, and to afford a furface, fafe and pleafant to the traveller, and friendly to the feet of tenderfooted animals.

On dry snow, the wind acts in the fame manner as on dust: the crown of a round road is among the laft places covered, and the firft bared, in a fnowy feafon.

Thefe being the principal facts and · reflections that have occurred to me refpecting the forms of roads, I put an end to this long, and to myfelf at leaft, tirefome article; which nothing but a defire of placing an important fubject in a juft light, could have induced me to have begun.

I confefs, however, that I do not regret the attention I have beftowed upon it; as the ftudying and digefting of it have brought to light truths, which otherwife I might not have feen, and which ferve to eftablifh ftill more firmly, than thofe I had hitherto adduced, the fuperiority of the CONVEX PRINCIPLE;—of roads moderately round, with a free open channel on either fide as a horfe path; with banks level on the top, as guards to the paths, and as refources, in wet weather, for footpaffengers; and, where the width of

VOL. I.   G   the

the lane will permit, with a fide road for fummer travelling.

By giving this form to roads, and by preferving it with due attention, fo as to keep
the furface free, as poffible, from water, and,
in a continuance of wet weather, from a fuperfluity of reduced materials; and by paying proper attention to the fide roads;—I am
clearly convinced that a very confiderable
proportion—perhaps one third—perhaps one
half—of the money now expended on the
roads of this kingdom might be faved.

And although the whole of the expence of
roads does not fall on the farmer; yet, confidering the toll he pays, in addition to the labour,
or the rate, he is obliged to furnifh, the principal part of it may be faid to fall on the occupiers, and of courfe, eventually, on the
owners of lands; a fact which will fully apo-
logize, I hope, if any apology be required,
for the length of thefe obfervations.

For an inftance of a rough fandy road being
fmoothed at a fmall expence, fee MIN. 71.

FENCES.

5.

F E N C E S.

IN A COUNTRY which, for some time past, has been changing from an open to an inclosed state, we may reasonably expect a degree of excellency in the art of hedge planting. It seldom happens that, under such circumstances, the art remains in a state of obscurity; but that the prevailing mode of execution is adapted to the given soil and situation.

This, however, is not invariably the case: in similar situations, on similar soils, and under similar circumstances, we find very different modes of performing the same operation: a proof that the rural arts are either very abstruse, or are not universally studied with due attention.

In Norfolk, where a deep free subsoil prevails, we see hedgewood planted by the side of a deep ditch, and perhaps near the top

of a high bank; and this notwithstanding
the substrata are naturally absorbent or dry.
While in this district, likewise having a deep
free soil and subsoil, the plants are laid into
a flat broad low bank, with a narrow shallow
ditch; a mere trench; and this notwithstanding the substrata are, in a manner invariably, retentive or wet; and the surface
waters, of course, have no other way of escaping, than by means of deep ditches. In
a recently inclosed common field, I have seen
ditches a foot deep, with water standing in
the furrows, hard by, not less than fifteen
or eighteen inches deep!

This error in practice, however, is rather
detrimental to the lands, than to the hedges;
which, in this district, are above par; and
their treatment, of course, requires attention.

The useful ideas, collected in this case,
fall under the heads,

Raising new Hedges;

Treatment of grown Hedges.

RAISING NEW HEDGES. The *species of
hedgewood*, whitethorn, with some instances
of

of crabtree *. At prefent, however, "garden quick" may be faid to be the univerfal
hedgewood; although there was, within
the memory of many men, no fuch thing in
ufe.

The rejection of nurfery plants, however,
did not proceed from ignorance in the method of raifing them, but from principle,
founded on a falfe notion that plants, pam-
pered in the rich foil of a garden, were of
courfe improper to be planted in a ditch
bank of common earth. No, no; the planters
of thofe days knew better. "Gather them
in woods, where they have been expofed to
hardfhips, and have learnt to live upon
coarfe fare, and, in that cafe, when they
come to be tranfplanted into hedges, they
muft thrive."

A gentleman near Tamworth was the firft
who ventured to plant garden quick on a
large fcale; and his fuccefs ruined the *bufi-*

G 3 *nefs,*

* HOLLY HEDGES. In this diftrict I obferved a
natural holly hedge flourifhing, as a fence againft every
thing, under very low-headed fpreading oaks: an
evidence of what might be expected from holly hedges
under oaks properly trained.

nefs, as it had long been, of quickgathering. The quantity now raifed, at Tamworth and its neighbourhood, for the Birmingham and other markets, is extraordinary. It is moftly tranfplanted. Its price, even at Tamworth, feven fhillings a thoufand : at Birmingham eight to ten fhillings : yet at thofe prices one gardener fells, even when no public inclo. fures are going forward, three or four hun. dred thoufands annually.

The moft judicious planter I met with in the diftrifts, and from whom, with the garden- er here alluded to, I had thefe particulars, chufes his plants at four years old, tranf- planted at two ; and cares not how rich a foil they are raifed in.

The *time of planting*, here, is not unfre- quently autumn. I had an opportunity of making a comparative obfervation, on a neighbour's practice, between plants fet in autumn, and others planted, in continuation of the fame hedge, in fpring. The autumnal planting, *in this cafe*, had a decided prefer- ence. But the fituation was fomewhat dry ; and the fpring and fummer proved fo like- wife :—under thefe circumftances autumnal planting will generally fucceed beft,

The

The *method of planting* has been said to be that of putting the plants into a broad flat mound : generally planting *two rows*, ten or twelve inches apart, and a similar distance from the brink of the trench, by the side of which they are planted.

The reason given for this mode of planting is, that a deep ditch makes a high heavy bank, and this " overloads the roots."

There is, no doubt, some truth in this reasoning. Plants never thrive so well as on level ground, provided they are not incommoded by standing water: see YORK. ECON.: and the disadvantages of a high heavy bank have been pointed out in the NORF. ECON.: but it is a fact, evident in various parts of the kingdom, and particularly in my own practice in three different and distant parts of it, that hedges may be raised with success in the front of a high bank ; and that its disadvantages are by no means equal to the advantage gained by a deep ditch and high bank, as a defence to the rising hedge.

Two rows of posts and rails are here the common guard : incurring an expence equal to twice that of a deep ditch

G 4   and

and banklet on one fide, and a high bank
and hedge on the other. If the hedge be
planted behind a fhelf of fufficient width,
and part of the mould of the ditch be applied in forming a banklet on its outer brink,
the load incurred by the remainder is little,
if any, impediment to the progrefs of the
young hedge.

For the method and expence of planting
a hedge in this manner, See MIN. 123.

The *nurfing* of young hedges, a bufinefs
which, in moft parts of the kingdom, is in
a manner totally neglected, is in many cafes
well attended to here. They are pretty generally weeded, and, in fome inftances, hoed :
in others, however, they are here, as in other
places, feen ftruggling among weeds ;—
principally of the following fpecies.

I enumerate them here, as I paid more
attention to hedgeweeds in this, than in
any other, diftrict : and though they vary,
in fome degree, in different places, they are,
upon the whole, very much the fame in all.

HEDGEWEEDS

Hedgeweeds of the Midland District.

Weeds of young Hedges.

Couch grass and other grasses *.
The thistles, particularly the spear thistle;
The docks;
The nettle;
Sowthistles;
Hawkweeds; and a variety of small weeds,
which rob the plants of their nourishment,
and ought to be cut off with the hoe, so
often as they rise.

The convolvolus;

The blue-tufted vetch, and other vetches;
and

The cleavers, and other climbing plants,
are a burden to the taller more upright
shoots.

In low moist situations,

The meadow sweet;

The

---

* I have seen, in this district, quick planted, across
a foul arable inclosure, in a bed of couch! Nothing can
be greater folly. The other grasses may be destroyed
with the hoe; but scarcely any art can free young hedge
plants from couch; which ought, at any cost, to be destroyed before the hedge be planted.

The wild angelica;

The willowherbs (epilobia);

The perficarias, &c. &c. are almoft certain fuffocation to weak plants, the firft and fecond years, if not repeatedly removed by hand, fo often as they threaten the injury of the infant hedge.

Weeds of older Hedges.

The briar;

The bramble;

The woodbine;

The bitterfweet (folanum dulcamara);

Black briony (tamus communis); and in fome places, the white briony (bryonia alba); and the

Traveller's joy (clematis vitalba); are very deftructive to hedges; efpecially if fuffered to grow up with them, either in the firft inftance, or after the hedge has been cut down.

They ought therefore, in both cafes, to be eradicated, or at leaft cut out and kept under, until the hedge be free from injury.

THE TREATMENT OF GROWN HEDGES. *Plafhing* may be called the univerfal practice of this diftrict. Neverthelefs, I have obferved a few inftances of cutting hedges,

that

that do not come within the defcription of plafhing.

In this practice; one row of ftems, if double quicked, is cut to the ftub, the other, hedge height; not level off, or all of the fame height, but in fuch a manner as to lean back, away from the ftubs of the fallen row; cutting thofe which ftand fore-moft the loweft, and fuch as lean or branch away from them, the higheft; leaving the back fpray on, to form a blind, and affift to make a fence.

Under this management, two rows of quick are evidently preferable to a fingle row; for although I have feen fingle quick treated fomewhat in this manner, efpecially in Derbyfhire, the effect is very different. In this cafe the ftools and the ftems are fed from the fame roots; the fame fet of fibres; and the ftems with the fpray left upon them, rob the lower fhoots, from which the new fence is to rife, of a great part of their fap. While in the other, the ftools not only ftand diftinct from the ftems, but have a diftinct fet of roots to fupport them, entirely inde-pendent of the ftems left ftanding as a tem-porary fence.

The

The *methods of plaſhing* are various : the
old and ſtill moſt prevailing method is to
leave paof the ſtems ſtanding, as " live
ſtakes"; between which the plaſhers are in-
terwoven, in the uſual manner.

Judicious managers, however, object, and
with good reaſon, to live ſtakes; which,
throwing out ſpreading heads, in the
pollard manner, overhang and deſtroy the
plaſhers, and prevent the ſhoots of the
ſtools from riſing : conſequently tending to
convert the hedge into a row of thorn pollard ;
in which ſtate old hedges, that have been
thus treated, are too evidently ſeen. On
the contrary, when the entire hedge is cut
down, or crippled as plaſhers, to the ſtub,
the plaſhers have no impediment, and the
young ſhoots are the leſs incommoded in as
much as the plaſhers ſhoot leſs luxuriantly
than the ſtakes. Still, however, the ſhoots
from the ſtools, the only offspring of the
old hedge from which a new one can
be expected, are greatly injured by the
plaſhers overſpreading them.

Hence an improvement has been ſtruck
out, in this diſtrict, which probably raiſes
the art of plaſhing to its higheſt degree

of

of perfection. This is effected, by driving the dead ftakes, not in a line with the ftubs, but fome foot or more behind them, and by winding the plafhers among them, and eddering them, according to the cuftom of this country, with brambles, leave the fhoots from the ftubs the fame air and headroom, or nearly the fame, as if the whole were cut down, and a dead hedge raifed behind them.

The advantage of this method of plafhing, compared with the practice of felling the whole to the ftub, is, that a live hedge, which improves by age, is raifed, inftead of a dead one, which grows worfe every year. The difadvantage, that of part of the fap (of fingle hedges) being drawn away from the young fhoots; which, in this cafe, are left lefs free and open, than when the whole of the ftems are cleared away at the ftub.

However, where there are a fufficiency of young pliable ftems for plafhers, and the ditch does not require much repair, the plafhing here defcribed may have, upon the whole, the preference; efpecially if the plafhers, when the young hedge has got up, be removed from their interference with the upright fhoots.

But,

But, where the hedge has been neglected, the ſtems are grown few and large, particularly where vacancies require to be filled up by layers or otherwiſe, and the ditch requires to be new made,—felling to the ſtub is indiſputably preferable.

It is obſervable, however, that in the diſtrict under ſurvey, the ditch is rarely remade, and but ſeldom ſcoured : even where the ſoil is retentive ; and a ditch, of courſe, neceſſary to good management.

The *reaſoning*, in this caſe, is the ſame as in that of planting by a narrow ditch : namely, the fear of " overloading the roots !" In that caſe there may be ſome ſhadow of truth ; but in this, in which the roots are feeding ſeveral feet from the bank, there is probably not the leaſt foundation. The practice, no doubt, originates in indolence or falſe economy.

This cenſure, however, is not intended to be paſſed indiſcriminately. There are many individuals, who are aware of the utility of open ditches, in freeing their lands from ſurface water.

REFERENCES

REFERENCES to the MINUTES on FENCES.

For the principles of *Gatehanging*, fee MIN. 36.

For obfervations on making *Sodbanks*, fee MIN. 49.

For further obfervations on *Hanging gates*, fee MIN. 54.

For an inftance of practice in *Hedgeplanting*, fee MIN. 123.

For a proof of the nuifance of *wide hedges*, fee MIN. 131.

For obfervations on water ftanding againft *live hedges*, fee MIN. 132.

For remarks on the *weeding of hedges*, fee MIN. 152.

For obfervations on the nature of the root of the *hawthorn*, and on *rippling hedge banks*, fee MIN. 159.

For a proof of the nuifance of *high hedges*, fee MIN. 160.

For further Obfervations on *high hedges*, fee MIN. 161.

For the probable origin of *crooked hedges*, fee MIN. 162.

HEDGEROW

6.

HEDGEROW TIMBER.

FEW DISTRICTS are lo thin of hedgerow timber as this. The old enclofed townfhips have a tolerable fhare, but the new inclofures, which, with the open fields that yet
remain, conftitute a principal part of the
Midland Diftrict, are as naked, to the diftant
eye, as the downs of Surrey, or the wolds of
Yorkfhire. LEICESTERSHIRE, more particularly, ftands in this predicament. There is not,
fpeaking generally, a young oak in the
county. If this error fhould not be rectified,
there may not, in half a century, be a tree
left in a townfhip.

This poverty in hedgerow timber has probably arifen, partly in neglect, but much
more in a rooted antipathy, among occupiers, againft trees in hedges. The mifchiefs
of the afh and elm, and low fpreading oaks,
having been experienced, all fpecies have
been indifcriminately profcribed.

The

The afh, the elm, and lowheaded oaks, are indifputably mifchievous in hedges—injurious to the occupier, and deftructive to the hedge.—But oaks trained in the manner which I have repeatedly recommended *,—while they enhance, in a very high degree, the value of an eftate, do, comparatively, little injury to the occupier, and but very little to the hedge.

The DISTRICT of the STATION furnifhes an inftance of the latter part, at leaft, of the above affertion. The road through an entire townfhip (I believe)—Grindon—the refidence of Lady Robert Bertie—has on each fide of it a line of tall ftemmed trees, moftly oaks, rifing in a trimmed hawthorn hedge; which, far from being deftroyed by them, flourifhes with extraordinary vigour; clofely embracing the ftems of the trees; a fence againft any thing.

The lowheaded *pollard* is feldom feen in the hedges of the old inclofures of this diftrict; which, however, fometimes exhibit a ftill more aukward object: a kind of tall, and moftly crooked ftump—a fomething between

* PLANTING and ORN. GARD. and NORF. ECON.

tween a tree and a pollard;—with frequently a fingle fmall bough, left on one
fide of its top! as if the owner, having re-
pented of his folly, were endeavouring to
convert the *object* into a tree again.

For the method of taking down, &c. fee ·
the next article.

For an inftance of practice in *training*
hedge oaklings, fee MIN. 155.

7.

WOODLANDS.

VIEWING THE MIDLAND COUN-
TIES generally, they are ftill fufficiently
wooded; although there has, within memory, been an undoubted decreafe.—Cham-
wood Foreft has not, figuratively fpeaking,
a ftick left in it; though, within the prefent
century, much of the ancient foreft remained.
Many fmaller plots of woodland, and townfhips of well wooded hedges, have been
cleared away, within the laft fifty years.

There

There is little danger, however, of the district suffering through a want of TIM-BER.—WARWICKSHIRE, STAFFORDSHIRE, and DERBYSHIRE, are still fully wooded; LEICESTERSHIRE, with the private woods scattered round the skirts of the forest, and on the borders of RUTLANDSHIRE, has *yet* a sufficiency left to supply its internal consumption.

But with respect to COPPICE WOOD, many parts of Leicestershire, more particularly, must even now feel a want, and experience many inconveniencies, which a distribution of coppices would remove. It is true, that many of these woodless parts are too valuable, as grass or arable land, to be converted, on a large scale, into coppice grounds. Nevertheless, there are, in most townships, cold patches of soil, less productive of corn and grass, and angles in the outline of every estate, which might be profitably planted with coppice wood.

The DISTRICT of the STATION is in a manner surrounded by woodlands, and, during my residence in it, I collected, through this and other circumstances, more information respecting their management, than in any

other

other I have refided in. The fubject, therefore, requires, in this place, efpecial attention.

The information obtained claffes under the
following fubdivifions :

1. Raifing.   4. Timber.
2. Selling.   5. Bark.
3. Taking down.   6. Coppice.

I. RAISING. It is more than probable, that
moft of the private woods, which we fee, at
prefent, fcattered over the ifland, have been
raifed by art ; and that they are not, as they
are generally fuppofed to be, remnants of
the ancient forefts, or native woods.

In the old woods of this quarter of the
kingdom, it is pretty generally obfervable,
that the north and eaftern margins abound
with afh, while the body of the wood is principally oak ; and it is believed that the afh,
being a quick-mounting tree, was propagated
there as a fcreen to the oaklings *. This is
a circumftantial evidence of their being raifed
by art : while the *evident veftiges of the plow*,
in other inftances, are proofs of the pofition ;
at leaft as to thefe inftances.

But

* But fee MIN. 166.

But the practice of PROPAGATING WOOD-LANDS (I mean ordinary woodlands of oak, afh, or other native woods) can be traced by circumftances only, in every part of this ifland I have obferved in, excepting NORTH WAR-WICKSHIRE; where the practice may be faid to be at prefent in ufe. Several young woods are now getting up from acorns and other tree feeds, fown by the hands of men now living. Yet their appearance to the eye, on the clofeft examination, is the fame as that which we obferve in cafes where the proof is lefs pofitive.

The MODE OF PROPAGATION is that of fowing acorns, keys, &c. with the feeds of corn; or of dibbling them into grafsland; as will more fully appear in MIN. 124.

II. SELLING TIMBER TREES. The prefent mode of difpofal is by auction,—as it ftands:—a mode always to be recommended, for reafons already given. See YORK. ECON. i. 241.

The method of VALUING timber. The only circumftance which requires to be mentioned, here, is that of valuing the timber and bark feparately;—keeping two diftinct accounts. This is done by the timber mer-

H 3   chant

chant when he fells the bark to the tanner
by fuch valuation: a practice which is not
uncommon: the tanner, of courfe, making
his counter valuation of the bark only. Vague
as this mode of valuation may feem, and various as the proportions between the timber
and the bark of different trees really are,
there are men, accuftomed to this mode of
eftimation, who, it feems, will come very
near the truth.

For inftances of the mode of difpofal,—
conditions of fale, &c ,fee the MINUTES referred to below.

III. TAKING DOWN TIMBER TREES,
Three methods of felling are here in ufe:

> Stocking,
> Axe-grubbing, and
> Axe-falling.

STOCKING (a provincial term for grubbing,
or digging with a mattock, &c.) is a kind of
partial grubbing. The roots are cut through,
a foot or more from the ftem; and, again, a
foot or more from the inner cutting; taking
up a fhort length of the thickeft part of the
roots, and digging a trench round the tree,
wide enough to come at the downward roots.

AXE-

AXE-GRUBBING is fimilar *to* the Norfolk *grubbing* (fee Norf. Econ.), only the end of the but is left larger here than in Norfolk.

AXE-FALLING is the common method of Yorkfhire and other places, of cutting off, aboveground, with the axe:—a method which is feldom practifed; except in fome few cafes, where another crop of timber or coppice wood is intended to be taken.

Stocking is the prevailing method;—the PRICE FOR TAKING DOWN varying with the fize of the tree: for a tree of two feet diameter, the price is about a fhilling; and about four pence more for cutting off the but; the ftocking and butting being generally let together.

PEELING BARK. The *Peeling Tool* commonly made ufe of, here, is of *bone*. The thigh and the fhin bone of an afs are preferred. The former (a two-handed inftrument) for the ftem and the larger boughs; the latter, for the fmaller branches. The handle, a crutched piece of wood, fixed in the end of the bone. The point once given, by the grinding ftone, or a rafp, keeps itfelf fharp by wear.

H 4   The

The ARMS or BOUGHS are cut up into
posts, rails, and " *cordwood*," for CHARCOAL.
The price for cutting and setting up cordwood is about two shillings a cord of " yardwood." A " statute cord" measures four
feet high, four feet wide, and eight feet
long. But four feet lengths being inconvenient to the charcoal burners, it is generally
cut into lengths of three feet; consequently
a cord of yardwood is only three fourths of
a statute cord *.

The SPRAY is generally formed into
fagots, provincially " kids,"—the price
for " kidding" a shilling a load of sixty
kids; or, if the workman finds bindings,
fifteen or sixteen pence a load.

IV. TIMBER. The consumption of the
timber grown in this central part of the
island (excepting the Banks of the Trent)
falls chiefly among inland dealers..

In a maritime country, the trees are carried bodily to the ship yard : here, they are
mostly divided, in the places of their growth,
into a variety of wares; hence, the business
of

* The STATUTE CORD of this country, therefore, agrees
pretty nearly with the STACK of the southern counties;
though their dimensions are very different.

of cutting up— provincially and properly termed "converting" timber,—is, here, conducted in a fuperior manner; a quick judgment of the proper wares, into which a given tree ought to be converted, requiring much practice.

The wares, into which the timber of this neighbourhood are converted, will appear in the MINUTES.

V. BARK. Oak bark is difpofed of in two different ways: one of them peculiar, perhaps, to this diftrict; in which, as has been faid, it is fometimes valued upon the tree; the wood merchant carrying on two valuations; one of the timber, the other of the bark; felling it to the tanner, who likewife makes his eftimate, by the lump.

The other mode of difpofal is the common one of felling it by the ton, in the rough: the method of weighing it, or rather of eftimating its weight, is, however, noticeable. The bark having been fet up in the ufual manner, but with more than common care as to evennefs of quantity, againft horizontal poles or treffels; and having ftood fome nine or ten days, more or lefs, according to the weather, until it be fit to

carry,

carry, the buyer choofes one, two, three, or a greater number of yards in one place, and the feller a like number in another. Thefe yards of bark are weighed, and the reft meafured and eftimated accordingly *,

VI. COPPICE WOOD. The two principal coppices, of the Diftrict of the Station, are thofe of Seal and Hopwas; the former in Derbyfhire; the latter in Staffordfhire.

The *age* at which coppice wood is cut in this part of the kingdom varies much with the intended ware. For *pofts, rails,* and *coal-wood,* twenty years or upward are requifite to bring the wood to fufficient fize. But for the fmaller wares, into which the produce of the coppices of this neighbourhood are chiefly converted, they are felled much oftener.

The prevailing wares are *ftakes, edders, hurdles, brooms,* and *cratewood*; the laft a fpecies of coppice ware I have not met with before; but which is here a confiderable article: the Staffordfhire potteries working up no fmall quantity of wood in making their various packages.

In

* The fame eftimation being taken by the tanner and the peelers.

In this quarter of the island; especially on the Staffordshire side of the district; where iron forges abound, CHARCOAL becomes an object of considerable magnitude to the woodman. I had an opportunity, here, of paying close attention to the process of burning it; as will appear in the MINUTES.

For the practice and profit of *cultivating oak woods*, see MIN. 124.

For instances of neglect in the *training* of *young oak woods*, 125.

For instances of *oak woods* being disfoliated by the *chafer*, see MIN. 126.

For the process of making *charcoal*, see MIN. 127.

For remarks on *seedling oaks* rising spontaneously in grassland, see 128.

For further obs. on the *chafer*, 129.

For the consequent *appearance* of the oak, see MIN. 130.

For obs. on the *growth* of the *ash*, 133.

For obs. on the *growth* of the *elm*, 134.

For obs. on the *growth* of the *poplar*, 135.

For an account of the *sale* of Merevale timber, see MIN. 136.

For obs. on the *rise of the sap* in old timber oaks, see MIN. 137.

For

For

For farther obf. on the *cultivated woodlands* of North Warwickſhire, fee 156.

For remarks on *banging woods*, fee MIN. 157.

For an evidence of the experience requiſite in the buſineſs of *converting* timber, 158.

For remarks on the advantage of woods on *rock*, fee MIN. 158.

For the *ſale* of Statfold aſh and elm, 163.

For remarks on adapting perennial plants to ſoils and ſituations, 164.

For inſtance of practice in *converting* oak timber, 165.

For remarks on the *age*, &c. of aſh and elm, 166.

For a defcription of the *Middleton oak*, 167.

PLANTING

8.

P L A N T I N G.

THE ART OF PLANTING is feparable from that of raifing woodlands in a more natural and fimple way, immediately from the feed. This is a fummary operation, like that of fowing a crop of corn, or laying down land with grafs feeds. The other a progreffive work; confifting of various nice and difficult operations; both in the NURSERY and in the PLANTATION. Neverthelefs PLANTING. is, at this day, the prevailing mode of propagating trees; whether for USE or for ORNAMENT.

With a view to mere utility, however, PLANTING, except in HEDGEROWS, can rarely be adopted with propriety. But where ornament is a joint, or the principal object, planting is in moft cafes eligible.

It is not my intention to introduce the fubject of RURAL ORNAMENT, in a work of

RURAL ECONOMY. Neverthelefs, the ART OF PLANTING, which is applicable, on many occafions, to USE as well as ORNAMENT, is profeffedly a branch of the prefent work.

Planting is indeed an art to which I have long been partial, and on which I have, at different times, beftowed confiderable attention.

Some years ago, I digefted my ideas on the fubject, and revifed them, in the prefs, during my refidence in this diftrict *.

Warm with the fubject, and wifhing to extend my practice, I undertook, while I was *improving* this eftate, to *ornament* it.

How far I have fucceeded, the place itfelf muft fpeak. What I purpofe to convey in thefe volumes are fome practical obfervations on PLANTING : an art which my fuccefs has led me to believe I have in fome meafure advanced.

But thefe remarks being on my own practice, they will appear with moft propriety in the fecond volume. See the MINUTES referred to below.

The

* See PLANTING and ORNAMENTAL GARDENING, a Practical Treatife ; in one volume octavo.

The plantations of this diftrict are few, and afford little information on the fubject.—Excepting thofe at Fisherwick, done under the direction of the late Mr. Brown, few have fucceeded well. But, in every part of the ifland, we fee fimilar mifcarriages in planting : a proof that the art is not generally underftood, or not fufficiently attended to.

The only circumftance that requires to be noticed, refpecting the practice of planting in this diftrict, is that of the nurferyman's *infuring* the plants the firft year. That is, if they do not grow, he furnifhes his cuftomers with frefh ones in their ftead : and this whether he plants them himfelf, or leaves it to others to put them in ; provided that in the latter cafe they follow his directions.

This practice, I underftand, was firft eftablifhed by a nurferyman of Coventry ; but has fince, through a kind of neceffity, been adopted by other nurferymen.

Where the nurferyman is employed to put in his own plants, this is a *reafonable* practice ; but, when we confider how much depends on the operation of planting, it can fcarcely be be deemed fuch to infure the fuccefs of others.

For a detail of my own practice in the fpring of 1785, fee MIN. 146.

For inftances of the want of fuccefs in planting in the dry fpring of 1785, fee MIN. 148.

For farther remarks on my own practice in 1785, fee 153.

For remarks on the advantage of planting fteep flope, fee 157.

For a detail of my own practice in the autumn of 1785, and the fpring of 1786, fee MIN. 168.

9.

F A R M S.

THE SIZE OF FARMS, throughout the MIDLAND DISTRICT, is large, confidering the quality of the foil.

The DISTRICT of the STATION contains fome capital farms. *Bramcot, Pooley, Alncot, Amington, Sievfcot, Hopfhill, Dunnimeer, Statfold, Thorp, Seckington,* &c. &c. lying immediately in *this* neighbourhood, rank among the firft clafs of farms in the kingdom. Moft of them three to four or five hundred acres of land, worth twenty to twentyfive fhillings an acre.

Thefe farms are fituated in the old inclofed parts of the diftrict. How they have been aggregated to their prefent fize is not obvious. Probably, they have never been in the ftate of common field. Formerly, much of them lay in large — " feeding pieces"—grazing grounds—of fifty or fixty acres each. This accounts for the prefent ftraightnefs of many

of

of the hedges. Some of them are extraparochial; and may be subdivisions of townships given, by the feudal lords, to their dependants. This, however, by the way.

The CHARACTERISTIC OF FARMS varies of course with their state as to inclosure. The open township, as well as those which have been recently inclosed, are mostly in a state of aration.

The farms of the older inclosures, of which only I shall speak, are much of them in grass; being subjected, in the manner which will be shown, to an alternacy of grass and arable.

10.

FARMERS.

EVERY DISTRICT has its leading men; its " capital farmers :" their proportionate number varying, in some degree at least, with the size of farms prevalent within it, and the state of husbandry at which it has arrived.

I 2   These

Thefe men confift either of TENANTS, whofe fathers, having profited by their good management, have left their fons fufficient capitals and knowledge to increafe them; or of the fuperior clafs of YEOMANRY, cultivating, in continuation, their paternal eftates.

This clafs of occupiers have many advantages over the lower orders of hufbandmen. They travel much; efpecially thofe whofe principal object is livestock. They are led to diftant markets, and perhaps to the metropolis. They fee, of courfe, various modes of management, and mix in various companies: confifting not merely of men of their own profeffion: men of fortune and fcience have, of late years, admitted them into their company: and to their mutual advantage.

Thus their prejudices are worn off, their knowledge enlarged, and their difpofitions rendered liberal and communicative, in a degree which thofe, who have not mixed and converfed freely with them, are not aware of.

The MIDLAND DISTRICT may boaft of a greater number of this defcription of men, than

than any other I have yet been over;
and we may, I apprehend, venture to add
without rifque, than any diftrict of equal extent in the kingdom. It is not only a large-
farm and grazing country; but the fpirit of
breeding, which has gone forth of late years,
has infufed an ardour and exertion among
them, unobfervable in other diftricts. Except in Yorkfhire, I have found the spirit of improvement now here fo high.

Befides thefe, many of the midland farmers have had other two, great advantages,
of which farmers in general are in want.

Formerly, and ftill in many diftricts,
yeomen and farmers, who were able and wil-
ling to educate their fons, did it folely with
a view to fit them for trade, or enable them
to follow one or other of what are emphatically termed the *prof-ffions.* Being educated,
they were of courfe incapacitated for farmers!

Not fo, however, in this country. There
are men, now at the middle age of life, who
have had a regular school education; and
who, inftead of being fent out of the country to a trade, or a " profeffion," have been

I 3 placed

placed as PUPILS, with superior farmers, at
some distance from their fathers' residences.
Thus not only improving their knowledge
by a double tuition, but breaking off, in
their tender state, those attachments to customs, right or wrong, which those, who have
seen only one mode of management, are too
liable to form.

Hence, we find this description of men
not only ADOPTING such IMPROVEMENTS as
have gained a degree of establishment, but
striking out others by EXPERIMENT, and still
farther enlarging their ideas by READING:
and this with little danger of being misled.
Their judgements are in a degree formed.
They have a basis to build on.

Among the rising generation, and in a
very few years, we may expect to find numbers of this class of occupiers. Almost every
substantial farmer, now, educates his sons,
and brings up one or more to *his own profession.*

If ever agriculture be brought near to
perfection, this is the class of men who must
raise it. MEN OF FORTUNE may, and ought
for their own interest, to *encourage* and *promote,* for with them, eventually, center the
profits

profits of improvement. But the SUPERIOR CLASS of PROFESSIONAL MEN muſt *ſuggeſt* and *execute* [*].

With reſpect to the LOWER CLASSES of HUSBANDMEN, who form the main body of occupiers, their buſineſs is to *follow*: and, if the men, whom they are in the habit of looking up to, lead the way, though it may be ſlowly, they are ſure to follow.

Thus improvements, ſtruck out and effected, by the ſuperior claſs of profeſſional occupiers, are introduced into common practice; while thoſe of unprofeſſional men, if they merit adoption, die for want of being properly matured; or, if raiſed into individual practice, ſeldom become ſerviceable to the community at large.

The great bulk of occupiers conſider every man who has not been bred up in the habits
I 4   of

---

[*] By PROFESSIONAL MEN, I do not mean thoſe, only, who have been bred up to huſbandry from their youth. There are men, in every quarter of the kingdom, who, having attended *perſonally*, and *cloſely*, during a courſe of years, to the *minutiæ* of huſbandry, *as a profeſſion*, are of courſe become PROFESSIONAL: and many MEN OF FORTUNE, who, having paid a ſimilar kind of attention to PRACTICE, have acquired, of courſe, a ſimilar kind of PRACTICAL KNOWLEDGE.

of hufbandry, or enured to them by long
practice, as a vifionary; and are more in-
clined to fneer at his plans, than adopt them,
though ever fo excellent.

Hence, probably, the inefficacy of the numerous SOCIETIES of agriculture, which
have been formed, in various parts of the
kingdom. There is only one, that of BATH,
which, from all the information that has
come within my knowledge, has been in any
confiderable degree fuccefsful; and the fuccefs of this, probably, has been, in fome degree at leaft, owing to the profeffional men
who belong to it.

Societies formed of PROFESSIONAL MEN,
encouraged and *affifted* by the LANDED INTE-
REST, could not fail of being beneficial, in
promoting the rural affairs of thefe kingdoms; and the MIDLAND COUNTIES, whether from centrality of fituation, or from
the number of fuperior managers in it, are
fingularly eligible for fuch a fociety.

But SOCIETIES, on the plan which has hitherto been adopted, though they were to
be formed of profeffional men under the patronage of the landed intereft, would ftill
be, in their nature, little more than *theoreti-
cal,*

cal. Mere focieties want the *fubject* before them. Their moft probable good effect could be that of affimilating, by frequent meetings, the fentiments of the PROPRIETORS and the OCCUPIERS of lands: thereby encrea-fing the neceffary confidence between them; and thus far, of courfe, becoming effentially ferviceable to their common intereft. But they fall far fhort of being the moft eligible inftitutions, for the advancement of rural knowledge.

In the Digeft of the MINUTES OF AGRICUL-TURE, on the fubject PUBLIC AGRICULTURE, I propofed an eftablifhment of AGRICUL-TURAL COLLEGES, to be diftributed in dif-ferent diftricts, as SEMINARIES of RURAL KNOWLEDGE.

It is now more than twelve years fince that propofal was written, during which time my attention has been bent, unremittingly, on rural fubjects. and the refult is, that I now fee, ftill more evidently, the want of RURAL SEMINARIES.

The feminaries there propofed are, however, on too large a fcale for any thing lefs than NATIONAL eftablifhment; and COMMERCE, rather than AGRICULTURE, appears to engage,

engage, at prefent, the more immediate
attention of GOVERNMENT; and this notwithftanding the prefent fcarcity of corn is
fuch, that we are afking, even the AMERI-
CANS, for a fupply; and notwithftanding a
very confiderable part of the CATTLE, which
now come to market, are the produce of
IRELAND. See MIN. 122.

I have already faid, in the courfe of this
work, that it is not my intention to obtrude
my fentiments, unfeemingly, on NATIONAL
CONCERNS; but poffeffed of the mafs of information, which, in the nature of my purfuit,
I muft neceffarily have accumulated,—no
man, *perhaps*, having had a fimilar opportunity,—I think it a duty I owe to fociety,
and an infeparable part of my prefent undertaking, to regifter fuch ideas, whether national or profeffional, as refult, aptly and fairly, out of the fubject before me : and, in this
place, I think it right to intimate the probable
advantage which might arife from a BOARD
OF AGRICULTURE;—or, more generally,
of RURAL AFFAIRS; to take cognizance,
not of the ftate and promotion of AGRICUL-
TURE, merely; but alfo of the CULTIVA-
TION OF WASTES and the PROPAGATION OF
TIMBER;

TIMBER: bafes, on which, not commerce only, but the political exiftence of the nation is founded. And when may this country expect a more favourable opportunity, than the prefent, of laying a broad and firm bafis of its future profperity?

The ESTABLISHMENTS, I am now about to propofe, might be formed by INDIVIDUALS, in various parts of the kingdom; and might readily be raifed into PRACTICE.

The SITUATION of an eftablifhment of this nature ought to be (though not necef-farily) upon a confiderable landed eftate; as five thoufand acres of tolerable foil.

The immediate SITE might confift of five hundred acres, more or lefs; laid out into TWO FARMS, or general divifions;—the one ECONOMICAL, the other EXPERIMENTAL *.

The ECONOMICAL divifion to be efta-blifhed, in the outfet, on the beft practice of the diftrict it may lie in; and to be con-ducted

* If the MANAGEMENT OF ESTATES, including PLANTING, RURAL ARCHITECTURE, &c. &c. fhould form parts of the eftablifhment, an ESTATE would be in a degree requifite. But, if it were confined to AGRI-CULTURE, folely, a FARM, only, would be wanted.

ducted on the most rigid principles of pe-
cuniary advantage.

The EXPERIMENTAL part to be appropriated, chiefly, to HUSBANDRY, with a
compartment for PLANTING, and another
for BOTANY.

The part appropriated to PLANTING to consist of a NURSERY GROUND, and such corner
or screen PLANTATIONS, as may be wanted
for the use of the estate: the intention being
that of making experiments on the propagation of WOODLANDS and HEDGES; as well
as that of raising NEW VARIETIES of trees
and hedgewoods.

The BOTANIC GARDEN to receive a collection of NATIVE PLANTS, as well as
of the several VARIETIES of CULTIVATED
PLANTS, whether native or exotic: its intended use being that of a SCHOOL of
BOTANY; as well as that of raising NEW
VARIETIES of the agricultural plants already
cultivated; and of endeavouring to discover,
among the uncultivated species, FRESH
PLANTS, fit for the purpose of cultivation.

The rest to be appropriated to EXPERI-
MENTS in HUSBANDRY; on the several departments of the ARABLE and the GRASS-

LAND

LAND management; as well as on LIVE-STOCK;—a moft interefting fubject of experiment; as will appear fully, under that head, at the clofe of this volume.

The ufe of this compartment requires not to be explained. It may, however, be proper to fay, that the general intention propofes, as the main purport of the eftablifhment, that, as an operation, a procefs, or a general principle, fhall be fully *proved* by experiment (but not before, however *plaufible* it may be in theory), it fhall be transferred to the part purely economical, and be there *regiftered* as an IMPROVEMENT of the eftablifhed practice.

The BUILDINGS of the two farms to be diftinct. Thofe of the economical, the ordinary farm buildings which may be fuppofed to be on the premifes. Thofe of the experimental to confift of

A FARMERY, or regular fuite of farm buildings, on the beft plan, and in the beft ftyle of rural architecture, at prefent known; endeavouring to unite, as far as fituation and materials will permit, fimplicity and conveniency with cheapnefs and durability.

A REPO-

A REPOSITORY OF IMPLEMENTS, and MODELS of farm buildings, fences, gates, &c. Not the ingenious fabrics of theory; but such as are admitted into the established practice of the different districts of the island; or such as have been, otherwise, *fully proved*, by a continued course of practice: in order, that, by bringing the whole under the eye, regularly arranged and duly classed, their comparative merit may be more readily ascertained; and the judgement be, of course, assisted, in selecting such as may be best adapted to a given soil and situation. With a MANUFACTORY OF IMPLEMENTS; for the more easy dissemination of those which are already proved to be superiorly useful; as well as for the construction of such NEW IMPLEMENTS as invention may suggest. And with a TRIALGROUND adjoining; for the purpose of testing new implements (when no other ground may be at leisure), and for regulating, and setting to work, those to be transferred to distant districts; that less impediment may arise when they reach the intended places of practice.

An EXPERIMENTERY, for analyzing SOILS and MANURES, investigating the VEGETA-
BLE

BLE and ANIMAL ECONOMY; and, generally, for the study of the more abstruse branches of the science.

A LIBRARY, for the reception of books on RURAL SUBJECTS; as well as of those on every other subject, which may serve to elucidate RURAL KNOWLEDGE.

A LECTURE ROOM, for the purpose of instructing PUPILS in the PRINCIPLES of the RURAL SCIENCE; whether they arise out of NATURAL or SCIENTIFIC KNOWLEDGE.

The PROFESSORS, requisite to such an establishment, would be a PRINCIPAL, to form and conduct, with such ASSISTANTS, as circumstances would readily point out, when the scale and the departments were determined.

But, Who would wish to have such an incumbrance upon his estate? and, What individual would be at the expence of such an establishment?

Such questions would be futile.

Rather let it be asked, Who would not wish to have the rural knowledge of the island collected upon his estate? and, What liberal mind, especially if bent to agricultural pursuits, would not be gratified in seeing improvements, in the first art and science the

human

human mind can be employed upon, growing daily under his eye? and, What man, who
regards the interest of his family, would not
wish to see the best cultivated farm in the
kingdom upon his estate; and, of course, in
due time, to be in possession of the best cultivated estate in the kingdom?

This, alone, might be a sufficient recom-
pence for the original expence; which would,
in all probability, be repaid, with still greater
interest, by the PUPILS which such an establishment would, with a degree of moral certainty, draw together.

The present premium given with a farm
pupil to an *individual*, varies with the ability
or character of the tutor, and with the treatment the pupil expects to receive. The usual
term is four years, and the premium forty to
two hundred pounds. With the first, they
are treated as a superior kind of *servants*; with
the latter, as *affistants*.

What man, whether of the superior class
of yeomanry or tenants, or of the superior
class of tradesmen or others, who are now
bringing up their sons to husbandry, would
not, after his son had gone through a course
of private tuition, and received the rudi-

ments

ments of inftruction, from himfelf or fome profeffional friend, wifh to perfect his education in a public feminary;—where he would have, not only an opportunity of feeing PRACTICE in its higheft ftate of improvement, and of converfing with PROFESSIONAL MEN of the moft enlightened underftanding; but where he would be duly initiated in the THEORY of rural knowledge: in the method of making, regiftering, and obferving the refult of EXPERIMENTS; of afcertaining the natural qualities of SOILS and MANURES; of improving the varieties of CULTIVATED CROPS, as well as of afcertaining the inherent qualities, and improving the various breeds, of LIVESTOCK; where he would fee order and fubordination, and learn the proper treatment of SERVANTS; and among a variety of other branches of ufeful knowledge, the form and method of keeping farm ACCOUNTS, and of afcertaining, with accuracy, the profit or lofs upon the whole and every part of his bufinefs; confequently, of bringing it as nearly, as in its nature it is capable of being brought, to a degree of certainty.

And what poffeffor of landed property would not wifh to have the heir of his eftate initiated, at leaft, not in the management of ESTATES only, but in the proper management of FARMS; without a knowledge of which, no man can be a judge of the proper management of an eftate: a part of education, as effentially requifite to an heir of landed property, as the acquirements of political knowledge are to the heir of a kingdom. Indeed, the more immediate happinefs of a principal part of every nation depends rather on the poffeffors of eftates, than on the poffeffor of the crown. And it is a fact incontrovertible, that, in either cafe, the refpectability and perfonal happinefs of the poffeffor will ever be reciprocal with thofe of *the people*; on which alone they can be built, with firmnefs and full fecurity. Surely, then, a branch of knowledge, which naturally leads the poffeffor of a landed eftate to live in the hearts of his tenants, can be no mean acquirement.

WORKMEN.

II.

WORKMEN.

DAY LABOURERS may be faid to be fcarce, in this diftrict.

Neverthelefs *wages* are moderate. In regard to difpatch, they are much below par; and in what may be termed the honeft pride of workmen, very deficient.

The YEARLY SERVANTS are, of courfe, proportioned to the number of labourers in the given neighbourhood.

Their *wages* are very low. Seven or eight pounds the ordinary wages of a man fervant; ten pounds the higheft. A woman three guineas. Not much more than half the wages given in Yorkfhire. But a want of exertion, and an extravagance in keep, efpecially in *beer*, more than counterbalance the difparity in wages.

The ridiculous cuftom of the cider country, in regard to a fuperfluity of beverage, has

been feen in the Rural Economy of GLOCES-
TERSHIRE. A cuftom, equally abfurd, and
much more *extravagant*, prevails in the MID-
LAND DISTRICTS.

In the cider countries, in a cider year, the
actual coft is inconfiderable. But here the
enormity of extravagance is annual, and in
a degree certain. The price of malt is much
lefs fluctuating than that of apples and pears.

The *quantity* of liquor wafted may be fomewhat lefs, here, than in Glocefterfhire: but in
quality and in *coft* of the beverage of farm
labourers, this diftrict far excels every other:
fee MIN. 22.

The TIME OF CHANGING fervants, here, is
Michaelmas.

The PLACES OF HIRING, " ftatutes."

For a defcription of *Polefworth ftatute*, fee
MIN. 11.

For calculations and remarks on *beer*, fee
MIN. 22.

For inftances of allowing labourers to plant
potatoes in the nooks of arable fields, fee 44.

For inftance of labourers being allowed
half the crop of *potatoes* for cultivating
it, fee 63.

For

For an inſtance of the *hard living* of farm labourers, ſee MIN. 94.

For the inconveniency of farm labourers living at a diſtance from the farm, ſee 101.

For a rare inſtance of ſtrong natural ability, induſtry, and honeſty, being united in a farm labourer, ſee 117.

12.

BEASTS OF LABOUR.

HEAVY HORSES have been, time immemorial, the beaſts of draught of this diſtrict.

Of late years, however, ſome few OXEN have been worked; and a ſpirit for working them appears to be gaining ground, apace, among ſuperior managers.

The HORSE TEAM of this diſtrict is grown to a ſhameful height of extravagance. The *pride of ſhow teams*, a folly obſervable more or leſs in moſt diſtricts, is here truly abſurd.

K 3　　　　The

The firſt coſt, the trappings, and the keep, are all equally out of character for *farm* horſes.

A *faſhionable* ſixyearold horſe cannot be purchaſed under thirty or forty guineas. Five horſes are conſidered as a team. A ſhow team, fit to be *ſeen*, cannot, therefore, be purchaſed for leſs than one hundred and fifty pounds.

The firſt coſt, however, is not more extravagant than the annual expence. A ſhow team is a ſhame to be ſeen, unleſs the horſes have three or four inches of ſat upon their ribs. To bring them to this exquiſite ſtate, they are of courſe limited in work, and unſtinted in provender. " A ſtrike a meal for ſix horſes is counted fairiſh feeding." Two meals a day : fourteen ſtrike a week ; near two and a half buſhels a horſe a week !

The harneſs, too, eſpecially the houſing, is truly ridiculous ; at once expenſive and unornamental : ſtanding up aukwardly high above the back of the horſe ; like the ſailfin of the nautilus ; as if it were intended to catch the wind, and accelerate or retard the motion of the animal.

With

With refpect to ATTENDANCE, however, the cuftom of the Midland Diftrict is economical, compared with the fouthern counties; where a man and a boy are allowed to each team of four horfes. Here, a man alone, ufually takes care of fix horfes (as a team and a faddle horfe) : " a waggoner" and his " lad," frequently of two teams.

As a fpecies of PROVENDER, *beans* are ftill in ufe ; though not fo liberally as they were formerly, when the fields were open, and beans of courfe more plentiful than they are now. They are pretty generally " kibbled"? —that is, crufhed in a mill ; whether for old or for young horfes. *Barley* which is not maltable, is fometimes given to horfes; but it is not a favourite, or rather not a fafhionable provender: it is apt to " *tan*" the horfes ! This, too, is frequently kibbled ; and fometimes *oats* are crufhed.

When *chaff* is not in plenty, all horfe corn ought, no doubt, in ftrictnefs of management, to be *crafhed.*

Another provender of horfes, which is in ufe in this diftrict, and in which, only, I have found it in ordinary practice, is " *cut meat :*" that is, oats in ftraw, cut into very fhort lengths,

K 4   in

in a chaff-box, and in a manner which will be fpoken of under BARN MANAGEMENT. This is an excellent horfe food, efpecially when hay is fcarce ; being in itfelf both *bay and corn*. The cutting, it is true, is fome expence ; but thrafhing and pilfering are thereby avoided.

13.

IMPLEMENTS.

THE SPECIES OF IMPLEMENTS, requiring notice in this place, are,

  The Waggon,
  The Plow,
  The Harrow.

The WAGGON is noticeable on account of its aukwardnefs, clumfinefs, unwieldinefs, and all together, in the prefent ftate of roads, its unfitnefs for a *farmer's* ufe. Its weight (with narrow wheels) a ton to twenty-five hundred weight. Its height, with the " geering" on, feven or eight feet (*when empty!*). The length
of

of the body fourteen or fifteen feet: from tug to tail twenty, or upward !—The height of the fore wheels four feet nine or ten inches; without any infection in the body of the waggon to receive them ! No wonder it should require near an acre of ground to turn it on; and a horse or two extra to draw it.

The gawkiness of its construction originated, no doubt, in the depth of the roads, at the time it received its present form :—a tall waggon was drawn on its belly *seldomer* than a low one. But, now, when the roads are rendered more passable, a more convenient carriage ought to be adopted.

If any leading man would introduce the GLOCESTERSHIRE WAGGON, he might be rendering his country an essential service. The superiority of a waggon which, when loaded with a full harvest load, is not much higher than the present waggon of this district, when empty, could not fail of being readily seen *.

The

* In this inland country, where *sail cloths* are not easily had, and where *tilts* are not yet in use for farmers waggons, *hair cloths* are common, for covering body loads, or spread occasionally along the middle of a top load. They come high, but are very durable.

The old PLOW of this diſtrict is ſimilar to that of Gloceſterſhire : a long heavy unwieldy implement : requiring five or ſix horſes to work it. At preſent, the prevailing plow is the modern plow of Yorkſhire; from whence it has not been many years introduced into this diſtrict : even the ſteep ridges of ſome of the common fields are now plowed, in common, with this light ſhort plow and three horſes.

But a ſtill more modern invention is the DOUBLE PLOW : an implement which took its riſe in this neighbourhood; and which has made the moſt rapid progreſs toward common uſe that any implement of huſbandry, perhaps, ever did.

Every circumſtance that leſſens the expence of tillage, without leſſening its efficacy, is of the firſt conſideration in huſbandry.

In Gloceſterſhire, we have ſeen the exceſſive coſt of plowing with an ill formed plow, and with five, ſix, or ſeven horſes to this one plow : a mode of tillage which heretofore has probably prevailed in moſt parts of the iſland.

In Norfolk, and in Yorkſhire, we have ſeen this folly done away by a better conſtructed plow,

plow, and two horfes, without a driver. And in the MIDLAND COUNTIES we find the fame abfurd practice now under eradication, by five, or perhaps only four horfes drawing two plows, without a holder.

Double and even triple plows I have feen in ufe, many years ago, by a moft ingenious hufbandman, Mr. DUCKET of Surrey. Thefe were formed with a *crooked beam*, and kept in an upright pofition, fo as not to require a holder, by means of an upright fpindle, paffing through the end of the beam and the bolfter, &c. of a pair of common plow wheels : fuch as are in ufe for the Norfolk and the turnwreft plows.

About twenty years ago, a farmer of this neighbourhood fetched a double plow out of WORCESTERSHIRE: but this, as Mr. Ducket's, did not " fhift ;" the bodies of the plows being fixed at fome certain diftance from each other, without any means of regulation.

The " DOUBLE SHIFTING PLOW" appears, evidently, to have been the invention (or rather perhaps an improvement of the Worcefterfhire,

cefterfhire plow) of one Bush, a wheelwright
of Hurley, in the north of Warwickfhire,
about feventeen years ago.

Some fourteen or fifteen years ago he *ad-
vertifed* it, and delivered printed directions
for ufing it; but never had, I underftand, a
patent for it.

This Bush is ftill (1786) the leading
maker; but double plows, of his conftruction, are now made by all principal plow-
wrights; and may be faid to be in the hands
of every farmer in the diftrict, who has
ftrength enough to work one.

The great merit of the invention lies in
introducing the ends of the two beams into
the axle, or what amounts to the axle, of the
wheels.   Thus giving at once firmnefs, ftea-
dinefs, and truth to the machine; and, at the
fame time, admitting of eafy means of regulating, at pleafure, the width of the furrows.

Its rapid progrefs into common ufe among
farmers of every clafs, who work horfes enow
to draw one, is beft accounted for, perhaps,
in the circumftance of its meeting the approbation of the " waggoners," who, to a
man, are partial to it; becaufe it requires
their *whole team*, and a long whip to drive it:

while

while they as uniformly difapprove of whip-
rein plows ; becaufe they break their team ;
wrefting part of their horfes from them ; and
fubject them, as they conceive, to the difgraceful tafk of both holding and driving
their plow. And the farmers with good
reafon approve of it ; becaufe, in fome cafes,
five horfes and one man, with a double plow,
will do as much or nearly as much work as
fix horfes, two plows, two men, and two
boys, ufually do with fingle plows.

On ftraight even ridges, and level ground,
the double plow makes very good work ; but
wherever the lands are crooked, or are wider
at one end than the other, or the ground
lies in hills and hollows, fuch work is frequently made, as a good plowman would, and
as every farmer ought to be afhamed of.

However, in level work, *when the land is
wet* (and liable to be poached by horfes
abreaft), the double plow gains an advantage over the two-horfe plow. Neverthelefs,
it is allowed by men in this diftrict, who
work both on a large fcale, that though the
double plow may, *in fome cafes*, be ufed with
fuperior advantage, two horfes abreaft are,
on the whole, the moft eligible plow team.

The

The fame principle of guiding by wheels, without a holder, has been of late years extended to the fingle plow. I have obferved one man and a boy driving and directing two of thefe plows, with three horfes at length in each. The man going firft, and having guided his own plow at the end, and entered it fecurely, drove out the boy's team; and, having feen that fairly entered, ftept forward to his own. This method applied to two double plows (to which it is equally applicable) is reducing the *manual labour* of plowing to the loweft degree: one man and a boy to four plows: and, in a clean foil, in good working order, with a level furface and long ftraight parallel lands, good work may in this way be made.

The HARROW, which requires to be particularly noticed here, is one of very large dimenfions (as fix feet by five and a half, with five bulls and twenty-five tines) very heavy, and with the tines very long and ftrong,— *hung behind a pair of wheels*,—with fhafts, fimilar to waggon fore wheels—and with a " *running bull.*"

This, in tearing up to the furface, and expofing there, the buried clods of a fallow,
after

after thofe on the furface have been reduced, is an excellent implement.

I do not mean to fpeak of a large fingle harrow as being peculiar to this diftrict ; but I have not elfewhere feen it drawn with WHEELS; which bearing up the fore part, renders it much more effectual than when it has not this fupport.

Nor have I feen, in any other diftrict, the " RUNNING BULL ;" an admirable part, whether of a fingle or the double harrow. It confifts, in the cafe under notice, of a ftring of iron, an inch or more in diameter, fixed on a crofs bar in the front of the harrow, reaching almoft, but not quite, from fide to fide ; the immediate corner of a harrow being an improper point of draught. On this bar or ftring of iron, a ring, with a chain paffing to the wheels, plays freely from end to end ;—confequently whichever way the team turns, whether to the right or to the left, the harrow, by the point of draught being at liberty to fhift from corner to corner, is not liable to be ftrained nor over-turned ; nor is the hind horfe fubjected to any unneceffary exertion at the ends.

A more

A more fimple, and equally effectual, method is to tenon the crofs piece, in front, into
the two outfide bulls, leaving the inner
bulls fhort, fo as to admit of a large iron
ring to play upon the crofs piece, made
round and fmooth for that purpofe, with an
iron pin a few inches from each end, to prevent the ring from running up quite to the
corners ; thereby giving, as has been faid, a
more eligible point of draught.

For inftances of large farms having each a
blackfmith's fhop, fee MI N. 48.

14.

WEATHER.

THE BAROMETER is here in good
efteem. 1 have found it nowhere fo well attended to as in Yorkfhire, and this diftrict :
and, what is obfervable, in thefe diftricts a
general fpirit of enquiry and improvement
is fingularly prevalent. For want, however,
of paying due attention to *other* circum-
                                    ftances

ſtances of the atmoſphere than its *weight*, diſappointment in the weather muſt of courſe frequently occur, in both diſtricts *.

During my two years reſidence in the MIDLAND DISTRICT, I paid an almoſt un-remitted attention to this ſubject; eſpecially during the HARVESTING MONTHS of *July, Auguſt,* and *September :* in which I kept a REGISTER OF THE WEATHER, on the plan of that formerly kept in Surrey †; noting with ſufficient accuracy the STATE OF THE ATMO-SPHERE, with reſpect to its *weight, moiſture, heat, motion,* and *appearances*; with the *quantity of rain,* or, more generally, the STATE OF THE WEATHER, which reſulted each day from the preſent and preceding ſtate of the atmoſphere; the only philoſophical baſis on which to found a foreknowledge of the weather.

Beſide theſe regiſters in ſummer, I marked the PROGRESS OF SPRING, and caught the characteriſtics of SEASONS; ſuch as, having ſeldom occurred, require to be regiſtered.

I therefore collect the whole together in this place; thereby rendering them more uſeful than they would be in detached Mi-

VOL. I.   L   nutes.

---

nutes. Beſide, the reader may, in this form,
read them, or paſs them over, as inclination
may direct. I publiſh them the rather, as
they contain a kind of information which,
though not difficult to collect, requires a degree of attention and perſeverance, to which
few men, who are not immediately intereſted
in the quality of ſeaſons, would ſubject themſelves ; and ſtill fewer, perhaps, of thoſe
who are, have leiſure and *patience* enough to
go through ſo tedious an employment ; or,
if they ſhould, have not perhaps an opportunity of rendering their collections uſeful to
the public.

STATFOLD, APRIL 28, 1784. The weather
of laſt ſummer was extremely hot ; as hot, perhaps, as has been known in this iſland ; more
diſagreeably hot than I remember to have felt
it in the Weſt-Indies. .

The 28th July the thermometer got up to
87° of Fahrenheit : the 2d Auguſt, at twelve
o'clock, in a north ſhade, it roſe to 89¼° : at
half paſt twelve the ſame day, to 90 degrees * !
　　　　　　　　　　　　　　　Autumn

* The firſt poſition I took myſelf : the two laſt were
taken by a man on whoſe accuracy I can ſafely rely.
I ſaw the thermometer, preſently after, in the ſituation
in which they were taken : a fair north ſhade : no reflection to add to the natural warmth of the atmoſphere.
　　　　　　　　　　　　　　　　　　I regiſter

Autumn was moderate; but winter and early spring extremely severe.

On Christmas-day a frost set in, which lasted without intermission (a day or two excepted) until the 20th February.   An EIGHT WEEKS FROST; with one of the deepest falls of snow that can be remembered. In some parts of Yorkshire the distress for fuel was such as has seldom, perhaps, been experienced, in any country.

Last month, as well as the present, have been uncommonly cold and peevish: this far, the backwardest spring I have known. The hazel did not begin to blow until the second week in March; and continued to blow until the middle of April!

It seldom happens that there are not a few genial days, in February or March, to bring out some of the earlier plants; but this year, even the coltsfoot and dwarf deadnettle did not *begin* to blow before 6th April! nor did the grosberry foliate until the 18th April! and the hawthorn hedges are still as naked as they were at Christmas.

L 2

Extra-

I register this incident the rather, as it evidences a degree of heat which, I believe, the atmosphere of this island rarely acquires.

Extraordinary ! the fwallow, this year, returned, and the grofberry foliated the fame day ! and notwithftanding the backwardnefs of fpring, the cuckoo began to call the 26th April, in a cold fharp white-frofty morning.

How various are the circumftances attending the progrefs of fpring, in different years ! in 1779, the grofberry foliated the 20th February, and the fwallow did not appear until the 8th May *.

PROGRESS OF SPRING 1784 †.

Hazel blowed March-April !
Grofberry foliated 18th April !
Swallow returned 18th April !
Cuckoo began to call 26th April.
Sallow blowed 27th April !
Poplar in pride 7th May.
Hawthorn foliated 9th May.
Blackthorn blowed 11th May.
Fine-leaved elm foliated 13th May.
Oak foliated 18th May.
Afh foliated 24th May.
Hawthorn blowed 31ft May.
Wheat fhot into ear 20th June.

JULY

* See NORF. ECON. ii. 337.

† In *this* neighbourhood: an early fituation. See page 5.

JULY 9. The firſt week in May ſummer ſet in ; ſo that, this year, there was no palpable progreſſion of ſpring : it might be ſaid to be winter one day and ſummer the next. Vegetation broke forth at once with unuſual vigour. During the principal part of May, and the firſt three weeks of June, it was rapid, perhaps, beyond example. But toward the wane of the month, either through too much moiſture and coolneſs, or from the powers of vernal vegetation having exhauſted themſelves, there was an evident check in vegetation, eſpecially of graſs. About the firſt of July the rains took up, and dry weather gave, at length, a looſe to haymaking.

AUGUST 1. The firſt eighteen days of July were fine ; excepting a thunder ſquall in the night of the eighth : the latter part of the month a continuance of wet weather.

The inferences reſulting from the laſt month's REGISTER OF THE WEATHER are theſe * :

L 3   The

____

* I forbear to publiſh the regiſter at large, leſt it ſhould be conſidered as an incumbrance to the generality of readers, to whom it would not be uſeful : the inferences, drawn at the time, will be of more general utility.

The *barometer*, during the former part of the month, was truly prognostic; portending the thunder storm with sufficient accuracy. But, during the rains at the close of the month, the barometer viewed separately, was deceptious; continuing at or above par, during the rainy weather. On the 30th, when a very heavy rain fell, it rose two degrees *.

But the *hygrometer* was, at that time, in the extreme of moistness. Therefore, the inference to be drawn, in this case, is, that 1° heavy is not able to support a very moist atmosphere: for, by the appearances, it was as moist upwards, as it was near the earth. But rising yesterday to 3° and today to 4°, the rain has ceased; notwithstanding the hygrometer and appearances remain moist.

The *thermometer* continued above par all the month: even during the rain it was 1° warm; and, on the hottest days, not more than 4°.

The

---

* The several instruments are graduated in this manner: the extreme points being ascertained, the mean between them is taken as par; from which ten equal degrees are marked toward each extremity. See EXPERIMENTS and OBSERVATIONS on AGRICULTURE and the WEATHER, page 115, and the PLATE of INSTRUMENTS there given.

The *wind*, during the former part of the month, kept to the northward of weſt; excepting two days preceding the thunder ſtorm, when it got back to the ſouthweſt and the ſouth : but what is remarkable, the rain came with a ſtrong northeaſt wind : and what is not leſs obſervable, the heavieſt of the rain, at the cloſe of the month, came with the wind at ſouth and a ſourheaſt.

Appearances, whether in high day, or at the cloſe, were ſingularly conſiſtent. Streamers (" mare's-tails," Surrey —" filley-tails," Yorkſhire—"hen-ſcratlings," Midland) and with ſmall livid clouds ſailing beneath them, were uniformly prognoſtic of foul or ſhowery weather. The ſetting ſun might be ſaid to be truly prognoſtic throughout. Brightneſs or with a degree of redneſs preceded fine, foulneſs or broken watery clouds portended foul weather *.

L 4   August

---

* It muſt be obſerved, however, that I was frequently deprived of the advantage of ſeeing the immediate ſetting (the great thing to be depended upon) through the want of a ſufficiently clear horizon. A ſerious inconveniency in the ſituation of a farmery.

AUGUST 12. 'An hygrometer in the houfe is not, invariably, a guide to the moifture of the air in the field.

Yefterday, two hygrometers, in the houfe, though expofed to a thorough air, ftood at 7 to 8° moift; while hay fpread upon the ground, as wet as rain could make it, dried fufficiently to be carried (à la Midland) about three o'clock in the afternoon.

To prove the comparative ftate of abforbency of the air within, and that without, placed one of the inftruments in the open air: it fell 5 or 6° in about an hour; while that in the houfe remained unmoved.

In this cafe, the probable reafon of fo great a difparity, was the local dampnefs of the fituation in the houfe; caufed by the unufual dampnefs of three or four days preceding; and which had not yet had time to efcape.

AUGUST 14. The ftring of a hygrometer fhould be gently ftretched, before the true ftate of the moifture of the atmofphere can be afcertained by it: more efpecially after the air has been remarkably moift, and is growing drier.

Notwithftanding the air, to day, is as dry as fun and wind can make it, and, to common appearances,

appearances, as dry in the house as in the field, the hygrometer in the former stood at 3° moist.

Being impatient to see the index fall, I pressed it down gently with the finger, some two or three degrees; and, to my surprize, it stood there. I then forced it down still lower; where it resisted the pressure, and, on being set free, rose deliberately to somewhat above par; where it still remains.

This incident led me to another instrument, placed in the sun and wind; and which stood at 4° dry: but after forcing down the index to the stretch, below the extreme point, it rested, and now stands, at almost extreme dryness.

Excessive moisture, on being dryed up, leaves behind it a gumminess (especially perhaps in a linen substance) which the weight of the index is not able to overcome. It is, therefore, as necessary to press down the index of a cord hygrometer, as it is to tap the case of the barometer.

AUGUST 15. The air is at length become thoroughly dry, as well in the house as in the field,

One

One hygrometer placed in the *wind* and *sun* (very warm ; 89° in the *sun* ; 77° in the *shade*) dropt to 8° dry. Removed it into the *shade*, but full, as before, in the wind,—it remained stationary for some time : but afterwards sunk 1° still lower. Replaced it in the *sun :* no perceptible variation took place.

A proof that the *sun*, when the *wind* is absorbent, is of little or no use in the *drying* of vegetable substances [*].

Another, which remained in the house, fell equally low ! and, on returning the portable one to its place in the house, it did not rise even a hair's breadth !

Proofs that when the *air* is highly absorbent, it has the property of drying quickly and thoroughly, without either *wind* or *sun.*

SEPTEMBER 1. The REGISTER OF THE WEATHER of AUGUST affords few inferences.

The month consisted of a mixture of fair and showery weather ; with one heavily rainy morning. Seventeen fair days ; fourteen more or less rainy.

The

---

[*] Nevertheless in what is termed the *weathering* of *hay*, &c. the *sun* may be most effective.

The *barometer* varied from par to 4° heavy; and, on the whole, acted with great truth; the 6th it got down to ½° heavy; the attendant circumstance was half an inch, at least, of rain: the 28th it stood at par; and the estimated quantity of rain not less than a quarter of an inch. The 31st it likewise got down from 1½° to ½° heavy; another quarter of an inch of rain fell.

The *hygrometer* did not act, last month, with equal sensibility. The former part of the month it was, in general, extremely moist: though we had several *fair* days: to its credit, however, we had few *bright* days: a sort of smokey, gloomy, overcast weather. The latter part of the month, from par to 5° dry; with nevertheless, a similar kind of atmosphere.

The *thermometer*, chiefly, from par to 2° warm.—The 15th it rose to extreme heat; with no remarkable attendant or consequent circumstance.

The *wind* varying, Upon the whole, and in almost every instance, north of west brought fair, south of west rainy weather: 5° due west brought light flying showers.

Appearances have been deceitful; even streamers with undersailers passed off without

out rain; were in one inftance fucceeded by
a fingularly fcorching hot harveft day. The
fetting fun, however, faved its credit; portending, with its wonted faithfulnefs, the
quality of the coming weather: in the inftances, I mean, in which I had a full opportunity of obferving its appearances.

Upon the whole, notwithftanding the change-
ablenefs of the weather, the indecifivenefs of
the inftruments, and the inconfiftency of
common appearances, I have not, refting
my judgement on the mafs of information,
committed one effential error, in the courfe
of laft month.

OCTOBER 4. From the firft to the nine-
teenth of laft month, hot parching harveft
weather. To this fucceeded ten days of
fhowery weather; but not fettled rain: and
to this a week of very fine fettled weather
for the feafon; and this notwithftanding fome
fevere *white frofts*: a rare incident.

During the eighteen days fettled fine weather, the *barometer* and *hygrometer* were unani-
mous: the former varying from $1\frac{1}{2}°$ to $3\frac{1}{2}°$
heavy; the other, from $2°$ to $6°$ dry. Dur-
ing the ten days fhowery weather, the barometer kept below par; but the hygrometer
remained

remained ftationary. Hence, perhaps, we
may fay, the weather was only fhowery, not
rainy : and that the barometer recovering its
elevation, and the air of courfe its weight, the
weather, in confequence, became fair and
firmly fettled.

With refpect to *appearances*, it is obfervable, that during the fine weather in the former part of the month, the fun frequently fet
with a degree of foulnefs ; occafioned, however, principally by that fpecies of SMOKEYNESS which is frequently feen in droughty
feafons ; and which was fo memorably confpicuous, throughout Europe, I believe, in the
dry fummer of 1783.

After the whole of this fummer's experience, I can fay, what I may not be able to repeat the next, that I have not, generally
fpeaking, been once *deceived* in the weather ;
that is, I have not once been *caught* in the
rain, either in hay or in corn harveft.

OCTOBER 13. A remarkable incident!
Today, there has been two or three fmartifh
SHOWERS ; with the *barometer* at 4° heavy,
the *hygrometer* at 4° dry, the *thermometer* at
temperate, and the *wind* at due north ! In this
instance,

inftance, *apprarances* alone portended them.
Notwithftanding the barometer and hygrometer have been ftationary for near a fortnight, with a remarkably bright fine atmofphere, this became, the day before yefterday, loaded with large heavy clouds, with
fmall livid fpecks failing beneath them ; and
yet without any alterations in the weight,
moifture, heat, or motion of the air, at the
furface of the earth. This, though no general inference, perhaps, can be drawn from
it, appears to me an interefting fact. The
quantity of rain has not been great, but what
fell came down freely, and from a loaded atmofphere.

NOVEMBER 18. From that day, the feafon continued remarkably dry for more than
three weeks. Wheats, which were fown the
beginning of October, lay in the ground a
full month, before they came up fo as to meet
the eye. The ground remained as dry as in
any part of fummer : even the fallows of the
common fields have been, until about a week
or ten days ago, too dry and cloddy to work ;
and whole ground much too hard to be
plowed with propriety.

The

The night before laſt there was thunder and lightning ! with a deluge of rain in the morning. Yeſterday fine, and part of the night froſty ; but, this morning, the rain returned, and has continued all day, raining very hard ; with every appearance of a rainy ſeaſon being ſet in. Nevertheleſs, the *barometer* ſtands between 1° and 2° heavy, and the *hygrometer* between 2° and 3° dry !

This rain, perhaps, may be accounted for in the lightning and the *wind :* which for the laſt week has been weſterly and ſtrong ; bringing with it a ſucceſſion of heavy clouds from the ſea. But the wind is now northeaſt ; bringing back the vapours, perhaps, in a compreſſed ſtate, ariſing from this *contrariety of winds.*

JANUARY 19, 1785. The ſecond of December a froſt ſet in, hard enough to ſtop the plow ; which has ſtood near ſeven weeks frozen in the ſoil : yeſterday being the firſt day (notwithſtanding we have had a ſingularly mild muggy air for the laſt ten days !) on which it could be ſet to work with propriety.

This has hitherto been an old-faſhioned winter : froſt and ſnow ſetting in, as of yore,

before

before Chriſtmas. But ſo much ſevere weather before that time has ſeldom, perhaps, happened in any age. A man who can recollect ſixty years, does not remember a ſimilar inſtance.

It is remarkable, that the *barometer* roſe during the thaw. The 5th and 6th, when it froze ſeverely, the glaſs was below par; the 9th, the air peculiarly mild and muggy, it ſtood firmly between 3° and 4° heavy; and the 10th, *roſe*, during the ſame moiſt ſtate of the air, to 4½° heavy! It is obſervable, however, that no rain fell.

FEBRUARY 10. Yeſterday, during a hard froſt, the *barometer* ſtood at 1° heavy. To-day, it has got up to 4° heavy, for a drizzling mild rain!

FEBRUARY 20. About a week ago the barometer ſtood at 2 to 3° heavy: the air froſty. But the air becoming mild, with a drizzling rain, it roſe (while it actually rained) to the unuſual height of 7° heavy!

It has ſince kept lowering gradually: the weather mild; with every appearance of a fall of rain. But inſtead of this a ſmart ſhower of ſnow took place; clearing up with a froſty
air;

air; freezing moſt intenſely all night, with the barometer at par; at which it ſtill remains : though laſt night, at ſix o'clock, the thermometer got down to 20° (of Fahrenheit), and at nine to below 16°, the loweſt I remember to have ſeen it *.

APRIL 24. The ſeaſon ſtill dry : not one-tenth of an inch of rain has fallen ſince the froſt. Nevertheleſs, the earth, even to the very ſurface, is moiſter than it was ſome weeks ago! and this with the air at the extreme of dryneſs! Oats come up as quick and as ſtrong as if the ground were full of rain! and the ſprings are all alive.

MAY 8. The barlies and the late-ſown oats produce a motley ſight; appearing in blotches : half up, half in the ground, as dry as when they were ſown.

MAY 17. Laſt night fell the firſt ſhower of rain we have had this ſpring. And even this is too inconſiderable to bring up the late-ſown crops.

JUNE 1. At length we have had ſome cool dropping weather; but yet no quantity of

---

* Yet during this paroxyſm of froſt the barometer ſunk to 2° light! *In winter*, the weight of the air ſhould ſeem to have no influence on the weather.

of rain. That which has fallen, however, has been sufficient to rouse a principal part, at least, of the latent barley.

June 30. The last winter and spring have been strongly marked; and the summer continues no less extraordinary. The frost, taken altogether, unusually long and severe; with but little snow; and this little drank up by the sun, or dissipated by the dryness of the atmosphere; a very small portion of it penetrated the soil. Yet not one drop of rain (some drizzling showers excepted) from November until the latter end of May, when the ground was moistened nearly plow deep. But, from that time to the present, the weather has been uniformly dry, and often excessively hot!

The early part of this spring advanced more slowly even than that of the last. For although it made an effort about the 20th of March, frost and snow returned the 22d, and continued till the beginning of April. The *coltsfoot* did not shew itself before the 5th of April; nor the *pilewort* disclose its blossoms till the 6th. And those of the *hazel* were never conspicuous: it might be said to blow about the first of April. The *grosberry* did

did not foliate till the 16th; before which I saw two *swallows* nesting !

PROGRESS OF SPRING 1785.

Hazel blowed about the 1st April.

Fieldfares singing their parting song 6th April *.

Water martins nesting 13th April.

Swallows nesting 14th April.

Grosberry foliated 16th April !

Sallow blowed (a pale sickly colour) 16th April.

Hawthorn foliated 26th April.

Poplar in pride 26th April.

Female wasps 26th April.

Cuckoo — uncertain —

Blackthorn blowed 5th May.

Oak foliated 12th May !

Ash foliated 24th May !

Hawthorn blowed 1st June !

Wheat shot into ear 24th June.

The foliation of trees was, this spring, singularly rapid. The elm, the maple, the sallow, &c. &c. *and the oak!* were all in a state of foliation at the same time ! the 7th May.

But the most observable circumstance in the progress of vegetation, this spring,—was

M 2   the

* But though in full chorus on that day, they did not take flight till some time afterwards.

the early *foliation* of the *oak*, compared with that of the *afh*, and the *blowing* of the *hawthorn* : the afh near a fortnight, and the hawthorn near three weeks, after the oak !

It is likewife remarkable that the *meadow trefoil* (the wild red clover) blowed, this fpring, with the *meadow foxtail* and *vernal!* beginning to blow the 12th of May : actuated, probably, by the fame law of nature as the oak : both of them tap-rooted, deep-ftriking plants : while the afh, the hawthorn, the foxtail, and the vernal are merely fibrous, and feed, comparatively, near the furface. Hence, admitting the principle of vegetation to be merely that of comparative rarefaction, thefe extraordinary circumftances may be accounted for in the different ftates of the earth and the atmofphere, at the time thefe circumftances took place.

AUGUST 1. REGISTER OF THE WEATHER in JULY. Much thunder, with heavy fhowers; but no long continuance of rain.

The *barometer* wavering from 2¼° heavy to 2° light; hovering much about par : of courfe no dependance could be placed in it, feparately confidered.

The *hygrometer* uniformly dry; varying from 4° to 8°. Hence, perhaps, no continued

tinued rain. None fell but what was pro-
voked, or ſtimulated, by thunder and lightning; which, frequently, were not able to
ſhake down a ſhower: owing, probably, to
the dryneſs of the atmoſphere. I never experienced the uſe of the hygrometer ſo much
as I have done laſt month.

Thermometer, uniformly warm: the air
ſometimes very hot: ſo high as 78° of Fahrenheit.

The *wind* various: the rain came chiefly
with the wind at ſouthweſt, or weſt. Thunder paſſed off without rain, with the wind at
north.

Appearances. Large dark indigo-coloured
clouds portended approaching thunder.
Livid clouds, forming whirlpools on a ſilvery
ground, immediately preceded remarkably
vivid beautiful lightning; running, ſerpen-
tinely, along the face of the clouds. The
ſcenery and the muſic equally ſublime!

AUGUST 7. On Wedneſday laſt, the 3d
of Auguſt, ended the DROUGHT OF EIGHTY-
FIVE.

Prior to that, partial thunder ſhowers
had quenched particular ſpots; but no general rain took place, in this part of the
M 3   iſland,

ifland, till that day,—when an inch of rain,
at leaft, fell. This, with fome fhowers, before and fince, have moiftened the foil to
the bottom ; and fully fatisfied the farmers;
who are now calling out for fair weather,
to get in their harveft.

A " DRY SUMMER" is a phenomenon to
the middleaged men of this country. Old
George Barwell * (feventytwo) fays no man
who cannot recollect forty years can know
anything of " dry fummers :" about forty or
fifty years ago, he fays, there were three or
four dry fummers, nearly fucceeding each
other ; and fpeaks of one about twenty years
ago : adding, that he never knew a dry
fummer which was not preceded by a fevere
winter, and fucceeded by great crops. He
foretold with great confidence, early in the
fpring, the drynefs of this fummer : faying
that he did not remember an inftance,
before laft year, of a long froft without a dry
fummer to fucceed it †.

The

---

* See MIN. 117.

† This year, 1789, is another exception. Laft winter was remarkably dry (fee GLO. ECON.) with a very
long froft ; and this fummer as remarkably wet. Not

more

The fummer after the "nine weeks froft," he fays, was dryer than this has been; and the crops of that fummer, particularly the wheat, did much worfe, than they have done this; owing chiefly to its being more injured by the froft. The price, the enfuing winter, got up to nine fhillings a "ftrike" (a bufhel). But the next year's crop was fo profufe, it got down to half a crown! and continued low for feveral years afterwards; the crops being remarkably good: owing in part, he thinks, to the froft; but ftill more to the drought. He feems to confider the rays of the fun as a fpecies of manure!

Be this as it may, his natural underftand-ing is remarkably ftrong, and his obferva-

M 4   tions

more than three weeks or a month's harveft weather, for both hay and corn. The early cut grafs and the late cut corns were in a manner wafted. Summer floods were perhaps never more mifchievous. In going down into Leicefterfhire, in July, I faw not only hay cocks, but waggons, floating in the meadows. And in return-ing, in October, by the way of Oxfordfhire and Berk-fhire, the bean crop almoft entirely, and much barley were ftill out. And by authentic information from Yorkfhire, the fame crops were then in a fimilar ftate, in November! when, on the lower lands, little wheat had been fown; nor any profpect of fowing it.

tions on rural matters generally clear, and frequently juſt.

To the DRY SUMMER OF EIGHTYFIVE I have paid ſome attention ; and it may be right to preſerve ſuch particulars reſpecting it as are now freſh in my mind.

It was *preceded* by a continuance of froſt without ſnow ; a remarkably dry winter ; and by the other circumſtances of the weather above recited.

The *attendant circumſtances*, beſide thoſe of the weather which appear above, were,

An overabundance of *inſects* : the oak and the apple tree have been in a manner disfoliated by a caterpillar (ſee MIN. 150.) The turnep, too, beſide the beetle and the tenthredo, has been peſtered, this year, by a new enemy—the bug (ſee MIN. 61 and 84). But, what is obſervable, the chafer (the common brown beetle) ſcarcely made its appearance, in this diſtrict *.

Vegetation, in the early part of the ſpring, though the ground was ſufficiently moiſt, was in general weak ; owing principally, perhaps, to

---

* See MIN. 147.

to night frosts; and, in the later part of spring
and in summer, it has been unable to exert
itself; the subterraneous moisture being exhausted, without being replaced by a supply from the atmosphere.

Pasture grounds were, of course, bare, and
meadows short. Nevertheless, it is observable,
that

Cattle, were their pasture ever so naked,
looked sleek and healthy. But, unless where
ground was understocked, cows gave little
milk, and "feeders" gathered little fat.

Even *horses* were distressed for want of
water. See MIN. 58.

Sheep alone did well. In a moist country,
dry weather is favourable to sheep. It *raises*
them to their natural situation.

Wheat, injured by the frost, got thin upon
the ground, in the spring: in some places,
so "gally"—so full of bare patches—as to
be scarcely worth preserving as a crop.

Spring corn, in general, came up partially.
Some, however, sown early and immediately
after the plow, came up well together, and
preserved a pretty good strength of vegetation.

Plantations, and fresh-planted hedges, fared
extremely ill, The frosts continued late;
and

and were immediately preceded by dry parching winds. See MIN. 148.

Fires were never so frequent : no less than two villages have suffered almost total destruction in the Midland Counties alone !

No *thunder* until last month, when it became very frequent : otherwise, in much probability, we should still have had a continuance of drought. For, generally speaking, we have had no rain which has not been shook down by thunder and lightning.

The *barometer* has been no certain guide to the weather. Thunder, alone, seemed to preside in the atmosphere.

Drinking pits were, of course, dry : many *springs* the same : and *rivers*, in consequence, unusually low. Millers, perhaps, never experienced a greater want of water than they did for some time before the late rains brought a supply to their pools. Even the

Price of wheat was affected by the circumstance : their mills being full, and their purses empty, the markets became crouded with samples, and a fall in price the natural consequence.

A re-

A remarkable *fall in the price of livestock.* In the spring, stock was unusually dear : not nearly enough in the country to supply the cravings of the graziers : owing, perhaps, not more to a real scarcity, than to a succession of good grazing years.   The rage for stock did not abate until the middle of May, when lean cattle began to drop, and continued falling in price until Tamworth fair, 26th July ; where store cattle could not be sold at any price.   Even pigs, which four months ago were worth fifteen shillings a piece, might, a fortnight ago, have been bought for ten. Horses, too, fell from the clouds.   Sheep alone kept up.

The *consequences*, so far as they are yet un-folded, are,

Fallows appear to have received an extra-ordinary degree of melioration.   The turnep fallow of No. 2. is in a state of tilth (friability, mellowness) in which I have not, I think, seen plowed ground before ; owing, perhaps, not more to the dryness of the summer, than to the frost in winter, when it lay in ribs, or nar-row single-furrow trenches.   The rootweeds appear to be totally annihilated ; and the

seeds

feeds of weeds, unlocked by the pulveriza-
tion of the foil, and now fufficiently moiftened
by the late rains, are fpending themfelves:
the furface green with feminal weeds.

Fallows that have this fummer received tolerably good management, will, it is highly
probable, communicate a degree of fertility
to the foil for fome years to come; and
it is equally probable, that foils not in a
ftate of fallow will receive a fimilar degree of
improvement, from their texture being
broken by the froft, and their crudities
drawn out or corrected, to an unufual depth,
by the fun. I fpeak more particularly of
ftrong and middle foils. There is indeed an
idea, which is probably of ancient date, as it
has grown into a maxim, that "a dry fummer
was never bad for England *."

No *turneps*, except a few patches which
were fown early, when the fpring moifture
was not yet exhaufted, and when their enemies—from what caufe is a myftery—perhaps

---

* The fummer of 1786 I fpent in London, and cannot fpeak, from my own obfervation, of its crops. The
fummer of 1787 fhewed fuch a ftrength of vegetation as
I never have, in any other fummer, obferved. See
York. Econ. v. i. p. 289.

haps for want of a shower to assist their exclusion—suffered the plants to rise without a
check. But the middle and the later sowings
have been cut off wholly by the *beetle* and
the *bug*; which would not suffer the *cater-
pillars*, though numbers of flies were among
them, to partake of the spoil; the plants being
commonly devoured before the eggs of the
tenthredo had time to be matured. I found
one nearly ready for exclusion, and another
half naked in its nidus; part of which had
been devoured by the rapacious beetle.

A scarcity of hay. Not one fourth of a common crop; including both meadows and upper lands. See MIN. 56.

An unevenness in corn crops : occasioned by
the wheat being injured by the frosts; and
the spring corn rising partially; through a
want of sufficient moisture, at the time of
sowing; appearing, throughout summer, in
two or perhaps three crops.

A plumpness of grain : especially of wheat,
and of oats that were sown early *.

A scarcity

---

* Mr. Baox, of Elford, on whose accuracy I can
rely, mentions a remarkable circumstance respecting his
wheat; which, this harvest, is so full in the ear, that
while

A scarcity of cheese. Not more, perhaps, than two thirds of the common make of factors cheese will go to market.

A scarcity of fat cattle. It is probable that half of the "feeders" in the diftrict are not of more value now than they were when turned to grafs; and ftill more probable, that not one in ten is what is termed good beef. See MIN. 53.

Upon the whole, this dry fummer is likely to produce, in the firft inftance, *a very bad year for farmers*; and all the confolation they have at prefent, is the hope of a fucceffion of better crops in future *.

AUGUST 21. The laft fortnight has been almoft continually rainy! no poffibility of carrying corn, in tolerable order, until to-day. And this day happens to be Sunday † I

Took

---

while the ftraw was yet underripe, the grain, affifted by the late fhowers and gleams, burft its bounds, fhewing itfelf to the eye as it ftood upon the ftalk; and fhedding, in the act of reaping, a quantity nearly equal to the feed fown!

* Great quantities of *mufhrooms*, and of *wafps*, were other confequences of the dry fummer of Eighty-five.

† Neverthelefs, fome farmers in the neighbourhood, I find, had good fenfe and gratitude enough to fecure a confiderable part of their wheat crops.

Took a ride in the morning to see the state of the corn crops. The wheat, mostly cut, and almost all standing in "shuck," except a few loads carried last night. *Barley*:—a good deal down, and very much discoloured, and some beginning to "sprit." *Crops*, in general, thin; in the common fields very thin; —barley, on a par, not half a crop. *Oats*:— some carried: many down: straw much injured: crop very bad:—especially in the common fields, scarcely worth mowing: the oat crop throughout not half a common crop. *Beans*:—mostly down. Crop, execrable! not beans, but the straw of catlock; whose seeds would lie thick enough to hide the surface, had not part of it been swallowed, before the rain, by the fissures or cracks; running down, perhaps, some feet deep! Yet succeeding generations may wonder how it came there.

AUGUST 30. Yesterday, in much probability, the *barometer* and *hygrometer* were instrumental in saving three times their cost. I had some wheat to carry, and some barley to mow. The wheat was in fine order, except the immediate buts of the sheaves; which, being set up when the ground was moist, the

bottoms

bottoms remained damp and dirty; the
straggling ears which happened to touch
the ground being some of them damaged.
It was therefore proper that the shucks
should be laid open, and the buts aired,
before they were carried; and my original
intentions were to have mown barley in the
morning, and to have carried wheat in the
afternoon; allowing the buts and the inner
sides of the sheaves all the forenoon sun and
air to dry them.

The three preceding days had been tolerable harvest weather, and the early part of
the morning was bright and fine: general
appearances, then, bespoke a fine day. But
the *barometer*, though high (31° heavy), was
sinking: the *hygrometer* getting moist. The
preceding morning had been marked by a
white frost (the first this autumn), and the
canopy the two preceding days had been frequently scattered with streamers. The *sun*,
too, began, as the day advanced, to lose its
splendor, and to play at hide-and-seek
among the clouds.

I therefore, at length, concluded to secure
the wheat; sending a boy before to open the
shucks, by laying the sheaves down gently
upon

upon their backs : by which means moſt of the buts had two or three hours wind and partial ſun to dry them ; and the ears having been uncapped the day before, the whole was carried in good order.

The laſt load was barely in the barn when it began to rain ; it has continued ſhowery ever ſince ; and now rains very hard !

But, thanks to the *barometer*, on which chiefly I reſted my judgement, and which is now below par ! the wheat is in the barn, and the barley ſtill ſtanding.

Auguſt 31.   A valley, with a river in it, *appears* to have an influence on *ſhowers*. It is a common obſervation in this country, that the Trent draws away ſhowers from this neighbourhood : and I have repeatedly obſerved that the Tame *ſeems* to have a ſimilar effect.

September 1.   Register of the Weather of Auguſt.   The laſt has been a rainy month ; with only one interval of fair weather.   No thunder, except once, at the beginning of the month.   Hence, perhaps, the weather has been influenced chiefly by the *weight* and *moiſture* of the atmoſphere ; and

The *barometer* and *hygrometer* have, of course, been truly prognostic : except in one instance, when a quantity of rain fell, without any other previous change in the atmosphere than a sensible *chillinefs*; which was sufficiently noticed by the *thermometer* ; but which made a still greater impression on the senses.

This chillinefs and the rain were brought by a brisk north *wind*, after a succession of southwest winds. The *clouds* of vapours were probably returning in a condensed state, and finding our atmosphere in a state comparatively rarefied, only $1\frac{1}{2}°$ heavy, they of course fell : and this, notwithstanding the air near the earth was $5°$ dry.

Hence, when the *barometer* is about par, no dependance can be had on the weather; not only *lightning*, but the *wind*, is able to influence it ; and, of course, every minute circumstance of the atmosphere should be attended to, with double diligence.

OCTOBER I. The REGISTER OF THE WEATHER of SEPTEMBER. Another rainy month ! with, however, several short intervals of fair weather. With frequent *fogs* ; and some

thunder

thunder and *lightning*, which always brought *rain*.

The *barometer*, about, or below, par; until the wane of the month, when it rofe from 3½° light to 3½° heavy in forty-eight hours! a moſt extraordinary rife. The confequence of which was, after a deluge of rain, three or four fair days.

The *hygrometer*, above par, the whole month; notwithſtanding the wetneſs of the weather! a moſt intereſting circumſtance.

The *wind*, wavering: principally fouth or fouthweſt; frequently ſtrong. Shifting round to the northeaſt, brought a fall of rain.

Appearances. Small livid underfailing clouds were pretty certain forerunners of heavy ſhowers. The ſetting ſun (when obſerved) generally foul.

GENERAL OBSERVATIONS. On the whole of this ſummer's experience, I have been leſs certain than on that of the laſt: owing principally to the barometer reſting about par; the atmoſphere remaining in equilibrium; ſuſceptible of the ſlighteſt alteration of moiſture, wind, lightning, or other impulſe.

N 2   Confidering,

Confidering, however, this circumftance, as well as that of my feldom having an opportunity of feeing the weftern horizon, during the fetting of the fun; and with thefe, the extreme wetnefs of the corn harveft; it is not, perhaps, lefs remarkable that I fhould have been *caught, only once*, this fummer, than that laft fummer I fhould efcape without an accident.

At prefent, I am clearly of opinion, that, by attending to the BAROMETER and the SETTING SUN, only, the weather may be foretold, frequently for three or four days, generally for twenty-four hours (a length of time effentially ferviceable to a farmer) with a degree of certainty: provided the atmofphere be not, in the mean time, agitated by thunder and lightning; againft which there appears to be, at prefent, no certain guard. They will fometimes forefhow themfelves for feveral hours, in the figure and colour of the clouds: but in general, *perhaps*, they are not there to be forefeen: and the grand defideratum now wanted is a prognoftic of lightning, as well as a teft of the prefence of the electrical fluid, or the matter of lightning; as it is more than probable that this has its in-

fluence

fluence on the atmosphere; though it do not show itself in lightning, or still more forcibly declare itself in thunder.

But supposing that even thunder, the most certain harbinger of rain, cannot be fore-known with any degree of certainty; this, considering its comparative unfrequency, ought to be no discouragement to the far-mer.

The sailor, though he cannot calculate the longitude, *with certainty*, is neverthelefs affiduous in making and regiftering his ob-servations.

To purfue the comparifon, a farmer without a barometer, in HAYTIME and HARVEST*, is a failor at fea without a quadrant. And,

N 3   in

* From general obfervation, as well as from the in-cidents regiftered aforegoing, the weather appears to be influenced, in fome degree at leaft, by different caufes, in different feafons : and although it may not be wrong to *obferve* thefe influences, in AUTUMN, WINTER, and SPRING; yet I am clearly of opinion, that the facts arifing from fuch obfervations, ought not, in drawing inferences, to be *mixed* with thofe collected in the SUM-MER MONTHS. For other remarks on this fubject, fee Exp. and Obs. on Agr. and the WEATHER, p. 155.

in the ſtrictneſs of good management, it is
not leſs requiſite to the latter, in that ſituation,
to be attentive to his log-book, than for the
former, in thoſe ſeaſons, to pay due attention
to his regiſter.

To the ſtudent, at leaſt, a REGISTER is in-
diſpenſibly requiſite : it is not merely a ſtimu-
lus to his attention, but, by preſerving what
no memory can retain, becomes an authentic
document of ſtudy: a record of reference
to a combination of facts: the pureſt fountain from which to draw practical knowledge.

GENERAL

15.

GENERAL MANAGEMENT

O F

F A R M S.

THE OBJECTS of the Midland huſbandry vary, in different quarters of the
GENERAL DISTRICT, as has been already
intimated, and as will more fully appear in
the courſe of this volume.

In the DISTRICT of the STATION, the
four grand objects are mixed in a ſingular
manner :

GRAIN of almoſt every ſpecies ;

BREEDING in all its branches ;

DAIRYING on a large ſcale ; and

GRAZING, both cattle and ſheep *.

N 4   The

* And to theſe might be added a fifth,——JOBBING;
which is not here, as in other diſtricts, confined to
what might be called profeſſional *dealers*, but enters,
more or leſs, into the buſineſs of *farmers* ; as will appear in MIN. 107.

The OUTLINES of management confift in keeping the land in *grafs* and *corn*, alternately, under a fingular fyftem of practice; and in applying the grafs to the *breeding* of heifers for the dairy, to *dairying*, and to the *grazing* of barren and aged cows; with a mixture of ewes and lambs for the butcher : all together, a beautifully fimple fyftem of management; and, being profecuted on large farms, and by wealthy and fpirited farmers, becomes a fingularly interefting fubject of ftudy.

In giving a detail of the ARABLE MA-NAGEMENT, I fhall attend folely to the IN-CLOSED TOWNSHIPS; which, whether the inclofures be new or of an older date, are cultivated under the fame courfe of manage-ment *.

REFERENCES

* The hufbandry of COMMON FIELDS is the fame in moft parts of the ifland; as if a general order or arret had, at fome early period, gone forth for their regulation. In Yorkfhire, in Glocefterfhire, and in the Midland Counties, one uniform practice prevails: uniform, I mean, in the *outline*: in the *minutiæ* differences are traceable; and as, in a few years, the common field hufbandry of this ifland will probably be no more, I endeavoured to catch thefe minutial differences in the MIDLAND COUNTIES, See MIN. 98.

REFERENCES to the MINUTES relating to the GENERAL MANAGEMENT OF FARMS.

For converfation and reflections on the *arable management* of this diftrict, fee MIN. 19.

For a caution to the occupiers of *extra-parochial farms*, 33.

For general reflections on the *bufinefs* of farming, 67.

For an inftance of impolitic management in an *outgoing tenant*, 76.

For obf. on *neatnefs* and *minutial* management, 78.

For an inftance of the ufe of *experiments* to farmers, 89.

For reflections on *jobbing*, 107.

For an inftance of the folly of *fpeculating* in hufbandry, 114.

COURSE

· 16.

COURSE OF HUSBANDRY.

NO circumstance belonging to the provincial practice of this kingdom has been, to me, a matter of more surprize, than the SUCCESSION OF CROPS, in the prevailing practice of this district.

The GENERAL PRINCIPLE of management is that upon which every middlesoiled district ought to form its practice: namely, that of CHANGING THE PRODUCE, from grass to arable crops, and from grain to herbage.

But whether the MINUTIÆ of practice, established in the district under survey, be eligible in every other middlesoiled district, I mean not here to say. I will endeavour to give a faithful register of the practice, and leave the reader to adopt the whole, or such part of it as may be found eligible in his own situation.

In

In the prevailing practice of the district;—
a practice whose origin I have not been able
to trace, having been prevalent in the inclosed townships, I understand, time immemorial;—the course of management is this:

The land having lain six or seven years in a
state of SWARD,—provincially "TURP,"—it
is broken up, by a single plowing, for OATS;
the oat stubble plowed two or three times for
WHEAT; and the wheat stubble winterfal-
lowed, for BARLEY and GRASS SEEDS;—letting the land lie, during another period of six
or seven years, in HERBAGE; and then, again,
breaking it up, for the same singular suc-
CESSION of ARABLE CROPS.

There are men, however, who object to
this practice, arguing that the soil cannot be
kept sufficiently clean under this course of management; and on the lighter lands, on the
forest side of the district, it is become prevalent to clean the soil, for barley and grass
feeds, by a TURNEP FALLOW; a practice
which has spread itself, more or less, over the
whole district. But the turnep crop, as will
be shewn under the head TURNEPS, is losing
ground, on the stronger soils; on which,

nine

nine acres of ten are kept as regularly under
the courſe of

> Turf,
> Oats,
> Wheat,
> Barley,
> Turf,

as the lands of Norfolk are under the Norfolk
ſyſtem of management.

For reflections on this extraordinary courſe,
ſee MIN. 19.

17.

SOIL and its MANAGEMENT.

THE SPECIES OF SOILS have already
been mentioned, in deſcribing the diſtrict at
large; the prevailing ſpecies being a DEEP
SANDY LOAM; varying, however, in ſtrength
and productiveneſs: but, taken throughout,
few diſtricts can equal the diſtrict of the preſent ſtation, in uniformity of ſoil; the va-
riations in productiveneſs being frequently oc-
caſioned by

The

The subsoil, which, though likewise remarkably uniform, is not altogether so. Beds of *sand*, and thin seams of *gravel*, are found in different parts of it; and a *red clay*,—provincially "marl,"—in others; but the prevailing subsoil is a *sandy loam* or brick earth; varying, like the soil, somewhat in strength.

This variation of subsoil is a natural cause of variation in the productiveness of the soil: water, imbibed by the absorbent strata, and checked in its course by the retentive, is pent up, and forced toward the surface; rendering the soil cold and ungenial.

Nevertheless, underdraining found its way, late, into this district. Its first appearance in it was upon *this* estate, about thirty years ago; when some men from the Morelands of Staffordshire, into which it is probable the art had travelled out of Lancashire, brought it into this country.

Its *establishment* here, was probably owing to a mere circumstance. A farmer in the neighbourhood, struck with this novel practice, prevailed upon one of his labourers, who was a clever fellow at a "dyche," to go and see these "foreigners" at work. He went,

went, caught their art and their tools in his eye; brought them both away with him; got tools made; commenced "fougher;" and still remains the moſt experienced of the diſtrict: though, from him, ſeveral others have taken up, and long followed, the buſineſs; ſo that, in the courſe of a few years, moſt of the principal farms have been " gone over :" that is, have received the benefits of this cardinal improvement.

Thus genius and judgement, when happily joined, are valuable, even in a ditch. OLD SAMUEL, who is ſurnamed CLEVERDYCHE, and from whom I have theſe particulars, is, in truth, a genius of the firſt caſt. See MIN. 106.

It is obſervable, however, that previous to the introduction of the preſent art, a ſpecies of underdraining had been practiſed in this diſtrict,—with THREE ALDER POLES; which have frequently been found, not by old Samuel only, but by other experienced foughers, buried in very wet boggy patches, one upon two, in the triangular manner; forming a kind of pipe in the center.

But it does not appear, by the ſituations in which theſe poles are found, that the modern

art of "killing fprings," as it is termed, was
known to the ancient foughers.

The MATERIAL of foughing made ufe of
by the Morelanders was *wood:* and old Samuel
continued to drain with this material for
many years. But finding, that, in the courfe
of twelve or fourteen years, the fprings broke
out again, he has not, for many years, ufed
wood; except in very difficult cafes; and
then not alone. He reckons twelve or fourteen years to be the longeft duration of wood
drains; let them be ever fo well made.

The ufes of wood were, therefore, fuper-
feded by *ftone;* pebbles—provincially "bowl-
ders,"—picked off the arable land; the only
ftone the country affords; and better ftones
for the purpofe need not be had. With thefe
ftones, the principal part of the effective
drains now in the country have been done.
The method of forming thefe drains will appear in MIN. 106.

Sod or "turf" drains have likewife been
introduced into this diftrict; but thro' a
different channel; and in a manner which
ought not to be paffed unnoticed; as it fhews
what may be expected from the experience
and

and example of the superior clafs of profeffional hufbandmen, affifted by the fpirited
encouragement of landed gentlemen.

Some twenty years ago, Mr. William
More of Thorpe, in *this* neighbourhood, having obferved, in a diftant diftrict, this method
of draining, mentioned it to his landlord, the
late Mr. INGE of Litchfield (whofe character,
as a landlord, and as a magiftrate, was an ornament to his country), and intimated his defire
to make a trial of it. The reply was,—" Send
for a man, and I will fet him to work ; and
if you think it will anfwer, you may then
employ him ; if not, I will allow you his expences." A man was fent for, and the foil
being found proper for this mode of draining,
he was employed fome length of time ; the
tenant paying his wages ; the landlord, the
expences of his journey.

From Thorpe this method of underdraining travelled into Leicefterfhire ; where Mr.
PAGET, a fuperior manager of the higheft
clafs of yeomanry, made himfelf mafter of
the art, taught it to his labourers, practifed it
on an extenfive fcale upon his own eftate, and
has fent young men, of his inftructing, into
various diftricts as fod-drainers : even *this*
neigh-

neighbourhood has, now, its fod-draining done by men from that quarter.

How fortunate for rural affairs, when genius becomes aſſiſted by ſcience and ſelf-practice! What may not be expected from profeſſional men of this deſcription!

The outline of the method of forming fod-drains, here, is this: The upper part of the trench is opened with a common ſpade, nine to twelve inches wide at the bottom, and to a depth ſuitable to the given ſituation; leaving it with a ſmooth, even bottom: in the middle of which a narrow channel is ſunk with a draining tool *, and cleared with a ſcoop, to a depth proportioned to the firmneſs of the ſubſtratum, in which it is made; leaving a fair even " ſhoulder" on either ſide; on which ſhoulders the firſt ſpit or fod is laid, with the graſsſide downward, and, being trod down firm and cloſe, the trench is filled up with the excavated mould.

If the ſubſoil be too tender to bear the fod, or of too looſe and crumbly a texture to ſtand firmly without " running in," the wide trench is ſunk down to the required depth, and ſhoulders formed with fods, cut ſquare, and ſet
firmly

* Sᴇᴇ Nᴏʀꜰ. Ecᴏɴ. ᴍɪɴ. 2.

firmly on each fide of the bottom of the trench; leaving a channel three or four inches wide between them; and laying the inverted fod upon thefe artificial fhoulders.

The *expence*, in either cafe, about a penny a yard; which, being the *whole* expence, is very low.

Neverthelefs, the *duration* of fod-drains, if the fubſtrata be fufficiently firm, appears to be much loager than thofe of wood, and, perhaps, equal, in fome fituaticns, to thofe of ſtone.

Mr. More fhowed me fome, which had been made upwards of twenty years, and which appeared to be quite perfect, acting, in wet weather, as well now as they did the firſt year. On cutting through fome of thefe old drains, and examining them carefully, he found the fod had united intimately with the mould of the fubfoil, into one firm mafs; forming a regular arch; the pipe, fo far from being warped up or even fouled, was wider than when it was made. Polecats and other vermin burrow in thefe drains:—this, reafon fuggefts, would, in making their inner chambers, be liable to clofe the pipe. Moles are, in theory, ftill more formidable enemies. But reafon and theory cannot fet afide facts.

Mr.

Mr. Pager, likewise, having occasion to make some additional drains in a ground which had been sod-drained, some ten or twelve years, found, in cutting acrofs the old drains, that they were in a state of high prefervation.

FALLOWING. The prevailing fallow of this diftrict is the *pin-fallow*, for barley (fee the article BARLEY) : the *fummer fallow* is rarely attempted ; and the *turnep fallow*, as has been intimated, is confined, at prefent, to the practice of a few individuals.

If fallowing can be difpenfed with in any cafe, it may be under the management of this diftrict, where only three arable crops are taken before the land be laid down again to grafs. But even under this management, much of the land is foul and unproductive, through the want of being fallowed.

And it is a fact, which ought not to be concealed, that one of the firft managers in the diftrict is averfe to the pin-fallow practice. His argument is ftrong. " See what a piece of feeds (raygrafs and the clovers) after a turnep fallow will do. It will require a cow and perhaps five or fix fheep an acre to keep it down ; efpecially in the fpring when grafs

it

is valuable. But look into a piece of ten or twelve acres of turf, after PINFALLOW, and you won't see, perhaps, more than five or·six cows and a few ſtraggling ſheep in it : with ſome parts eaten as bare as a common, and others ſcarcely touched."

For an inſtance of practice in *ſummer fallowing*, ſee MIN. 18.

For a propoſed improvement of the *pinfallow*, ſee MIN. 19.

For the origin and cauſe of *high ridges*, ſee MIN. 21.

For an inſtance of practice in *ſurface draining*, 32.

For inſtance of practice in the reclaiming of pit places, 35.

For inſtance of practice in *underdraining*, ſee 106.

For inſtance of the efficacy of *ſod drains*, ſee 109.

MANURES

18.

MANURES

AND THEIR

MANAGEMENT.

THE SPECIES OF MANURE made ufe of, here, are DUNG, LIME, and what is called "MARL *."

DUNG is become, in this neighbourhood, an extravagant fpecies of manure. I have found it nowhere elfe fo highly valued. Half a guinea a load is not an uncommon price. The load, however, is large : that of a waggon, with five horfes. Neverthelefs, the price

O 3   is

* The CORES OF HORNS, crufhed in a mill, have been ufed in this diftrict ; but with what fuccefs I have not learnt. As an animal production, there can be little doubt of their efficacy : the only objection to them lies in the difficulty of reducing them.

is a ftrong evidence of the ftrength and fpirit
of the farmers of this diftrict.   The gardens
of Tamworth * may, however, be, in fome
meafure, the caufe of this extreme dearnefs.

In the MANAGEMENT OF DUNG, one circumftance, chiefly, requires to be particularized ; the method of *fpreading* it on the land.

In the ordinary practice of the kingdom,
dung is fet upon the land in hillocks, and
fpread, afterward, by a man ftanding on the
ground.   But, here, the prevailing cuftom is
to fpread it out of the carriage, as it is brought
into the field ; by a man or men, ftanding on
the carriage.

For the minutiæ of this practice, fee MIN. 12.

For farther obfervations on it, fee MIN. 18.

LIME is, here, in high eftimation, among
farmers in general ; though fome few individuals object to it.

In the ordinary practice of the diftrict, a
fallow is feldom made without being dreffed
with lime ; under an idea that it " mellows"
the foil and makes it " work well," while in tillage ; and " fweetens," improves the *quality*
of the herbage, when laid down to grafs.

Unfor-

Unfortunately, however, for the diſtrict of the ſtation, no calcarious ſubſtance has yet been diſcovered within it, to ſupply it with lime, in quantity as a manure *: for which purpoſe it is fetched, into *this* neighbourhood, eighteen or twenty miles.

There are two *ſpecies of lime* in uſe : the one burnt from a ſtone of ſingular hardneſs, the other from more common limeſtones : the firſt is of ſingular ſtrength as a manure ; the latter of a more common quality. The one, I believe, is peculiar to ſome hillocks in Derbyſhire, on the northern ſkirts of the Charnwood hills ; the other is common to that quarter and to the weſt of Staffordſhire : the former is called *Breedon* lime, the latter *Ticknall* or *Walſal* lime, from the names of the places in or near which they are principally burnt.

The nature of the BREEDON LIME is a fit ſubject of enquiry.

A general deſcription of it will appear in MIN. 2. and an experiment made with it, in MIN. 100. All that remains to be given in

O 4

this

---

* Limeſtone is found on both ſides of the Anker, in the neighbourhood of Tamworth ; and by a proper ſearch, might perhaps be found in ſufficient quantity to be profitably burnt into lime.

this place, is a minutial defcription, and the analyfis, of the ftone.

The prevailing fpecies, of which the lime may be faid to be made, is of this defcription: The *colour*, of the furface formed by the natural feams or fiffures, is a red or ftrong flefhcolour; of that of old fragments, a lighter flefhcolour; of frefhbroken fragments, a lighter blufh. The *contexture* uniform; breaking with rough furfaces; extremely hard, and *clofe*, refifting acids in an extraordinary manner; the muriatic acid ftanding fome time on its furface, before it take effect! and, when pounded, diffolves flowly and *quietly*. Neverthelefs, under the hammer it flies as the St. Vincent ftone. See GLO. ECON. *

One hundred grains contain only three grains of indiffoluble matter,—a red brickduftlike powder, with a few ruftlike fragments. Neverthelefs, the tincture of galls produces no effect on the folution; nor does the fmell, in diffolving, detect any thing of a chalybeate

---

* It is a noticeable circumftance, however, that notwithftanding the refemblance between thefe two foffils, the LIME from one is *white* as fnow, from the other (now under notice) the colour of *wood afhes!* and this notwithftanding the *redrefs* of the ftone.

chalybeate quality: an alkaline folution throwing down a pure white calcarious matter.

Another fpecimen of a ftill higher red—a direct ruft colour—and which is fufpected to be a fpecies of iron ftone, proves, under analyfis, to be of the fame quality as the main rock; except that it contains a greater proportion of indiffoluble fragments.

Hence, it is more than probable, the idea, that Breedon lime contains fomething of an iron quality, is void of foundation: an idea, however, which deters fome fenfible men from ufing it.

The MANAGEMENT OF LIME, in this diftrict, is entitled to fingular praife. In the common practice of the diftrict, the load heaps are generally *watered*, as they are thrown down from the waggon; and always *turned over*, to complete the falling more effectually. See YORK. ECON. vol. i. p. 350.

For an inftance of this practice, fee MIN. 3.

Another economical practice, in the management of lime, is equally entitled to notice. If a quantity of lime be fetched in autumn or the early part of winter, to be ufed in the fpring, when team labour is more valuable, it is thrown up into a regular rooflike

heap

heap or mound, and *thatcht* as a ftack ! a
fmall trench being cut round the fkirts to
catch, with an outlet to convey away, rain
water.   By this admirable precaution the
furface of the heap, perhaps to a confiderable
depth, is prevented from being run to a mor-
tarlike confiftence by the fnows and rains of
winter, and thereby rendered in a manner ufelefs as manure. See YORK. ECON. v. i. p. 349.

· · MARL.   The red earth which has been
fet upon the lands of this diftrict in great
abundance, as " *marl,*"—is much of it in a
manner deftitute of calcarious matter ; and,
of courfe, cannot, with propriety, be claffed
among MARLS.

Neverthelefs, a red foffil is found, in fome
parts of the diftrict, which contains a proportion of calcarious matter.

The marl of CROXALL (in part, of a
ftonelike or flatey contexture, and of a
light red colour) is the richeft in calcariofity :
one hundred grains of it affording *thirty
grains* of calcarious matter; and feventy
grains of fine impalpable *redbarklike* powder *.

And

* This marl is fingularly tenacious of its calcarious
matter ; diffolving remarkably flowly. One hundred
grains.

And a marl of ELFORD (in colour and contexture various, but refembling thofe of the
CROXALL marl) affords near *twenty grains* :

Yet the marl of BARTON—on the oppofite
fide of the Trent—though fomewhat of a fimilar contexture, but of a darker more dufky
colour—is in a manner deftitute of calcariofity ! one hundred grains of it yielding little
more than one grain—*not two grains* of calcarious matter.   Neverthelefs the pit, from
which I took the fpecimen under analyfis,
is an immenfe excavation, from which many
thoufand loads have been taken.

· And the marls of THIS NEIGHBOURHOOD
(which moftly differ in appearance from
thofe defcribed, having generally that of a
bloodred clay, interlayered, and fometimes
intermingled, with a white gritty fubftance)
are equally poor in calcariofity.

One

---

grains, roughly pounded, was twentyfour hours in diffolving ; and another hundred, though pulverized to
mere duft, continued to effervefce twelve hours; notwithftanding it was firft faturated with water, and afterward fhook repeatedly.   The Breedon ftone, roughly
pounded, diffolved in half the time ; notwithftanding
its extreme hardnefs.

One hundred grains of the marl of Statfold—(which I believe may be taken as a
fair fpecimen of the red clays of this quarter
of the diftrict) afford little more than *two
grains* of calcarious matter *.   Yet this is faid
to be "famous marl;" and, from the pits
which now appear, has been laid on in great
abundance.

I do not mean to intimate that thefe clays
are altogether deftitute of fertilizing properties, on their firft application. It is not likely
that the large pits which abound, in almoft
every part of the diftrict, and which muft
have been formed at a very great expence,
fhould have been dug, without their contents
being productive of fome evidently, or at
leaft apparently, good effect, on the lands
on which they have been fpread.

I confefs, however, that this is but con-
jecture; and it may be, that the good effect
of the marls, firft defcribed, being experienced, the *fafhion* was fet; and, the diftinguifhing quality being unknown, or not attended

* Lodged, not in the fubftance of the clay; but in
its natural cracks or fiffures.

tended to, marls and clays were indifcriminately ufed.

The moft interefting fact that can be brought
home, refpecting thefe clay pits is, that they
were made, chiefly, by the laft generation;
and that the prefent generation are ex-
periencing, or believing that they experience,
an evil effect arifing from their produce : the
fertilizing quality of which (if it ever exifted)
being now fpent, the dead clay remains a
clog to the native foil ; rendering it tenacious,
and difficult to work.

This is at leaft the opinion of intelligent
profeffional men; and the idea, I believe, is
founded in fact. LIME is found to do away
this evil effect; and this may account for the
fpirit of liming in the prefent generation.

On the fouthern banks of the Anker, is
found a GREY MARL; refembling, in general
appearance, the marl of Norfolk, or rather
the fullersearth of Surrey. In contexture, it
is loofe and friable.

This earth is fingularly prodigal of its calcariofity. The acid being dropped on its
furface, it flies into bubbles as the Norfolk
marl. This circumftance added to that of a
                                   ftriking

ftriking improvement which I was ſhown as
being effected by this earth (ſee MIN. 89.) I
was led to imagine that it was of a quality
ſimilar to the marls of Norfolk.

But, from the reſults of two experiments—
one of them made with granules formed by
the weather, and collected on the ſite of improvement, the other with a ſpecimen taken
from the pit—it appears that one hundred
grains of this earth contain no more than
ſix grains of calcarious matter ! the reſiduum
a creamcoloured ſaponaceous clay, with a
ſmall proportion of coarſe ſand.

Hence it is evident, that the acid applied
ſuperficially, as a TEST, *is no guide whatever*
to the intrinſic quality of calcarious ſubſtances.
The marl of Hall End appears, by the acid
of ſea ſalt, uſed as a TEST, to be of tenfold
ſtrength to that of Croxall ; but, by the ſame
acid, uſed as a menſtruum, the latter proves
to be of fivetimes the ſtrength of the former :
while the Breedon ſtone, which appears to be
noncalcarious to the acid, as a TEST, proves,
on ANALYSIS, to be almoſt purely calcarious[*].

For

[*] This by way of caution to thoſe who may have
occaſion to ſearch for calcarious ſubſtances. The
Breedon

For an account of the *Breedon lime*, fee
MIN. 2.

For an inftance of practice in the *management of lime*, 3.

For the method of *fpreading dung* out of
carts, 12.

For an *experiment* with *dung* on fallow for
barley, 18.

For obfervations on *fpreading dung* out of
carts, 18.

For an incident of *plowing in turneps* as a
manure, 34.

For an inftance of *dung* being *too dry* to
digeft, 45.

For an inftance of *watering* a *dung beap*, 47.

For practice and price, of *mixing manures*,
&c. 50.

For reflections on *growing aquatic manure*, 52.

For another inftance of *watering dung*, 57.

For an inftance of collecting *compoft*, 86.

For an account of the *marl* of North Warwickfhire, 89.

For

Breedon ftone by merely touching its natural furface, in
the ufual way, with the acid, might be paffed as noncalcarious. It is obfervable, however, that if the furface
be fcraped, fo as to loofen fome of the particles into a
powder, it inftantly yields to the acid.

For inftance of growing turneps on a *foil
heap*, 95.

For *experiment* with *lime* for barley, 100.

For further obfervations on *Breedonlime*, 103.

For inftance of *lime* ufed as a *topdreffing*, 108.

For the effect of *aquatic manure* on turneps,
fee MIN. 111.

19.

SEMINATION.

IN THE SEED PROCESS of this diftrict,
though there is nothing particularly cenfur-
able, there is little to praife. *Broadcaft*
may be faid to be the univerfal mode of
SOWING : though, of late years, *drilling*, a
procefs *new* to *this* quarter of the kingdom,
has been tried by a few individuals. With
refpect to PLANTING or SETTING, by hand,
I met with only one inftance, and that with
beans.

In finally ADJUSTING the furface after
fowing, the Midland farmers are entitled to
com-

commendation. Barley lands are *clotted,* with clotting beetles; which, on ftrong land, are perhaps much preferable to a roller: and oatlands " *turfed* :"—that is, the fods torn off the plits by the harrows, and lying on the furface, probably with their grafs fides upward, and of courfe in a ftate of vegetation, are thrown, by hand, or with forks, into hollows, with the grafs fide inverted: thus tending to neatnefs, cleannefs, and the relief of the infant crop; while the expence is inconfiderable *.

For a convenient method of *preparing the furface* of a whole-furrow feed-plowing, fee MIN. 20.

For an inftance of *mice* hoarding the *feed,* 26.

For an evidence of the propriety of *fowing the whole furrow* the day it is plowed, 40.

For obfervations on *fowing by the trees,* 82.

For further obfervations on the *fame* fubject, 90.

For opinions on the *change of feed,* 91.

VOL. I.　　　　P　　　　CORN

20.

C O R N   W E E D S.

THE VEGETATING PROCESS of the MIDLAND DISTRICT confifts, merely, in HANDWEEDING; the ufe of the HOE being in a manner unknown to farm labourers, and never attempted by their wives or children (fee GLO. ECON.). Turneps are the only crop which is hoed; and this is generally done by gardeners; or by men who make a trade and myftery of it. See the art. TURNEPS.

The ARABLE WEEDS moft noxious, in this diftrict, are the following. They are divifible into three claffes, agreeably to the ftates of aration, in which they are, refpectively, moft confpicuous; as thofe of

   Fallow, Corn, New ley.

FALLOW WEEDS.

Provincial.	*Linnean.*	*Englifh.*
Twitch,—*triticum repens*,—couchgrafs.		
Black twitch,—*feftuca duriufcula*,—hard fefcue.		

         Running

Provincial.   *Linnean.*   *Englifh.*

Running twitch,—*agroftis alba,*—creeping
    bentgrafs.

Common thiftle,—*ferratula arvenfis,*—com-
    mon thiftle.

Boar thiftle,—*carduus lanceolatus,*——fpear
    thiftle.

Docks—*rumex crifpus* *,—curled dock.

CORN WEEDS.

Rough cadlock,—*finapis arvenfis* †,—wild
    muftard.

Smooth cadlock,—*braffica napus,*—wild rape.

Fathen, or wild fpinage,—*chenopodium viride,*
    redjointed goofefoot.

Dea nettle, or wild hemp,—*galeopfis tetrait,*
    wild hemp.

P 2   *carduus*

---

* In this country, an inftance of practice occurred to
me, which is well entitled to a place in this regifter:
that of employing a woman to follow the plow, efpecially in FALLOWING, to pick up the root weeds expofed in the furrow ; more particularly the DOCK.
When root weeds are abundant, the practice is evidently eligible : the expence is no object, and the benefit, in fome cafes, may be almoft invaluable. MAJOR
BOWLES of Elmhurft, near Litchfield, is entitled to the
honor of this *thought.*

† With a few plants of the WILD RADISH, *raphanus
raphaniftrum.*

Provincial.　　　*Linnean.*　　　*English.*

　　　　carduus lanceolatus,—spear thistle.

　　　　serratula arvensis,—common thistle.

　　　　carduus palustris,—marsh thistle.

　　　　rumex crispus,—curled dock.

Dog fennel,—*anthemis cotula,*——maithe-
　　weed, or stinking camomile.

———, *matricaria suaveolens,*—sweetscent-
　　ed camomile.

Sow thistle,—*sonchus oleraceus,*——common
　　sowthistle.

Hard iron,—*ranunculus arvensis,*—corn crow-
　　foot.

Lap love,—*convolvulus arvensis,*—corn con-
　　volvulus.

———, *polygonum convolvulus,*—climbing
　　buckweed.

Corn mint,—*mentha arvensis,*—corn mint.

　　　　carduus crispus,—curled thistle.

Tare,—*ervum hirsutum,*—twoseeded tare.

———, ———*tetraspermum,*—fourseeded tare.

Hairof,—*galium aparine,*—cleavers.

Willow weed,—*polygonum pennsylvanicum,*—
　　pale persicaria.

Goose tansey,—*potentilla anserina,*—-silver-
　　weed.

　　　　tussilago farfara,—coltsfoot.

　　　　　　　　　　　　Nettles,

Provincial.   *Linnean.*   *Englifh.*

Nettles,—*urtica dioica*,—common nettle.

Poppy,——*papaver dubium*,——longfmooth-headed poppy.

Golds,—*chryfanth. fegetum*,—corn marigold.

Cockle,—*agroftemma githago*,—cockle.

Mellilot,—*trifolium mellilotus*,—mellilot.

Groundfil,—*fenecio vulgaris*,—groundfil.

       thlafpi burfa paft.—fhepherdspurfe.

Begars needle,—*fcandix peften-veneris*,——fhepherds needle.

Chicken weed,—*alfine media*,—chick weed.

       cuphrafia odontites,—red eyebright.

       thlafpi arvenfis, common mithridate.

       fcabiofa arvenfis [*],—corn fcabious.

CLOVER WEEDS.

       filago germanica,—common cudweed.

       ceraftium vulgatum, —— common moufe-ear.

P 3

geranium

[*] This inveterate enemy of arable crops (fee YORK. ECON.) is not common to the diftrifl. SUTTON AM-BION, the bloody fcene on which the brunt of the battle of BOSWORTH FIELD was probably fought, is the only fpot on which I have found it; and there it is fingularly prevalent. The wheat crop, in 1785, was in a manner deftroyed by this weed, encouraged in its mifchiefs by the drynefs of the feafon.

Provincial.	Linnean.	English.
	geranium diffectum, jagged cranesbill.	
	carduus lanceolatus,—spear thistle.	
	rumex crispus,—curled dock.	
	sonchus oleraceus,—common sow-thistle.	
	serratula arvensis *,—common thistle.	

For an instance of the mischievousness of " *black twitch*," see MIN. 59.

For observations on the *couchy softgrass*, 73.

For an instance of the shameful predominancy of *thistles* and *docks*, 76.

For an instance of *weeding* a wheat *stubble*, 77.

HAR-

* I met with an instance in this district, and in the practice of the first manager in it, of the COMMON CORN THISTLE being *drawn* out of new leys, with a docking iron, such as docks are usually drawn with; and although this operation is not found to be a *radical cure*, the first drawing, yet it weakens the roots very much; and, by continuing the practice a few years, is said to extirpate the plants. This I mention by way of hint to those who wish to ascertain, on their own particular soils and situations, the most eligible way of overcoming this most formidable enemy.

21.

HARVESTING.

THE CORN HARVEST of this diſtrict, though it cannot be called, emphatically, a *corn country*, is not got in without ſome foreign aſſiſtance from whom are termed "peakrils" and " low country men :"—namely, men, and ſome women, from the Peak of Derby-ſhire, and the Morelands of Staffordſhire. The wheat is much of it cut by theſe itinerants.

The HARVEST LABOURERS, of the diſtrict, are not hired for the *harveſt month*, as in Surrey, &c.; nor for the *harveſt*, be it ſhort or long, as in Norfolk; but work by the day, as at other ſeaſons of the year; and for the ſame *wages*, a ſhilling a day; but with the addition of full *board*, ſo long as the harveſt laſts: and, in addition to this, each labourer who has been conſtantly employed through the ſummer, has a right, by cuſtom, to the *carriage of a load of coals*, in autumn. It is

alſo

alſo a pretty common cuſtom for farmers to
let their conſtant labourers have their bread
corn ſomewhat below the market price;
more eſpecially when corn is dear.

The *hours of work*, too, like the wages,
are the ſame in harveſt as in leſs buſy ſeaſons;
and the ſame ſlow pace is too generally obſerved. No coming at four in the morning;
no trotting with empty waggons; nor any
perſonal exertion, whatever, betokening
harveſt; ſaving ſuch as are ſtimulated with
ale as ſtrong as brandy!

The method of harveſting SHEAF CORN,
whether *wheat* or *oats*, is, in this diſtrict,
above par. In part it is new to me: REAP-
ING being generally done by the " *threave:*"
—ſeldom by the *acre*.

A threave is twentyfour ſheaves; each ſheaf
meaſuring a yard round, in the banding
place; the ſtring croſſing the band in meaſuring. A better ſized ſheaf, for ſeaſons and
crops in general, could not, *perhaps*, well be
fixed upon (ſee GLO. ECON. art. WHEAT.)

The great difficulty, in reaping by the
threave, lies in not being able to get the
ſheaves made up to the ſtandard. The deviation,

viation, however, is on the right side : whereas, in reaping by the acre, it will always be on the wrong. For, in that case, it is the interest of the reapers to make large sheaves ; having thereby fewer bands and less binding. On the contrary, in reaping by the threave, it is their interest to make small sheaves.

Another conveniency arises from reaping by the threave : any number of hands may be scattered over a piece of corn, as circumstances may require, without the extraordinary trouble of measuring the land in this case. Each man sticks to his " throo," whether it consists of one or more lands, and sets up his own sheaves in one row of shucks, of twelve sheaves each : so that the trouble of ascertaining the number of threaves is inconsiderable.

The *price*, for *wheat*, is fourpence a threave, with beer; provided the crop be tolerably good : if very thin, fivepence or sixpence is sometimes given: or such thin wheat is sometimes reaped by the acre; at about six or seven shillings an acre. For *oats*, threepence is the common price.

In

In CARRYING sheaf corn, there is usually a loader to each pitcher. The buts are laid outward all round, as in Surrey and Norfolk; forming the load, not into a long square, but into a figure between that and an oval; binding it across and across, in three or four places.

The method of harvesting LOOSE CORN, whether *oats* or *barley*, is reduced, here, to the lowest degree of simplicity.

In Yorkshire, barley and oats are mown *inward*, against the standing corn, and harvested in sheaf.

In Kent and Surrey, they are mown *outward*, with a *cradle*, laying them so straight and neatly, they might be bound after the sithe; but are harvested loose. In cocking them, the Kentish farmers make use of *corn forks*; laying the ears all one way; preserving the same neatness and regularity, even to the stack; the outside course of which is laid with unbroken pitches, with the buts outward, having thereby a security nearly equal to that of sheaf corn.

In Norfolk, they are mown *outward*, with *bows*, fixed to the heels of the sithes; which,

which, however, do not lay them fo neatly as cradles; but ftill the heads, if the crop ftand anyway fair, lie one way, and the tails the other. There, too, the *corn fork* is ufed.

Here, they are mown *outward* with *naked fithes!* and cocked, or rather rolled into rough bundles, with common *hay forks!* and this, generally, two or three days before they be carried!! a crop of clover, a crop of barley, a crop of peas, a crop of oats, and a crop of beans and vetches, being harvefted very much in the fame manner.

Mowing barley and oats with naked fithes, and pulling them about with hay forks, have, to ftrangers, a flovenly and wafteful appearance. But with refpect to cocking loofe corn before the day of carrying, fomething, perhaps, may be offered in its favour.

It is true, that, in other diftricts, it is confidered as very bad management to leave even a few cocks remaining only one night; under an idea that, if loofe corn once get wet in cock, it is difficult to get it dry again, without a great wafte of labour and corn. Neverthelefs, experience fhows that even a very heavy fhower has not that evil effect in the practice of this country.

An

An incident in my own experience convinced me of the fact: I had, through neglect, a few oats in cock left out all night.
Next day, much rain fell; but the succeeding day proving fine, they were got into very
good order again, in this manner. The tops
were first dried, by raising them up, light and
porous, with the tines of a fork; so as to let
the sun and air into them; and, when the
tops were dry, the bundles were turned over,
to air the bottoms.

In this manner, and without greater trouble,
corn cocks are generally dried; though sometimes it will happen that they require to be
pulled to pieces: in which case, there is,
of course, considerable waste.

The Midland farmers have one very good
plea for harvesting *oats* in this manner. For,
by cocking them a few days before carrying,
the labour and waste of turning is saved:
besides, by being cocked while a portion
of the sap remains in them, they are not so
liable to be shed in cocking, as when they
are disturbed in a dry parched state.

This practice, probably, took its rise in
open common fields. Formerly, much of the
                                        district

diftrict lay in that ftate; the foil being raifed
into high rooflike ridges. The furrows and
fkirts of the lands lay, of courfe, proportionably
low; and the corn being thereby frequently deprived of the benefit of the fun and wind, it
was found, by experience, moft eligible to
gather the corn into heaps, and place them
upon the tops of the ridges.   And this is the
prefent practice of "field farmers." In a
few days after cutting, the whole crop may be
feen ftanding in pitchcocks, placed in clofe
order, like ftrings of beads ftretched along
the ridges.

But notwithftanding this practice may be
eligible where corn is mown with the naked
fithe, and rolled up into rough porous bundles,
it does not follow that it fhould be univerfally
adopted. Were a Kentifhman to leave his
unruffled clofe piles expofed even to one
heavy fhower, he would find fome difficulty
to get them thoroughly dry again, without
fpreading them abroad.

An evil attendant of the Midland method
of harvefting loofe corn is, the increafe of
bulk which corn harvefted in this way acquires, comparatively with the fame quantity
of

of corn harvested in the Kentish manner.
More barnroom is of course wanted, and a
greater number of loads are to be carried.
Four loads an acre is no uncommon crop :
five loads are talked of, and are sometimes
carried. But the method of *loading*, and that
of *barning*, both of them tend to increase this
evil.

The method of CARRYING loose corn,
here, differs from that of other districts, in
having only *one* loader to *two* pitchers ; and in
loading, not with the *arms*, but with a *fork* ; the
loader standing in the centre of the load, and
piling the corn loose and light around him.
Thus the entire process tends to encrease the
number of loads.

And the method of HOUSING is not calculated to do away the inconveniency. I never
met with an instance, in this district, of a
horse, or any other *animal*, being used on a
mow.

RICKING, however, remedies the evil ; and
in this district, where barnroom is more con-
tracted than in some other, loose corn is
pretty generally put into ricks.

In the *method of ricking loose corn*, nothing is
noticeable ; excepting the last finish. To
endeavour

endeavour to fecure the ftems from the pil-
laging of fparrows, and other fmall birds,
they are, generally, either " tucked" or
" pared :" that is, either the loofe ears, expofed on the outfide, as many unavoidably
are, in the method of harvefting above defcribed, are doubled back, and thruft into
the ftem; or the entire ftem is fhaved with a
fithe laid longway in the handle, or fome
other fimilar inftrument : in fome few inftances I have feen the ftems thatched, as the
roofs.

On *ricking fheaf corn* a few particulars may
be mentioned. Though built on a fquare
frame, the ftem—provincially the " wall,"—
is not carried up fquare, as in Surrey and
Norfolk; nor round, as in Glocefterfhire; but
in a form between the two; the corners of
ricks being rounded off, as thofe of loads.

Large ricks being fafhionable, and it being
cuftomary, in carrying up the ftems, to *bind*
with the ears, inftead of the buts of the
fheaves, they are of courfe liable to *flip*. This
has taught the Midland rickers an admirable
expedient, when any fymptom of flipping, in
carrying up the ftem, is perceived, to prevent

vent the mifchief; namely, that of laying *long green boughs* acrofs the part affected : an excellent thought.

In fetting on the *roof* of a fheaf corn rick, the Midland rickers are above par : laying the laft courfe of the ftem fo as to project a few inches, and form a kind of cornice for the eaves of the thatch to reft upon, and to carry the drip clear of the ftem. The middle is then filled in full and round ; fo that the buts of the outfide fheaves hang downward.

This, though not peculiar to the diftrict, is a rule which ought always to be obferved, in forming a roof : for, in this cafe, if rain fhould happen to penetrate through the thatch, there is little fear of its doing, even the roof of the rick, much injury : every ftraw becoming a conductor to lead it to the furface.

Another commendable practice, in forming the roof of a fheaf corn rick, and which is new to me, is that of carrying it up without a *pitching hole*. A man fticks his heels into the roof, and ftands with great eafe and fafety. This might well be copied by other diftricts : holes are dangerous ; unlefs great care be

ufed

used in making them up, and in thatching them securely. For if water enter, in this part, it finds its way directly into the heart of the rick.

The method of *securing corn ricks*, in a catching season, previous to their being thatched, is likewise entitled to notice. It is effected with " battins"—small trusses of straw—which are afterward used as thatch. A row being laid close, and pegged *securely* along the eaves, with their buts downward, others are laid (firmly but without pegs), as tiles or slates are laid on a roof, with their heads downward ; spreading the ears (without untying the bands) so as to prevent the rain water from getting through between those which lie below : continuing, thus, till the ridge be reached.

Having plenty of these battins, in corn harvest, ready at hand, to cover a rick with, in catching weather, is a very great conveniency. A rick of " 200 threave," eighteen or twenty loads, may be secured in a few hours : or, with plenty of hands, in half an hour.

The method of *thatching ricks* is also peculiar in this district, and requires to be men-

tioned.   Inftead of thrufting the ears of the
ftraw into the roof, and fpreading the buts
outwardly as a fecurity ; the ftraw, in thatching, is laid on as the battins, with the ears
downward, and of courfe outward (excepting
the firft courfe at the eaves), and is fecured
in its place, by pegs and hay ropes * ; paffing horizontally from end to end of the
roof; at the diftance of twelve or fourteen
inches from each other †.

For obfervations on *fhucking* fheaf corn, 10.

For remarks on *reaping* by the threave, 75.

For reflections on *gleaning*, 80.

For further obfervations on *fhucking*, 81.

FARM

* Sometimes thatch is bound with *ofier twigs*, which
are much more lafting than hay bands (that are only
annuals), in a fimple ingenious manner. The fmall end
is formed into an eye, like that of a with, and the thick
end run into the roof, as a peg, thro' the eye of the
fucceeding twig.

† An inconveniency attends this method of thatching.
A rick cannot be thatched, with propriety, until the
roof has done fettling. For if it fetle after it is thatched,
the ftraw is raifed into puckers between the bands, and
the water, of courfe, let in.

22.

FARMYARD MANAGEMENT.

ON THE BARN MANAGEMENT of this diſtrict little requires to be ſaid. The ſouthern method of *thraſhing*, and the *ſail fan*, are in univerſal practice. I have, however, met with ſome two or three *machine fans*; and theſe, in the practice of the very firſt managers of the diſtrict: neverthelefs, even the ſuperior claſs of farmers, in general, ſtill remain in the old duſty path.

CHAFCUTTING, as it is pretty generally termed, but here provincially "*ſtrawcutting*," —is in great uſe. Not, however, the ordinary practice of cutting *hay* and *ſtraw* into what is, in moſt places, called *chaf* or *cutchaf*, but, here, more properly "CUTMEAT;" but by reducing *oats, in ſtraw*, into this ſpecies of ſodder; which is given, not to horſes only, but to cattle; eſpecially fatting cattle.

It is thought to give, not only fatneſs, but a fineneſs of ſkin, to all ſorts of ſtock.

The CHAFBOX made uſe of, here, is of a peculiar conſtruction. It unites, in ſome meaſure, the old ſingle-hand machine, and the modern one with a wheel of blades. This, in uſe here, has a long upright knife; but feeds itſelf; by which means the cutter has both hands at liberty, for the knife. It is made at or near Birmingham, and ſold at moſt of the market towns of the diſtrict. It is, however, ſomewhat complex; and fitter for a man who makes a buſineſs of. " ſtraw cutting," than for a farmer's ſervant.

The *price* of cutting, three farthings a heaped buſhel; but it is cut extraordinarily fine.

The STRAWYARD MANAGEMENT, here, falls between the northern and the ſouthern practices: *cows* are pretty generally *houſed*, in the ſheds that have been deſcribed : but *young ſtock* ſtill remain in *open yards*; and ſome are kept out, in the *field*, a principal part of winter.

MARKETS.

23.

MARKETS.

THE PRINCIPAL MARKETS of the immediate DISTRICT of the STATION, are *Tamworth*, *Lichfield*, *Burton* (on Trent), *Ashby* (De la Zouch), *Atherston*, *Bosworth*.

The three firſt are good markets ; the laſt is almoſt in difuſe ; though ſituated in the center of a fertile diſtrict ; a charming plot of country. But there is no manufactory, no navigation, nor any great road, within ſeveral miles of it ; its own road very bad ; with Aſhby and Atherſton on either ſide of it ; and LEICESTER within reach.

But the *metropolitan* market of the diſtrict is BIRMINGHAM, with the manufacturing towns of its neighbourhood. The produce of *this* diſtrict, whether of live ſtock or grain,

grain, may be said to center eventually in Birmingham; which bears a similar relation to the market-towns of the country round it, as London does to those in its neighbourhood *.

The more southern parts of LEICESTERSHIRE and WARWICKSHIRE, NORTHAMPTONSHIRE, &c. are influenced by the grand vortex. The fat cattle and sheep of these districts go chiefly to SMITHFIELD.

It may be right in this place, to take notice of a dispute which arose, during my residence in the district, between the townspeople of Tamworth and the hucksters of Birmingham: the dispute arising to little less than riot: the townspeople driving the hucksters out of the market.

This is an interesting subject. Markets are, or ought to be adapted to the mutual benefit of the producers, and the consumers at large:

* Lately, a weekly market has been established at ROTHERHAM, in Yorkshire, to which fat stock is driven from the northern parts of LEICESTERSHIRE, &c. The buyers at this market are the butchers, not of the manufacturing towns of Yorkshire only, but of Lancashire.

large: but more particularly to thofe of the given town, and its neighbourhood. Mere market towns have no huckfters to fupply them. They depend entirely upon the marketday for their fupply: and if, in times of fcarcity, huckfters from large towns repair to a country market, they may, in a few minutes, clear the market; and leave the townfpeople deftitute of a week's provifions.

On the other hand, if huckfters be wholly precluded from buying up even the furplus of a country market, the market itfelf, and of courfe the townfpeople, eventually, will be injured. The producer will, of courfe, endeavour to find out a market, where he can fell his produce, *on a certainty*; without running the rifque of having it to bring home, or of felling it at an under price to the *monopolizers* of the town. The market of courfe becomes badly ferved, and the ware, in confequence, inferior and dear.

The markets of Lichfield and Walfal (with many others in the kingdom) are therefore wifely regulated. They *open at eleven* o'clock; but no HUCKSTER is permitted to buy until

twelve:

twelve: so that the TOWNSPEOPLE have an hour to supply their wants. By this judicious regulation the markets are, eventually, served; and this, without injuring the town, in the first instance, by rendering its inhabitants liable to circumstances.

For a description of Belton fair, 1.
For a description of Fazeley fair, 13.
For a description of Tamworth fair, 15.
For remarks on the delivery of corn, 31.
For a description of Ashby stallion show, 37.

24.

WHEAT.

THE SPECIES prevalent, here, is the " RED LAMMAS;" the ordinary red wheat of the kingdom.

Of late years, the " ESSEX DUN,"—similar to the *Kentish white cosh* of NORFOLK, and the *Hertfordshire brown* of YORKSHIRE, —has been making its way into this district.

Those

Thofe who have given it a fair trial, like it, on account of its giving a great produce: but the millers are not yet reconciled to it; though they give no fufficient reafon for their diflike. But fo it was in Norfolk, on its firft introduction there: fee NORF. ECON. vol. 1. p. 202.

CONE WHEAT was formerly grown in this diftrict; but is, at prefent, out of ufe.

SPRING WHEAT (*triticum æftivum*) is here cultivated, and with fingular fuccefs; owing principally to the *time of fowing:* the wane of April!

This proves that it is a fpecies widely diftinct in its nature from the *winter* wheats.

In the practice of a fuperior manager * it was difcovered, that by fowing early, as the beginning of March, the grain was liable to be fhrivelled, and the ftraw to be blighted; while that fown, late, as the middle or latter end of April, or even the beginning of May, produced clean plump corn! effects directly oppofite to thofe of winter wheat.

However,

* Mr. PAGET of Ibftock.

However, it appears to be at prefent (1789) growing into difrepute: the quality of the grain is found to be lefs valuable than that of Lammas wheat. Neverthelefs, in fome fituations, and under fome circumftances, I am clearly of opinion it may be highly eligible: more efpecially in a *turnep* country. It appears to me to be well entitled to the attention of the Norfolk farmers.

SUCCESSION. In the ordinary practice of the country, wheat *fucceeds* oats! Perhaps, nine tenths of the wheat grown in the diftrict is what is termed "brufh wheat:" is fown on *oat ftubble*—provincially "oat brufh"— with a fmall proportion of "*barley brufh*." A fact which a ftranger riding through the diftrict, previous to harveft, and feeing the fine crops of wheat which it produces, would not readily credit.

I met with a few inftances of wheat being fown on *turf* of fix or feven years leying; and with feveral on *clover ley* once plowed: alfo fome of wheat after *turneps* *. But the beft

crops

---

* Weftward of the Tame—the foil a light fandy loam,—it is the prevailing practice to fow wheat after turneps, fed off with fheep in autumn.

crops which this, or almoſt any other diſtrict produces, are ſown after *ſummerfallow*. The practice, however, is confined principally to one leading man ;—Mr. PRINCEP of Croxall.

Neverthelefs, viewing the diſtrict generally, the univerſal matrix of wheat may be ſaid to be OAT STUBBLE; of which, only, I ſhall treat.

TILLAGE. The ſoil procefs varies in the practice of different individuals. Some plow *once* lengthway, as the old turf was plowed for oats. Others plow *once* acrofs, cutting the plits of the old turf at right angle ; afterwards gathering a bout, that is, laying two plits back to back ; in each interfurrow ; to drain more effectually the wide ridges, in which the lands of the diſtrict are chiefly laid. Others break the ground (provincially "work their bruſhes"—) by *two* plowings—the firſt acrofs, the laſt lengthway : and ſome few by *three* plowings; lengthway, acrofs, lengthway.

The firſt is a filthy-looking, ſlovenly buſinefs; though a common practice. The ſecond, with the ſame labour, is infinitely preferable ; and, in a wet autumn, may be more eligible than breaking the ground by a greater number of plowings. When the seafon and other circumstances will permit, the last is, no doubt, to be preferred.

MANURE. The manure procefs likewife varies. If the turf has been recently manured, previous to the oat crop, or the foil otherwife in good heart, the wheat is frequently fown without manure. When manure is ufed, *dung*—provincially " muck" —is the prevailing fpecies. If the ground be only once plowed, the muck is generally laid upon the stubble, and plowed under, with the one plowing. If the ground be broken, it is common to lay it on the crofs plowing, and plow it under with the feed plowing.

One circumstance in the manure procefs for wheat requires to be noticed. It is common, though not univerfal, to fet the muck upon the land in a raw long ftrawy ftate; carrying it immediately from the yard to the field, without having been previoufly turned up and digefted. This is probably a dreg of the common field hufbandry; in which the yard muck was, perhaps judicioufly, left unmoved; with the intent that its ftrawinefs might prevent the too fallowy mould of land, fummerfallowed every third year, from being run together by heavy rains (fee MIN. 21).

But,

But, in pinfallowed inclofures, the twitch alone is too frequently more than adequate to this intention ; and to throw additional incumbrances in the way of the harrow is certainly reprehenfible.

Sowing. The *time of fowing*—October. Little is fown before new Michaelmas : and if the feafon be favourable, little after the clofe of October.

Preparing the feed is not univerfally attended to. Much feed is fown without preparation; which, I underftand, is of modern date, as a practice, in this diftrict. The preparation, in the beft efteem, is the common one of fwimming in brine, and candying with lime.

The *mode of fowing*, broadcaft, and generally above furrow ; the foil being feldom got fine enough to plow in the feed.

The *quantity of feed*, pretty univerfally, three bufhels an acre ; without much regard to the time of fowing.

Vegetating Process. *Handweeded:* no *hoing* of wheat in this diftrict.—For opinions on *eating* wheat with fheep, and on *barrowing* wheat in the fpring, fee XIN. 113.

Har-

For an incident on *sowing* the whole furrow of a *clover ley*, 40.

For remarks on the nature of *blights*, 65.

For an inftance of *blight*, 74.

For remarks on *reaping* by the threave, 75.

For an inftance of *weeding* wheat *ftubble*, 77.

For remarks on *gleaning*, 80.

For further obfervations on *fhucking*, 81.

For the effect of *sowing* wheat on clover ley immediately after the plow, 96.

For opinions on *eating* and *harrowing* wheat, fee MIN. 113.

25.

B A R L E Y.

THE SPECIES OF BARLEY in cultivation, here, are

HORDEUM *zeocriton*; LONGEARED BARLEY.
HORDEUM *diftichon*; SPRAT BARLEY.

The latter is the old ftock of the country; the former of late introduction; of not more, I underftand, than about fifty years ftanding. The fprat is deemed more hardy, and requires

quires to be fown more early; the longear
to be the better yielder. The fprat is thought
(by maltflers) to make the beft keeping
beer; the longear to be " freer"—to operate
quicker—both in the malthoufe and the
cellar.

The longear is not unfrequently had out
of Kent, under the name of THANET BAR-
LEY; which, at prefent, is in the firft eftimation.

SUCCESSION. In the ordinary practice of
the diftrict, barley fucceeds *wheat*. Where
turneps are grown, it fucceeds that crop.

It is obfervable, however, that on the
ftrong lands of *this* diftrict, the crop, after
wheat, is lefs productive, and much lefs *certain*, than it is after turneps *. But the fame
circumftance is obferved in Norfolk, where
the foil is much lighter. See NORF. ECON.
v. i. p. 237.

Barley is likewife fown, and of late years
not unfrequently, on *turf*; and with good
fuccefs †.

TILLAGE.

* On the lighter lands, on the fkirts of the Foreft, it is
faid to anfwer perfectly well after turneps. See MIN. 92.

† One fuperior manager has fown barley on turf, for
more than twenty years; getting extraordinary crops
from this practice.

TILLAGE. *After wheat*, the foil is winter-fallowed,—provincially " pin-fallowed *"—by three plowings : the firft, lengthway, in November, &c.; the fecond acrofs, in March, &c.; the laft, the feed plowing, lengthway. Between the two laft plowings the foil is harrowed, and the twitch fhook out with forks, and left, loofe and light, on the furface, to die ; being feldom, in common practice at leaft, either burnt or carried off. If the weather prove dry and parching, this may be an eafy way of *checking* the foulnefs.

After turneps—the foil has generally three plowings : for the turneps being moftly folded off with fheep, the foil, naturally of a clofe texture, is thought to receive a degree of compactnefs, ill fuited to the fibrils of this delicate plant, until it be broken, and rendered porous, by tillage.

SOWING. The *time of fowing*, if the *weather* will permit, is the two laft weeks in April and the firft in May : the Midland farmers going entirely by the ALMANACK—if they can—not by the SEASON.

The

---

* PIN-FALLOW. The origin of this term I have not learnt : it appears to be fynonymous with WINTER-FALLOW, or BARLEY FALLOW.

The *quantity of feed*—two bufhels and a half
to three bufhels an acre; and, in the practice
of fome men, fo much as four bufhels;
though, perhaps, unneceffarily.

The *method of fowing*—broadcaft; moftly
above; but fometimes, if the land be got
very fine, the feed is plowed under.

Adjufting. If the harrow leave any clods
unreduced on the furface, they are broken
with the clotting beetle by women, &c.; and
if any twitch be pulled up in harrowing, it is
fhook out loofe, with forks, and left on the
furface to wither. Both of them eligible
operations—where they are wanted.

The WEEDING,

The HARVESTING, and

The YARD MANAGEMENT of barley appear, aforegoing, under thefe general heads.

MARKETS. The *Burton* breweries; and
the *manufacturing towns*; where incredible
quantities of malt are faid to be confumed.

PRODUCE,—extraordinarily large. *Seven*
quarters an acre is no unufual crop: *eight*
quarters have been grown. One fuperior
manager frequently grows fix or feven quarters round. *Four* to *four and a half* quarters
an acre may be taken as the par produce.

For

For an experiment with barley on *clover ley*, see MIN. 9.

For an incident on *plowing in feed* barley, 41.

For instances of barley badly *harvested*, 83.

For a detail of my own practice, 90.

For observations on the *time of sowing*, 90:

For instances of barley miscarrying, *after turneps*, 92.

For instance of frost's *ripening* barley, 93.

For a further detail of my own practice, 102.

For the result of this practice, 117.

For instances of the bad quality of barley, see MIN. 117.

26.

O A T S.

THE SPECIES OF OAT at present in esteem is the " DUTCH OAT"—the same or similar to the *Friezland oat* of Yorkshire. The POLAND OAT, which was the favorite, is going out of repute; on account of the thickness of its skin.

R 2   The

The SUCCESSION, uniformly, *turf,—oats.*

The TILLAGE,—one plowing in February, March, or April.

SOWING. *Time of sowing,* latter end of March and beginning of April. *Quantity of seed,*—four to five bushels. The same observation, with respect to the seed of oats, has been made here as in Yorkshire; the produce being in proportion to the quantity of seed: hence six or seven bushels are sown in the practice of some individuals. *Sow* broadcast: —*cover* with the harrow; *adjust* by turfing. See general head SEMINATION.

For WEEDING,—HARVESTING, and YARD MANAGEMENT, see the general heads.

MARKETS. Notwithstanding the quantity of oats grown in the district, a principal part of them is expended on *farm horses!* others go to the *inns* of the district, and the surrounding country.

PRODUCE. Sward being the matrix, no wonder the produce is abundant. *Six quarters* an acre may be considered as the par produce of oats on turf, in the Midland District.

For observations on the *time of sowing,* see MIN. 82.

For remarks on *harvesting,* 82.

PULSE.

27.

P U L S E.

IN THE INCLOSURES of the Midland Diſtrict, little of this claſs of grain is cultivated.

BEANS and DILLS (a ſpecies of large vetch; the Yorkſhire *fitches*. See YORK. ECON.) are the prevailing crop.

The only circumſtance of their culture which is entitled to notice, belongs to the SEED PROCESS.

In every other diſtrict, in which I have hitherto obſerved, BEANS are either ſown on the whole plit, and *harrowed in*, or are ſet or *planted* by hand; but, here, the prevailing practice, at preſent, is to *ſow them on ſtubble*— generally wheat ſtubble—and to *plow them under!* with a thin *flat* furrow: afterwards ſowing the DILLS, and harrowing them in.

If beans alone be the crop, the ſurface, in

the practice of fome, is neverthelefs harrowed, as fine as if they had been fown
abovefurrow ; in others, the plits are left
whole.

If the ground be broken, as a pin-fallow,
—the beans and dills are fometimes both of
them fown *underfurrow*, and plowed in together.

It is obfervable that beans, plowed under
whole furrows, rife principally in the feams;
but fome of them through the furrows or
plits. They have even been obferved to force
their way through a footpath, though trod-
den as firm as a plafter floor!

The difadvantage of plowing beans under
whole furrows arifes principally, it is underftood, in their lying hollow ; thereby fpending their firft and main effort in running under the furrows ; never, in this cafe, reaching
the furface. Hence the ufe of turning the
furrows as *flat* as poffible. When the feafon
will permit, *rolling* would, under this idea,
be of effential fervice,

For HARVESTING beans, fee the general
article, HARVESTING LOOSE CORN.

POTATOES.

28.

POTATOES.

THE SPECIES, or rather VARIETIES of, potatoes have, of late years, undergone a total change, in this diſtrict.

The old varieties, formerly in cultivation, dwindling in produce, and being, at length, in a manner deſtroyed, by the diſeaſe of CURLEDTOP,—two new varieties were introduced,—under the names of GOLDFINDERS and GOLDENDABS;—the former a yellow kidneylike root (but with a ſcurfy rind, not unlike that of the old ruſſet potatoe); the latter of a ſimilar colour but of a different form, being ſomewhat bellſhaped.   The conſequence has been, the diſeaſe vaniſhed with the old ſorts, and is now (1786) and in *this* neighbourhood, where no other ſort is in ordinary cultivation, in a manner forgot.

In 1789, I met with a ſimilar inſtance in *Leiceſterſhire*; where the " old red ſort" was
R 4   entirely

entirely worn out with the difeafe ; while a white fort, now in cultivation, was " *never known to curl.*"

In *Rutlandfhire* I had ocular evidence of the fame nature. Obferving, in a large piece of potatoes, two ftripes which were almoft wholly curled, while the reft of the piece appeared to be free from the difeafe, I enquired into the caufe of difparity ; and received in anfwer, without hefitation, that the healthy plants were " manleys," and the difeafed ftripes " rednofed kidneys ;" which, heretofore, was the prevailing fpecies ; but being no longer to be cultivated with any degree of fuccefs, a *new fort* was, fome years ago, introduced under the name of the " manley," which ftill remains free from the difeafe.

Thefe are evidences, and ftrong ones, that the difeafe of CURLEDTOP is *incident to varieties* ; and the circumftance of the *old* forts, which have been in cultivation from the firft introduction of potatoes into the ifland, being now almoft wholly cut off by it,—renders it *probable* that the difeafe is incident to *declining varieties* of POTATOES ; as the *canker* is to declining varieties of FRUIT. See GLO. ECON, See alfo YORK. ECON. ii. 52.

The

The CULTIVATION of potatoes, in this diſtrict, though it does not require to be given in detail, throughout, is entitled, in ſeveral particulars, to notice.

SUCCESSION. Contrary to the practices of moſt other diſtricts, potatoes, here, ſucceed *turf*: are planted, almoſt invariably, on *graſs-land*.

SOIL PROCESS. The *plow* is ſeldom, if ever, uſed, here, in the cultivation of the potatoe crop. The ſoil is broken up with the *ſpade*: ſometimes in two ſhallow ſpits, throwing the ſward and the dung, if any be uſed, to the bottom; covering them, in the gardener's manner, with the under ſpit: but, generally, in one full ſpit; merely inverting the ſward; fitting the ſpits to each other; leaving a ſmooth even ſurface of clear free ſoil.

PLANTING. On this ſurface the plants are *dibbled* very thick, about the middle of April *.

The

* Potatoes are ſometimes grown two years together on the ſame land; and, in this caſe, *it is ſaid* to have been found that dibbling in the ſets, on the ſtale ſurface, as left, on taking up the firſt crop, or only levelled with the harrow, without a previous plowing or digging, is the moſt eligible method of putting in the ſecond crop: this, however, by way of hint.

The VEGETATING PROCESS confifts in *ho-ing*, once, twice, or as often as circumftances may require; the crop, throughout, being moftly, though not always, managed in a gardenly manner.

The crop is TAKEN UP with *forks*, in the gardener's method, about the middle of Oc-tober: the *price* of taking up is according to the crop; generally, I believe, from 1d. to 2d. a bufhel.

PRESERVING. The method of laying up potatoes, here, is, univerfally, that of "camp-ing" them: a method which requires to be defcribed.

"CAMPS" are fhallow pits, filled, and ridged up as a roof, with potatoes; which are covered up with the excavated mould of the pit.

This is a happy mean between burying them in *deep pits*, and laying them upon the *furface*. See YORK. ECON. v. ii. p. 62.

Camps are of various fizes; being too fre-quently made in a longfquare form, like a corn rick, and of a fize proportioned to the quantity to be laid up. It has, however, been found, by experience, that, when the quantity is large, they are liable to heat and fpoil:

spoil : much damage having sometimes been sustained by this imprudence.

Experienced campers hold, that a camp should not be more than three feet wide : four feet is, perhaps, as *wide* as it can be made with propriety ; proportioning the *length* to the quantity : or, if this be very large, forming a range of short ones, by the side of each other.

The usual *depth* is a foot.

The bottom of the trench being bedded with dry straw, the potatoes are deposited ; ridging them up, as in measuring them with a bushel. On each side the roof, long wheat straw is laid, neatly and evenly, as thatch ; and over this the mould, raised out of the trench, is evenly spread : making the surface firm and smooth with the back of the spade. A coat of coal ashes is sometimes spread over the mould ; as a still better guard against frost.

It is needless to observe that a camp should have a dry situation ; or that the roots ought to be deposited in as dry a state as possible.

These camps are *topped* at the end ; some battins, or a quantity of loose straw, being thrust close into the opened end, as a *bung* or safeguard,

MARKET

MARKETS and EXPENDITURE. Birmingham, the other manufacturing towns, and the
collieries are conftant markets for this valuable crop. And befide what go to market,
great quantities are expended, in a plentiful
year, on the fatting of fwine; and fome few
have been given to cattle.

The *price*, in a plentiful year, very low;
feldom more than a fhilling a bufhel: in
1785, they were fold, at the time of taking
up, at ten pence: in December, they were
fold at a fhilling; and warranted to weigh
80lb. a bufhel. How cheap, as an article of
human food!

PRODUCE. Extraordinary large. By information, that I have no reafon to doubt,
and in two or three different inftances, fix
hundred bufhels an acre have been produced!
feven ftrike a "rood" (of eight yards fquare)
has, not unfrequently, been grown. Four
to five ftrike a rood, or three to four hundred
bufhels an acre, is reckoned a fair good
crop.

For the practice of planting the nooks of
corn fields, fee MIN. 44.

For an inftance of the mafter and his men
going halves in a potatoe crop, 63.

TURNEPS.

29.

TURNEPS.

THE TURNEP CROP, though cultivated in a good manner by a few superior managers, does not enter into the ordinary practice of *this* diftrict. At prefent, not one acre in a hundred, taking the diftrict throughout, is fubjected to the turnep culture. I have rode through a fucceffion of townfhips without feeing an acre of turneps; and, of thofe that are fown, few are cultivated in a hufbandly manner.

Neverthelefs, there are, here and there, on *this* fide of the Tame, a patch of turneps to be feen, fet out and cleaned in a hufbandlike ftyle.

Weft of the Tame, where the foil is light, and the fubfoil abforbent, the turnep crop forms the bafis of the prefent hufbandry : and this notwithftanding the proper management

ment of the crop may be faid to be new to this quarter of the kingdom. The hoing of turneps has not been eftablifhed, as a practice in *hufbandry*, more, perhaps, than twenty years. To the MARQUIS TOWN-SHEND, who fent hoers out of Norfolk, the country, I underftand, is indebted for its eftablifhment.

There may be two reafons why the turnep culture does not become prevalent in this diftrict.

Grafs can be had at will; the whole diftrict being prone to it; while the foil and the fub-foil, except in fome particular fituations, are, *perhaps*, ineligible for this crop. One ftrong evidence, at leaft, may be produced in corroboration of this idea. One of the largeft farmers in the diftrict grows no turneps; and gives this as a reafon for his conduct.

The firft year his father gave up the ma-nagement of his farm to him; fome twelve or fifteen years ago; he grew a piece of turneps : the firft the farm produced. The crop turn-ed out pretty good; and he began, agreeably to the common practice of the country, to fold them off with fheep. But the piece
lying

lying flat, and the weather proving wet, his
sheep did "sadly;" and what was worse to
a young farmer, his father laughed at him.
He littered them in the close, with straw;
but this would not remedy the evil: at last
he drew the turneps; and threw them to the
sheep on an adjoining piece; but even
then, they did no good upon them. In
short, he speaks of eating turneps upon the
ground with sheep as a thing impracticable!

I do not mention this circumstance to throw
a damp on the culture of turneps; but to
endeavour to assign them their proper soil and
situation; by showing, in striking colours,
the difficulties to which the crop is liable,
on strong retentive land.

The other circumstance which has tended
to check the cultivation of the turnep crop,
was the devastation of the turnep caterpillar
in 1782: (See Norf. Econ.) since which
time its culture has been declining, rather
than gaining ground.

On a light dry turnep soil, in an upland
situation, this crop is in a degree *neceffary*; and,
there, little difficulties are struggled with,
and miscarriages soon forgot. Here, on the
contrary,

foil is in heart; the crop of barley good, and the furface of courfe *clean*; that is, free from the *herbage* of weeds; this may, fometimes, on a fheep farm, and under particular circumftances, be a valuable expedient. If the attempt mifcarry, the feed, only, is loft. The *thought*, at leaft, is worth preferving; efpecially as the inftance which came more particularly to my knowledge, occurred in the practice of a judicious manager.

Sowing. The deviation to be noticed is in the *method of fowing*: inftead of delivering the feed from between the two fingers and the thumb, as is ufually done, the feedman (fome feedfmen at leaft) lets it fall back into the palm of his hand, and delivers it from thence, in the manner corn is fown. It is obfervable that in this method of fowing, it is neceffary to keep the fingers clofe; otherwife, the feeds of turneps being fmall, they are liable to fly out between them. I mention this as a deviation, rather than a fuperior excellency. I have feen turneps come up very even from this method of fowing; but not evener, than I have feen them rife in Norfolk, from the common method.

For obfervations on HOING, in this diftrict, fee MIN. 6.

EXPENDITURE. The expedient I have
feen practifed, in this ftage of the turnep
culture, is that of drawing the turneps, at
the fetting in of a froft, or to clear the ground
in the fpring, and loading them upon waggons; leaving them in the piece, where
they are fafe, and ready to be drawn to
whence they may be wanted.

For obf. on the Midland practice of *hoing*, fee MIN. 6.

For obf. on *bandweeding*, 16.

For an inftance of *plowing in* turneps as a
manure, 34.

For an inftance of young turneps *thriving*
in drought, 43.

For inftances of the *enemies* of turneps,
61.

For an inftance of *hoing* clufters, 79.

For further obf. on turnep *infects*, 84.

For general obf. on the turnep *culture*, 87.

For practical obf. on *hoing*, 87.

For inftances of turneps being unfriendly
to *barley*, 92.

For obf. on *turneping* in froft, 115.

CABBAGES.

30.

CABBAGES.

THE SOILS of this diftrict are better adapted to CABBAGES, than to *turneps*. Confidering the facility of the culture of this crop, and the great produce it yields when a proper fort is planted on a fuitable foil, and confidering the length of time cabbages have now been cultivated as a crop in hufbandry, it is remarkable that they have not entered more freely into the general practice of *this* diftrict; to whofe foil and fituation they are peculiarly well adapted.

At prefent, the quantity grown is inconfiderable: I have feen, however, feveral fmall patches in different parts of the diftrict; and, from the manner in which the value of thefe is fpoken of, there is fome probability of cabbages becoming a prevalent crop.

Among

Among the rambreeders of *Leicestershire*, &c. they may be said to be already established as such ; and there is one man within *this* district, Mr. PAGET of Ibstock, who is the greatest cabbage grower I have any where observed *. He has grown ten, twelve, or fourteen acres, a year, for many years past.

On the CULTIVATION of this crop so much has been said, the public could receive little useful information from a recital of the practice of this district.

Indeed, the art of CULTIVATING cabbages is so extremely simple, and so well understood by every farmer, gardener, and cottager in the kingdom, it, perhaps, of all other operations in husbandry, requires the least explanation.

Much, however, depends on the SPECIES or sort for field culture. Not more on the *size*, than on the *nutritiveness* of quality and *hardiness*, in resisting the severity of winter.

There is, in this country, a valuable sort—a large green cabbage—propagated,

if

---

* Excepting, perhaps, Mr. BAKEWELL of Dishley.

if not raifed, by Mr. BAKEWELL, who is not more celebrated for his breed of rams, than for his *breed* of *cabbages.*

Great care is obferved, here, in RAISING THE SEED; being careful to fuffer no other variety of the braffica tribe to *blow* near feed cabbages; by which means they are kept "true to their kind." To this end, fome, it is faid, plant them in a piece of wheat: a good method; provided the feed in that fituation can be preferved from birds.

The principal advantage of largenefs in fize of field cabbages is, that of being able to plant them wide enough from each other to admit of their being cleaned with the plow; and yet to afford a full crop.

The PROPER DISTANCE, therefore, depends in fome meafure on the natural fize of the fpecies, and the ftrength of the foil. The thinner they ftand, the larger, no doubt, they will grow; but the clofer the more numerous: and I am of opinion that cabbages, as turneps, are frequently fet out too thin. Mr. PAGET's diftances are four feet by two and a half: a full diftance, in my opinion, for large cabbages on a rich foil.

S 3   The

The EXPENDITURE of. cabbages, here, is chiefly on *sheep*; but *cattle* and *swine* have a proportion. But, what is extraordinary, I have not in this, or any other district, met with an instance of cabbages being given to *horses*: and yet it is more than probable, that, either alone or mixed with chaf or "cutmeat," they might be rendered a valuable species of horse food.

. For ample observations on the culture of this crop, see MINUTES of AGRICULTURE in SURREY; DIGEST, p. 95, and the MINUTES thence referred to.

CULTIVATED

31.

CULTIVATED GRASSES.

THE PERENNIAL LEY is seldom the object of cultivation, in this district; the culture of grasses being confined to TEMPORARY LEYS; and chiefly to one species, which may be said to be peculiar to the district; and which, though of long duration, compared with the temporary leys of other districts, cannot be deemed perennial; its continuance being limited to six or seven years: and, in distinction, I shall term it SEXENNIAL LEY: beside which the ANNUAL or CLOVER LEY will require to be noticed.

CLOVER. It appears, by the COURSE OF HUSBANDRY already given, that the practice of growing wheat on a clover ley, agreeably to the modern practice of the kingdom at large, is not prevalent here. Nevertheless, the practice is sometimes used; more especially

S 4   cially

cially in the common fields, where it has been introduced, in feveral inftances, as a fubftitute of the bean crop.

When wheat is fown on the firft year's ley, it is ufual to mow the clover twice : under an idea, that a full crop of clover mown twice in the feafon, fmothers weeds of every kind ; even couch! It no doubt gives them a great check.

It is obfervable, however, that, in the common field practice, by fowing clover every third year, the crop, though abundant for awhile, foon begins to fail ; even in fo fhort a time as twelve or fifteen years. See alfo NORF. ECON. on this circumftance.

This circumftance is not introduced, here, as an evidence againft the cultivation of clover ; which is evidently, on a noncalcarious foil, by much the moft valuable *leaf grafs* (if the term were admiffible) agriculture is at prefent acquainted with ; but to put thofe, who have frefh ground in their poffeffion, on their guard in its cultivation.

TURF; or SIX YEARS LEY. In the inclofed townfhips, this is the prevailing and almoft only ley : furnifhing, in its different ftages, the two grand crops ; CLOVER and GRASS.

In

In the ordinary practice of the country, the method of cultivating it is merely that of sowing about ten pounds of RED CLOVER, at the time of sowing the barley.

To the red clover, some judicious managers, in *this* part of the district, add a small quantity of clean RAYGRASS, with a few pounds of WHITE CLOVER.

There are, however, men, and those of the first abilities, on the lighter lands, round the skirts of the Charnwood hills, who, though advocates for raygrass, think white clover unnecessary; finding, that whether they sow any or none, their leys are equally full of it.

When this is the case, it would, indeed, be folly to throw away the seed: but there are few lands that are blest with so desirable a quality as that of affording, naturally, a turf of white clover. By manuring highly, this valuable herb, especially on light free lands, may generally be obtained in sufficient quantity; and it is by those who generally manure their young leys on such land, that white clover is omitted to be sown.

In the MANAGEMENT of YOUNG SEEDS it is observable that, in the common practice of the district, and I understand universally, they

are

are *eaten off with sheep* in autumn. This I mention, not as a pattern to be copied implicitly, but as a circumstance in provincial practice. If they be eaten off in dry weather, and not too closely, the effect, it is possible, may not be so prejudicial as is generally conceived.

The first, and sometimes the second year, the young leys are *mown*, as CLOVER: the laft four or five, they are *grazed*, as GRASSLAND.

The CLOVER of young leys is seldom mown more than once * ; but, contrary to the practice of other districts, it is frequently suffered to run up, into head, as if for mowing a second time, before ftock be turned upon it.

In

* A very superior manager of this district paftures, in the spring, his clover leys which are intended to be mown for hay;—sometimes fo late as the beginning of June: and gives a threefold reason in support of his practice. The feedage of clover, in May, is valuable: a full crop of clover is made with difficulty and uncertainty: and the hay of such a crop, he conceives to be lefs valuable in quality than what he calls half a crop: and, upon his land, his reasoning may be conclusive; a rich free loam, in high cultivation, recently inclosed, and the clover crop new to it; the crops of course prodigious.—On a lefs productive soil, however, and this already exhausted by clover, even half a crop could not be obtained, with any degree of certainty, by that management.

In this state, stock of every kind are admitted; particularly rams, as will hereafter appear : but horses *, and even cattle, are turned into clover belly-deep ! and this without apprehension of danger : it being found, by experience, that it is less dangerous to cattle in this, than in a younger state.

For an instance of drawing the common thistle out of young leys, see art. CORN WEEDS.

For the AFTERMANAGEMENT of these TEMPORARY LEYS, see the next article; they being considered, in practice, after the second year, as analogous with older GRASSLANDS.

* For an instance of clover in this state being affected by and friendly to horses, see MIN. 17.

GRASSLAND.

32.

G R A S S L A N D.

THE SPECIES OF GRASSLAND, in the DISTRICT of the STATION, are, chiefly,

LOWLAND GRASS, or " MEADOW ;" and

MIDDLELAND GRASS, or " TURF :" there being no UPLAND GRASS or SHEEPWALK within it; except some heathlets, toward the Derbyshire margin.

MIDDLELAND GRASS, or " TURF." This includes the principal part of the grasslands of the district. It confsists chiefly of the TEMPORARY LEYS mentioned in the last article; with a slight intermixture of OLD GRASSLAND, —provincially " OLD TURF :" namely, lands that have lain, some centuries perhaps, in a state of grass; many of them being now over-run, as such lands too often are in other districts, with anthills and other encumbrances; some of them as full of anthills as a forest, and almost as rough.

In soil and situation, these OLD GRASSLANDS are similar to those of the temporary leys of the arable lands; and their management is

the

the fame.' All, therefore, that requires to be
faid of them is, that they ought not to remain
any longer a difgrace to the hufbandry of the
diftrict; but ought either to be fubjected to
the general management of the country, or to
be rendered productive, as grafsland, by
clearing them from their prefent encumbrances.

The GENERAL MANAGEMENT of this clafs
of grafslands is that of keeping them con-
ftantly in the ftate of PASTURAGE; as grazing
or dairy grounds.

In the MINUTIAL MANAGEMENT of PAS-
TURE GROUNDS, a few *particulars* require to
be noticed: though taken *all together*, the practice of this diftrict (nor indeed that of any
other *individual* diftrict I have yet feen) cannot be held out as a pattern. See the RURAL
ECONOMY OF YORKSHIRE; in which the
fubject of GRASSLAND is treated of analytically, and its feveral departments explained.

In the *fpring management* of *paftures*, a practice prevails, in this neighbourhood, which I
have not met with elfewhere.

In grounds which are fed in winter, cattle
are induced to fly to the hedges for fhelter,
and there to drop their dung. And it is the
cuftom, here, to fet women to collect the
dung,

dung, thus partially and superfluously scattered, into heaps; and to cart it into the
middle of the piece, and then spread it upon
the parts which most require it : while some
individuals pile it in large heaps, to be set
about in winter; objecting to the practice of
spreading it over the grass in the spring, as
tending to foul it : and, under the same idea,
object to spreading the dung, dropt in the
area of the piece,—late in the spring : esteeming it better management to collect and carry
it off, to be set about in a more suitable
season.

The whole of this practice, so far as relates
to the collecting of dung on pasture lands,
more especially *old* pasture lands, may be
eligible. But I am of opinion, that dung
thus collected, ought not to be set upon
pasture ground; especially such as, having been
long in a state of pasturage, may be in a degree satiated with this species of manure; but
should be carted to the dungyard for the use of
the *arable land*, or piled in heaps for the use of
mowing grounds : not, however, to be set on in
winter—the worst season possible—but immediately after the hay is off : refreshing the
                                                pasture

pasture grounds, if they require it, by some *change* of manure *.

For the *stocking* of *pastures*, see the article GRAZING.

In what may be termed the *winter management* of *pastures*, this district furnishes an instance of practice, which is well entitled to a place in this register: namely, that of shutting up pasture grounds, in autumn, for a supply of SPRING FEED.

Mr. PAGET of Ibstock, in whose superior management I more particularly observed this admirable stroke of practice, shuts up

from

---

* MOLES.   A remarkable circumstance in the present state of agriculture of this district is the scarcity of moles.   A mole hill is rarely seen.   There are perhaps entire townships without a single mole in them.

Two reasons may be assigned for this circumstance. There are in this district few *old hedgerows*, and still less *woodland :* both of them nurseries of moles.   And while they are thus destitute of shelter, it is the practice for townships to join in their destruction.

The price, in a township which has been neglected and the number of moles considerable, is about a penny an acre a year: afterwards not more than a halfpenny an acre: not more than two guineas perhaps for a middlesized township: and this, under due attention, becomes in a few years a mere sinecure : except near woods ; where they can seldom be wholly overcome.

from the middle of September to about old Michaelmas, as the age of the grafs, the feafon, and other circumftances fuit; making a point of eating the ground level and bare, previous to its being freed from ftock; from which it is kept free, until it be wanted for ewes and lambs; or, if it be intended for cattle, until the firft fhoot of grafs in the fpring; which, mingling with the autumnal fhoots, the herbage is found to be more nutritious to ftock than either of them are feparately. As a *certain* and *wholefome* fupply of food for ewes and lambs, in early fpring, this PRESERVED PASTURE is depended upon as the fheet-anchor; in preference to turneps, cabbages, or any other fpecies, whatever, of what is termed SPRING FEED.

For obfervations on PRESERVING AFTERGRASS, as a fupply of fpring feed, fee YORK. ECON. v. ii. p. 148.

LOWLAND GRASS, or " MEADOW." The meadowlands of this diftrict confift of the banks of rivers, and of the bottoms, or dips of vallies, fcattered over almoft every part of it.

Thefe meadows are moftly kept as MOWING GROUNDS; and the particulars, belonging to their

their MANAGEMENT, which will require to be noticed, fall under the heads

> Draining,
> Watering,
> Hay harveſt,
> Aftergraſs.

DRAINING. This operation, whether with reſpect to *underdrains* or *ſurface drains*, is well attended to, here; better, I think, than in any other diſtrict which has fallen under my obſervation.

Underdraining has been already mentioned under the article SOIL PROCESS; and all that requires to be ſaid of *ſurface draining* is, that it is generally done in the proper ſeaſon :— autumn, or the beginning of winter. See NORF. ECON.

For inſtances of practice in draining meadow lands, ſee the MINUTES referred to below.

WATERING MEADOWS. The watering of meadows cannot be ſaid to have yet entered into the common practice of this diſtrict. Nevertheleſs, it has made ſome conſiderable progreſs toward it. Many of the ſuperior claſs of occupiers have, already, evinced their

VOL. I. T ſpirit,

ſpirit, at leaſt, in proſecuting this CARDINAL
IMPROVEMENT.

There are, indeed, a few inſtances, in which
the art has reached a degree of perfection,
equal, perhaps, to that which it has attained
in any other part of the iſland.   But as I ſtill
hope to ſee this department of rural affairs on
what may be termed its own native ſoil, the
MORE WESTERN COUNTIES, where it appears
to have been firſt practiſed, in this iſland, and
where, only, I believe, it has been received
into common practice,—I ſhall forbear giving a *detail* of it in this place.   Nevertheleſs,
there are *circumſtances*, in the practice of this
diſtrict, which require to be noticed.

The ORIGIN of meliorating graſslands with
water may be traced, pretty evidently, in this
diſtrict.

The benefit of NATURAL FLOODS, to the
graſslands they occaſionally overflowed, being
evident, and in ſome inſtances great, the
means of producing ARTIFICIAL FLOODS,
and of ſpreading them over lands, not liable,
in their natural ſituation, to be overflowed,
would become, of courſe, a deſirable object.

The moſt *obvious* effect of floods, or over-
flowings of rivers and brooks, on the lands

over

over which they fpread, is that of *depofiting their earthy particles*; thereby operating as a VEHICLE OF MANURE. It is likewife evident to common obfervation, that foul waters, as thofe of floods, let fall their fediment moft freely in a *ftagnant ftate*. And it is alfo equally evident, that the ftate of ftagnation of the waters of floods, or a ftate that approaches it, is caufed by fome obftruction of the current, below the place of ftagnation.

Thefe circumftances being feen, and they could not well be miffed by any one who gave the fubject a fecond thought, the means of manuring lands with water, artificially, were given : in fituations, I mean, which would admit of the requifite obftructions.

The dips or vallies which abound, more or lefs, in every quarter of the kingdom, and which are mentioned above, were moft apt fubjects for flooding, artificially, with foul waters, on the principle of MANURING the land with their SEDIMENT.

A bank or dam being made acrofs the valley, below the part to be manured, the rivulet, which always accompanies a valley of this kind, efpecially after heavy rains, the

T 2   only

only time when flooding on this principle
could be practised, would of course be ob-
structed; and its waters, fouled, perhaps,
with the richest particles of arable lands,
would be spread over the bottom of the valley, to an extent proportioned to the height
of the bank, and its own flatnefs; a valve or
floodgate being fixed in the bed of the rivulet,
to let off the waters, when the *whole* of their
foulnefs were depofited: thus gaining a principal advantage over natural flooding; in
which the groffer particles, only, are let fall;
the finer, and perhaps most valuable, efcap-
ing to the river, and thence to the fea, before
they be precipitated.

On thefe principles, it is evident, fome of
the meadow lands of this diftrict have formerly been flooded * : and it is not probable
that fo evident a method of improving meadow lands fhould have been confined to
this diftrict; but may have been common to
other parts of the ifland.

But the ANTIENT METHOD of meliorating
grafslands, by the means of STAGNANT WA-
TER, could no longer prevail, than until the
                                          fupe-

---

* See MIN. 27.

superior effects of RUNNING WATER, on such lands, were difcovered and afcertained.

This important difcovery muft have been made, by *obfervation*, on the comparative effects of running and ftanding water, in the natural or artificial flooding above fpoken of ; and muft have been afcertained, by a long courfe of *experience :* it is not likely that *reafon* fhould have had any fhare, in ftriking out the MODERN METHOD of improving grafslands, by RUNNING WATER. For even now, when the reality of the improvement appears to be fully eftablifhed, there feems to be no fatiffactory *theory* to account for it. The *warmth*, communicated by running water to the grafs it flows over, is the beft account that the moft enlightened in the art can give, of the good effect of running water, on grafsland.

Even after the difcovery was made, and the effect fully eftablifhed, it would be fome length of time, before the art arrived at its prefent high degree of perfection. It may, in its prefent ftate, be fafely deemed the moft fcientific operation that has entered into the common practice of hufbandry.

To the memory of the inventor or inventors be the higheft praife !

If the art, as it now stands, were struck out on PRINCIPLE, it must have been on that of ANIMAL CIRCULATION; to which the operation of meliorating grafslands with water, through the means of FLOATS and DRAINS, is perfectly analogous.

The *floats* are *arteries*, conveying the circulating fluid to every part of the fubject; imbuing every atom : the *drains*, *veins*, collecting the fcattered fluid, and conveying it back to its natural channel.

In lefs figurative language, the floats are trenches, receiving, by the means of floodgates, as occafion requires, the waters of a river, brook, or rivulet, and conveying it along the upper margin, and upon the tops of the natural or artificial fwells of the field of improvement : the drains, counter trenches, ftretching along the lower margin, and winding in the dips and hollows, to receive the water fpread over the furface by the floats.

Each fet of trenches, whether of floats or drains, bears more or lefs refemblance to a tree, with its trunk and branches : the branches of the floats increafing in number, and diminifhing in fize, as they proceed from the river or other fource; thofe of the drains, on the

con-

contrary, diminishing in number and increasing in size, as they approach the receptacle.

When the water is at "work" (as it is properly enough termed) the entire surface (supposing the operation to be *perfect)* is covered with one continued SHEET OF LIVING WATER; purling evenly over every part, some inch or more deep. If the grass be very short, the water is seen; and has a beautiful as well as a profitable effect: if not, it steals unseen among the herbage; or shows itself partially: it being impossible, in practice, to render the sheet, throughout, of a uniform depth or thickness.

From this general idea of the method of watering grasslands, on the modern principle, it is evident, that a *dead flat*, a *perfect level*, is, of all other, the worst adapted to the practice.

A perfect level, however, seldom occurs in nature: inequalities, sufficiently to promote a circulation of water on turf, may generally be discovered, if judiciously sought.

In the MIDLAND COUNTIES, I have seen, in the practice of a superior manager, a beau-

tifully

tifully simple expedient practised, to find out the inequalities of a piece of ground, nearly flat: that of covering it with water; and preserving the level by the means of " levelling pegs :" stumps or piles driven down, in various parts, to a level with the surface of the water; so that after the water was let off, the level still remained. The parts last covered were, of course, the proper ground for the floats ; the parts last freed, for the drains: art being used, where wanted, to give additional advantage to the natural inequalities.

Situations, in general, abound sufficiently, with inequalities of surface : natural, as the *swells and hollows* of lands lying out of the way of floods, and having never been plowed : artificial, as those which have been raised by the plow into *ridge and furrow: in this* case, the ridges receive the floats, the furrows the drains : in *that,* the level (the spirit level, or perhaps only a plummet) is the guide to the floats ; the water they throw out, to the drains.

In this district, I have seen the *side of a hill* watered with rain water from a road running along the top of it : the same trench, in this

case,

case, acting as float and drain; running, a zigzag, along the face of the slope; the lower folds catching the water spread out by the upper.

I have likewise observed, in this district, several instances of *ridges and furrows* being watered from similar sources. In these cases, whether the natural descent of the lands were little or great, the floats were opened upon the ridges, with clods of turf, cut out of the trenches, placed, at distances proportioned to the descent, to check the current sufficiently, to force the water out of the trench above, yet leaving it a sufficient passage, to suffer it to carry down a supply to the parts below.

In this district, also, I have met with one or more instances in which *ridges and furrows* have been *levelled!* at an excessive cost, by paring off the turf, throwing down the ridges by hand, and replacing the turf! giving the surface one regular gentle descent: and this, notwithstanding it is allowed, by those who may be styled masters in the art, that THE QUICKER THE CIRCULATION, THE MORE BENEFICIAL THE EFFECT.

Upon the whole, it appears pretty evidently, that the operation, though *scientific*, can seldom be rendered *mechanical*.

Straight

Straight lines and plain furfaces can feldom
be had, but at a great and, frequently, an unneceffary expence.   The given fituation of
the ground fhould be confulted, and maturely
ftudied, before the work be fet about.   Every
fite may be faid to require a different arrangement of trenches.   Of courfe, no man ought
to fet about a work of fo difficult a nature,
until he has ftudied its principles, and made
himfelf mafter of its *theory* : nor, then, without the affiftance of *practice*, in himfelf or
others.

To expatiate on the UTILITY of watering
grafslands would be a wafte of words.   In
fituations where a *fufficient fupply* of water, of
a *fertilizing quality*, can be commanded, *at
all feafons*, it ranks, indifputably, among the
higheft clafs of improvements.

Much, however, depends on the QUALITY
of the water : not on its *colour*, or *clearnefs*,
but on the fpecific quality of its *fufpended
particles*.   Waters, in their natural ftate (not
purified by diftillation), more efpecially
fpring waters, though perfectly tranfparent
and pure to the eye, are various in quality,
as foils are : owing to earthy and other particles being fufpended in them, imperceptibly

to

to the eye; requiring the aid of chemiſtry to deteƈt them. Hence hard water, ſoft water, wholeſome waters, and medicinal waters. For a ſtriking effeƈt of clear ſpring water, ſee MIN. 39.

But although much may depend on the quality of water, for the purpoſe of melio‐ rating graſslands, ſtill more, perhaps, de‐ pends on the QUANTITY ; on having a *ſufficient ſupply at all ſeaſons.* With this, there are, perhaps, few waters which might not be ren‐ dered beneficial to graſsland, if thrown over it at proper ſeaſons, and in proper quantity : without it, the benefit, it is poſſible, may not be adequate to the expence. The *greateſt,* at leaſt the *moſt obvious,* advantage of water‐ ing graſslands ariſes in a dry ſeaſon ; and if the ſupply fail in ſuch ſeaſons, as frequent‐ ly happens, in many ſituations, the inten‐ tion is in part fruſtrated : the early ſpring waterings being, in this caſe, all that can be commanded.

This, however, by way of caution : not as a diſcouragement to the practice. There are, in this iſland, ſituations innumerable, in which the advantages ariſing to the prac‐ tice, properly conduƈted, would far exceed

the

the expence of obtaining them : and to afcertain them is an object of the firſt magnitude to . the owners and occupiers of graſslands.

Thus, having endeavoured to convey a
general idea, to thoſe who are unacquainted
with the ſubject, of the nature, the operation, and the effect of watering graſslands,
on the principle of circulation, I will mention
a few intereſting circumſtances of practice,
which occurred to my obſervation, in this
Midland diſtrict.

Mr. BAKEWELL of Diſhley ſtands firſt, in
this quarter of the kingdom, as an improver
of graſslands by watering.

Formerly, a ſuite of meadows, lying by
the banks of the Soar, received conſiderable
benefit from the water of the river being
judiciouſly ſpread over them, in the times
of floods. But, now, not only theſe meadows, but near a hundred acres, I believe,
of higher land, lying entirely out of the
way of natural floods, are watered on the
modern principle.

Mr. Bakewell, like a man of experience in
buſineſs, before he ſet about this great work,
ſtudied the art in the principal . ſcene of
practice;

practice; the west of England; where he spent some days with the ingenious Mr. Boswell, who, some years ago, published a treatise on the subject *.

The great stroke of management, in this department of Mr. Bakewell's practice, which marks his genius in strong characters, is that of diverting to his purpose a rivulet or small brook, whose natural channel skirts the farthest boundary of his farm; falling, with a considerable descent, down a narrow valley; in which its utility, as a source of improvement to land, was confined.

This rivulet is therefore turned, at the highest place that could be commanded, and carried, in the canal manner, round the point of a swell, which lies between its natural bed and the farmery: by the execution of this admirable thought, not only commanding the skirts of the hill as a site of improvement by watering; but supplying by this ARTIFICIAL BROOK (see YORK. ECON. i. 174.) the house and farm offices with water: —filling

* Mr. BOSWELL'S TREATISE, ON WATERING GRASSLANDS, cannot be too strongly recommended to those who wish to become acquainted with the practice.

—filling from it a drinking pool, for horfes and cattle;' a wafh pool, for fheep; and converting it to a multitude of other pur- pofes * : acquifitions which many other fituations in the ifland are capable of fur- nifhing.

Mr. B,'s improvements, in this depart- ment of rural affairs, are not only ex- tenfive, but high; and are rendered the more ftriking, by " proof pieces" (a good term for experimental patches) left in each fite of improvement. Mr. Bakewell is, in truth, a *mafter* in the art ; and Difhley, at pre- fent,

---

* One of which is too valuable to be paffed with- out diftinction. Three years ago, Mr. B. I remember, was endeavouring to invent a flatbottomed boat, or barge, to navigate upon this canal; for the purpofe, moft particularly, of conveying his turneps from the field to the cattle fheds. But finding this not eafily practicable, his great mind ftruck out, or rather caught, the beau- tifully fimple idea of launching the turneps themfelves into the water; and letting them float down fingly with the current! " We throw them in, and bid them meet us at the Barn End!!!" where he is now (October 1789) contriving a refervoir, or dry dock, for them to fail into; with a grate at the bottom to let out the wa- ter; but retaining the turneps; which will there be laid up, clean wafhed, and freightfree, as a fupply in frofty weather!

fent, a *fchool* in which it might be ftudied
with fingular advantage.

Mr. Paget of Ibftock is alfo a proficient
in the fcience and art of watering grafslands, on the modern principle. He cuts a
confiderable quantity of hay, annually, from
lands which have received no other *manure*
than *water*, during the laft forty years. A
ftriking inftance, this, that water is not
merely a *ftimulus* or *force*, as fome men conceive it to be; but communicates fome actual
nutriment to the herbage *.

Mr. Moor of Appleby has executed a
confiderable work of this kind, and in a judicious manner; cutting a frefh channel, on
one fide of the fite of improvement, for a rivulet which winded through its middle; in order to prevent its overflowing at an improper
feafon; and converting the old channel
(partially filled up) into a main float: an
expedient which may frequently be practifed with good effect.

And

* One circumftance which occurred in Mr. P.'s practice ought to be mentioned, by way of caution. By
watering an ORCHARD with the wafhings of the ftreet
and yards of a neighbouring village (a defirable fpecies
of water) the fruit trees were greatly injured: and in
Mr. B.'s practice, a fimilar circumftance took place.

And Mr. WILKS of Meeſham, among his various and extraordinary exertions of genius and ſpirit, has not neglected the watering of grafslands: a ſpecies of rural improvement which he is proſecuting with, perhaps, unexampled ardour.

In *this* neighbourhood, there are two inſtances of practice, which form a ſtriking contraſt: one was done at a great expence, with an uncertain ſupply of water: the other at a trifling coſt, with an abundant ſupply, at all ſeaſons. But as the comparative effect of theſe two incidents of practice will appear, under ſtriking circumſtances, in the MINUTES, it is unneceſſary to ſay more on the ſubject, here.

HAYING. The harveſting of *herbage* is among the firſt concerns of huſbandry. The quality, and of courſe the value, of hay depends, in a great meaſure, on the ſtate in which it is laid up. *Grain*, though liable to damage, by a long continuance of unfavourable weather, is much leſs hazardous than herbage.

Neverthelefs, in many, or moſt, parts of the kingdom, we find HAYMAKING, notwithſtanding it is one of the oldeſt operations

in

in hufbandry, the leaft underftood, or the moft neglected. In this diftrict, it is found in a ftate of the loweft neglect.

The ordinary practice of the diftrict is this : —the fwaths are fpread immediately, or prefently, after the mowers, with little or no regard to the weather : fuffering the grafs to lie abroad, no matter how long, until the top be dry. It is then turned ; and, the other fide being dried, it is raked into rows ; and carried, as it becomes dry ; beginning the rick, perhaps, as foon as one load is ready; letting it lie abroad, continuing to add load after load, until it be topped up. During the two hay harvefts I was in the diftrict, I do not recollect to have feen, in its practice, a HAYCOCK, *of any fize or form*; fome bundles of clover hay excepted.

But a main ftimulus to good management, emulation, appears to be here wanting, in this cafe. It is no difgrace to make bad hay. Every thing is attributed to the weather. All the praife of hay-making is given to him who has done firft; and all its difgrace falls on him who finifhes laft.

In 1784, a difficult feafon, a firft-rate farmer *bragged* of his having made, that year, all

VOL. I. U forts

forts of hay ; as cow hay, ſtirk hay, and
" pig hay :" namely, ſome ſo bad as to be fit
for litter only.

In 1785, when hay was four or five pounds
a ton, I have ſeen a very induſtrious pains-
taking farmer tedding his hay while it actually
rained : giving as a reaſon for his conduct,
that it muſt be ſpread about, and it might as
well be done ſooner as later.   Yet I had heard
this very man offering, only a few days before, a ſpeculative price of four guineas a ton
for " *good*" hay, to be delivered the enſuing
winter for his own uſe ! Nevertheleſs, the
hay under notice lay ſeveral days abroad, before it was deemed ſufficiently dry on the top
to be turned !

These circumſtances are not mentioned ill-
naturedly ; but to ſhew, the laſt more particularly, which occurred in the practice of one
of the ſhrewdeſt beſt managers in his neighbourhood, that the art is not ſufficiently underſtood : though, in the practice of ſome
few individuals, it may be ſuperior to the ordinary practice of the diſtrict.

For practice in SURREY, ſee MIN. of AGRIC.

For the practice of YORKSHIRE, ſee YORK.
ECON.

For

For the practice of GLOCESTERSHIRE, see
GLO. ECON.

AFTERGRASS. The management of aftergrafs, here, is in general judicious. It is generally suffered to get up to a full bite, before
it be broken: not turned in upon, as in GLO-
CESTERSHIRE, as soon as the hay is off: nor
suffered, as in YORKSHIRE, to stand until
much of it be wasted. For further remarks
on this subject, see MIN. 62.

In the *stocking* of lattermath, likewise, the
Midland graziers are judicious: esteeming it
bad management to overstock it. A cow an
acre, on well grown aftergrafs, seems to be
considered as full stock.

REFERENCES to the MINUTES on GRASSLAND.

For observations on the ancient method of
flooding grafsland by " floating upward," see
MIN. 27.

For instance of practice in *surface draining*,
see MIN. 32.

For the practice of *burning dead grafs*, and
the dangerous consequences, 38.

For the effect of *calcarious water* on land,
see MIN. 39.

For observations on the *water of the Dove*,
&c. 42.

U 2   For

For an inftance of great profit by *watering*, fee MIN. 46.

For the propriety of cutting *furface drains* where fods are wanted, 49.

For experience and the expence in mowing off the *weeds* of *pafture grounds*, 51.

For lifts of *graffes* and *weeds*, and obfervations on *agricultural botany*, 55.

For obfervations on *haying in drought*, and on the fmall *produce* of hay in 1785, 56.

For remarks on eating *lattermath*, 62.

For practice in fpreading the mould of *furface drains*, 64.

For practice and expence of clearing *drinking pits*, 66.

For practical obfervations on *watering ridges*, 68.

For farther obfervations on fpreading the mould of *furface drains*, 69.

For opinion that *geefe* are eligible in *pafture grounds*, 72.

For obfervations on the *meadow foftgrafs*, fee MIN. 73.

For obfervations on the *creeping crowfoot*, 85.

For inftances of *haying* in September, 88.

LIVESTOCK.

33.

L I V E S T O C K.

A DISTRICT, rich in foil, and much of it in a ftate of herbage, naturally abounds with LIVESTOCK.

In the MIDLAND DISTRICT, the four principal fpecies are found in peculiar plenty, and in a fingular ftate of improvement. The other three I fhall pafs over. RABBITS cannot be deemed an object of the rural economy of this diftrict; and with regard to POULTRY and BEES, nothing fufficiently ftriking has occurred to me in it, to require particular notice *.

Therefore, this divifion of the prefent work will be confined to

Horfes,	Sheep,
Cattle,	Swine.

U 3　　　A country

* Except that GAME FOWLS are, here, in the firft eftimation, as a fpecies of POULTRY; as producing more eggs, and being, themfelves, better *fleſhed* and better flavoured than fowls in general.

A country that has defervedly obtained fo much credit by its management of liveftock, efpecially the three fpecies firft mentioned, and which has carried on the improvement of the feveral fpecies, more particularly thofe of cattle and fheep, with a fpirit unknown before, and has raifed them to a height unattained, perhaps, in any age or nation, is entitled to every attention. It would, indeed, be unpardonable, and altogether inconfiftent with this undertaking, to pafs over its practice in a fuperficial manner. The fpirit of improvement is now in the zenith, and the improvement itfelf, taken in a general light, is now, probably, at its height. The breed of horfes of this diftrict is allowed to be on the decline. Its breed of cattle are probably at its height. And its fheep are at prefent fo near perfection, that it is not *probable* they fhould hereafter receive *much* improvement. Befide, the grand luminary of the art has paffed the meridian, and though at prefent in full fplendor, is verging toward the horizon.

It muft not, however, be underftood, by thofe who are not locally acquainted with this diftrict, that Mr. BAKEWELL, though he has been

been long, and moft defervedly, confidered as
the principal promoter of the ART OF BREED-
ING, and has for fome length of time taken
the lead, is the only man of diftinguifhed
merit in this department of rural affairs, in
the diftrict under furvey. It abounds, and
has, for many years, abounded, with intelligent and fpirited breeders. I could mention
fome fifteen or twenty men of repute, and
moft of them men of confiderable property,
who are in the fame department, and feveral
of them eminent for their breeds of ftock.

Neverthelefs, it muft be and is acknowledged, that Mr. BAKEWELL is at the head
of the department;—and, whenever he may
drop, it is much to be feared, and highly
probable, that another leader, of equal fpirit,
and equal abilities, will not be found to fucceed him.

Having faid this, however, it will be proper
to apprize my readers ftill farther, that the
following account muft not be underftood as
a detail of the practice of Mr. BAKEWELL;
but as a more enlarged regifter of the practice
at prefent eftablifhed in the MIDLAND COUN-
TIES. For notwithftanding I have been repeatedly

peatedly favoured with opportunities of making ample obfervation on Mr. BAKEWELL's practice; and have, as repeatedly, been favoured with his liberal communications on rural fubjects; it is not my intention to deal out Mr. B.'s *private* opinions, or even to attempt a recital of his *particular* practice, any other than as it conflitutes a valuable part of the practice of the diftrict under furvey.

In regiftering this practice, it will be requifite, befide a feparate account of the feveral BREEDS and their IMPROVEMENT, to defcribe the methods of BREEDING and REARING each fpecies, and to detail the bufinefs of GRAZING, and the DAIRY MANAGEMENT.

To give full fcope to the enquiry, it will be neceffary to take a feparate view of each fpecies of liveftock, that are here the objects of attention; and, previoufly; to convey fome general ideas refpecting the PRINCIPLES of IMPROVEMENT, which have, here, been laid down, and the MEANS, by which they have been fuccefsfully, and rapidly, raifed into practice. The fubject is new, at leaft to this work, and will therefore require a degree of attention adequate to its importance.

The

The moſt·general principle is BEAUTY OF FORM ;—a principle which has been applied in common to the four ſpecies. It is obſervable, however, that this principle was more cloſely attended to at the outſet of improvement (under an idea, in ſome degree falſely grounded, that BEAUTY OF FORM and UTILITY are inſeparable) than at preſent, when men who have been long converſant in practice, make a diſtinction between a " uſeful ſort," and a ſort which is merely " handſome."

The next principle attended to is a PROPORTION OF PARTS, or what may be called UTILITY OF FORM, abſtractedly conſidered from the BEAUTY OF FORM: thus, of the three edible ſpecies, the parts which are deemed OFFAL, or which bear an INFERIOR PRICE at market, ſhould be ſmall, in proportion to the better parts. This principle, however, appears to have been differently attended to in different ſpecies; and will require to be re-examined, in taking the ſeparate view of each ſpecies.

A third principle of improvement, which has engaged the attention of the Midland
breeders,

breeders, is the texture of the mufcular parts
—or what is termed FLESH: a quality of
liveftock which, familiar as it may long have
been to the *butcher* and the *confumer*, has not,
perhaps, been attended to by *breeders*, whatever it may have been by *graziers*, until of
late years in this diftrict; where the "FLESH"
is now fpoken of with the fame familiarity as
the hide or the fleece; and where it is clearly
underftood, that the grain of the meat depends wholly on the BREED, not, as has been
heretofore confidered, on the SIZE of the
animal *.

But the principle which, at prefent, en-
groffes the greateft fhare of attention, and
which, above all others, is entitled to the *grazier's* attention, is FAT,—or rather FATTING
QUALITY: that is, a natural propenfity to acquire a ftate of fatnefs, at an early age, and,
when at full keep, in a fhort fpace of time:
another quality which is found to be hereditary;—

* It appears, however, in the practice of YORKSHIRE
(vol. ii. p. 183.), that circumftances led the breeders of
that country to pay fome attention to the flefh of cattle:
and I have been informed, by a gentleman converfant
in the HEREFORDSHIRE breed of cattle, that fimilar
circumftances took place, and probably about the fame
time, in that quarter of the ifland.

tary;—depending, in some considerable degree at least, on BREED, or what is technically termed BLOOD: namely, on the specific quality of the parents.

Thus it appears, that the Midland breeders rest every thing on BREED; under a conviction, that the *beauty* and *utility of form*, the quality of the *flesh*, and its propensity to *fatness*, are, in the offspring, the natural consequence of similar qualities in the parents. And, what is extremely interesting, it is evident from observation, that these four qualities are compatible; being frequently found united, in a remarkable manner, in the same individuals.

Without admitting, or endeavouring to confute, in this place, that the four qualities, here explained, are the only ones necessary to the perfection of the several species of live-stock now under review, we pass on to the MEANS, whereby those principles have been applied, in attaining the degree of perfection, at present, observable in the district under survey.

The MEANS OF IMPROVEMENT, in the established practice of the kingdom at large, are

are thofe of felecting females from the native ftock of the country, and crossing
with males of an alien breed ; under an opinion, wh:ch has been univerfally received,
that continuing to breed from the fame line
of parentage tends *to weaken the breed.*

Rooted, however, as this opinion has been,
and univerfally as that practice has prevailed,
there is little doubt of the fact, that the fuperior breeds of ftock of this diftrict have been
raifed by a practice directly contrary ;—that
of breeding, not from the fame *line only,* but
the fame *family :* a practice which has now
been fo long eftablifhed, as to have acquired
a technical phrafe to exprefs it : " BREEDING
INANDIN " is as familiar in the converfation
of Midland breeders, as CROSSING is in that
of other diftricts *, The fire and the daughter, the fon and the mother, the brother and
the fifter, are, in the ordinary practice of fuperior breeders, now permitted to improve
their own kind ; and through the affiftance of
this

* BREEDING INANDIN. This term, however, is
not, I underftand, of Midland origin ; claiming *New-
market* as its birth-place ; the idea it reprefents, being
ftruck out, and the practice in a degree eftablifhed, by
the *gentlemen of the turf.*

this practice, as will appear, the *bold* leader
of thefe improvements produced his celebrated flock.

The argument held out in its favour is,
that there can be only one *beft* breed; and
if this be *croffed*, it muft neceffarily be with
an *inferior* breed; the neceffary confequence
of which muft be an *adulteration*, not an *improvement*.

How far this novel practice may, in a general light, be confidered as fuperiorly eligible, would be improper to be difcuffed in
this place; in which I mean to convey, only,
a general idea of the prefent practice of the
diftrict; in order to fave repetition, and to
enable the reader to follow me through the
feveral parts of the enquiry with greater
eafe.   To this intent, it muft likewife be underftood, that although much has probably
been done by BREEDING INANDIN, much
alfo has been done by CROSSING; not, however, by a mixture of alien breeds, but by
uniting the fuperior branches of the fame
breed.

The degree of excellency obtained, however, through thefe means, is not more remarkable than the rapidity with which the
                              improve-

improvement of the feveral breeds has been carried on, and extended; not over this diftrict only, but to various parts of the ifland.

But thefe circumftances, likewife, have arifen principally out of a mere point of practice; which, though not peculiar to this diftrict, is nowhere, I believe, equally pre-valent (except in Lincolnfhire), and enters not, in any degree, into the practice of the ifland at large : in which breeders of every clafs *rear* or *purchafe* their MALE STOCK.

Here, on the contrary, breeders moftly HIRE THEM BY THE SEASON,—of a few lead-ing men, in the line of breeding males for this purpofe ; returning them, at the end of the feafon, to their refpective owners ; who, during the time of letting, have their SHOWS or exhibitions, to which dairymen, graziers, and ftallion men repair, to choofe and hire males for the coming feafon.

Befide thefe private exhibitions, there are, annually, PUBLIC SHOWS, in different parts of the diftrict, for the fame purpofe : thus ASHBY has its *ftallion fhow* ; LEICESTER its *fhow of rams* ; and BOSWORTH has its *fhow*

of

of. bulls: not, however, merely for letting, but likewife for fale.

The practice of letting male ftock, by the feafon, is a department of rural affairs not known to the kingdom at large ; forming a *new* fubject in the rural fcience.

In practice, however, it generally happens that a breeder of male ftock—provincially, for want of a better term, called a " TUP-MAN," is likewife a DAIRYMAN, and frequntly a GRAZIER ; Mr. BAKEWELL being the only man, in this diftrict, who confines his practice folely to BREEDING and LETTING.

It muft not, however, be underftood that dairymen and graziers univerfally, throughout the diftrict, hire their males of thefe fuperior breeders. Many of them ftill go on in the old track of rearing, or of purchafing of each other, agreeably to the practice of other diftricts.

The practice of LETTING OUT MALE STOCK by the feafon being a fubject new to this undertaking, it will be proper, in this place, to examine it with due attention.

Its ORIGIN does not clearly appear. It has probably arifen in the letting of STALLIONS
for

for the fpring feafon. A domeftic induftrious
man has a good horfe ; but is too attentive
to the ordinary bufinefs of his farm, to follow
him every week to three or four markets, and
too diffident to fet him off to advantage, and
to enter into contefts and unavoidable fquab-
bles with ftallion men : while, to a man of
more lelfure and lefs modefty, a loofe calling
is moft agreeable. Thus both parties are
ferved : the letter by receiving a fum certain
and his horfe again ; the hirer by getting a
greater number of mares than the owner
could have got. This mode of difpofal would
of courfe give a loofe to the breeding of
ftallions ; for the breeder not only got rid of
the difagreeable part of the bufinefs ; but if
his own neighbourhood were overftocked, he
could, by this means, fend them to other
diftricts. Similar circumftances might lead
to the letting of BULLS and RAMS.

Be this as it may, the letting of RAMS has
long been the practice of Lincolnfhire ; and
the letting of HORSES has probably been
practifed, on a fmall fcale, in many diftricts.
But the letting of male ftock, viewed in the
general light we are now viewing it, was
never applied, generally, to the three principal

pal fpecies, until of late years in this diftrict. Mr. BAKEWELL, though he cannot be deemed the projector, has certainly been the principal promoter, of this branch of rural bufinefs.

The EFFECT of letting male ftock has, probably, been greater than was forefeen. The great improvement which has been made in the ftock of this diftrict is ftriking; but may be accounted for in this practice. A fuperior male, the beft for inftance, inftead of being kept confined within the pale of his proprietor, or of being beneficial to a few neighbours only, became, through this practice, a treafure to the whole diftrict: this year in one part of it, the next in another. Hence, even one fuperior male may change confiderably the breed of a country. But, in a year or two, his offspring are employed in forwarding the improvement. Such of his fons as prove of a fuperior quality are let out in a fimilar way; confequently the *blood*, in a fhort time, circulates through every part, and every man of fpirit partakes of the advantage.

The METHOD of conducting this department of rural affairs, and the PRICES given, will appear under each fpecies of ftock.

VOL. I.   X   HORSES.

34.

HORSES.

THE SPECIES of horfe bred in this diftrict, is the BLACK CARTHORSE ; for which the Midland Counties have, for fome length of time, been celebrated. Therefore, notwithftanding a full conviction in my own mind, of the unprofitablenefs of this breed of horfes, as beafts of draft in hufbandry, it is neceffary to the due execution of this work, and for other reafons which will appear, to regifter the leading facts belonging to the prefent improved variety of the Midland Counties.

This variety is generally and well underftood to have taken its RISE in fix ZEALAND MARES, fent over from the Hague by the late LORD CHESTERFIELD, during his embaffy at that court.

Thefe

Thefe mares finally refting at his lordfhip's feat at BRETBY, in the Derbyfhire quarter of this diftrict, the breed of that quarter became improved, and DERBYSHIRE, for fome time, took the lead, in this fpecies of ftock.

But, in courfe of time, LEICESTERSHIRE (into which this improved breed had travelled) either through better fortune, or better management, got the lead,—and kept it: Derbyfhire having been, for fome years, indebted to Leicefterfhire, for their beft ftallions: fo much depends on fortune, or management, or both, in breeding.

But although this may be deemed the origin of the prefent Leicefterfhire breed, the FORM has been very much altered fince its firft eftablifhment. During the laft thirty years, the long forend, long back, and long thick hairy legs, have been contracting into a fhort thick carcafe, a fhort but upright forend, and fhort clean legs: it having been at length difcovered, by men of fuperior penetration, that ftrength and activity, rather than height and weight, are the more effential properties of farm horfes: and there appears to be, at prefent, fome hope of men

X 2   in

in general gaining their fenfes *fo far*, as to fee them in the fame light.

The *handfomeſt* horfe I have feen of this breed, and perhaps the moſt *piĕurable* horfe of this kind ever bred in the ifland, was a ſtallion of Mr. Bakewell, named K. He was, in *reality*, the *fancied* war horfe of the German painters; who, in the luxuriance of imagination, never perhaps excelled the natural grandeur of this horfe. A man of moderate fize feemed to fhrink behind his forend, which rofe fo perfeĕtly upright, his ears ſtood (as Mr. B. fays every horfe's ears ought to ſtand !) perpendicularly over his fore feet. It may be faid, with little latitude, that, in grandeur and fymmetry of form, viewed as a piĕturable objeĕt, he exceeded as far the horfe which this fuperior breeder had the honor of fhowing to his majeſty, and which was afterwards fhown, publickly, fome months ago in London, as that horfe does the meaneſt of the breed. Nor was his form deficient in utility. He died, I think in 1785, at the age of nineteen years.

But the moſt *ufeful* horfe I have feen of this breed is a much younger horfe of Mr. B.

whole

whofe *letter* * I do not recollect. His carcafe
thick, his back fhort and ftraight, and his
legs fhort and clean : as ftrong as an ox ; yet
active as a poney ; equally fuitable for a cart
or a lighter carriage :—a fpecies of animal,
which, if it were fafhionable as human food,
would be full as eligible, for a farmer's ufe,
as an ox, of equal ftrength and activity.

Another comparative advantage of the
prefent improved variety, over the great
loofe heavy fluggifh forts of this breed, is its
hardinefs: its thriving quality : its being
able to carry flefh, or ftand hard work, with
comparatively little provender.

Among faddle horfes, this diftinction, in
individuals at leaft, is very obfervable ; and
there is no doubt of its belonging to diftinct *breeds* of horfes ; and may, in much probability, belong to *varieties* ; may be hereditary ; may defcend with fome degree of certainty from parents to their offspring.

If hardinefs of conftitution ; if the natural propenfity of thriving on a compara-
X 3 tively

* Mr. Bakewell has adopted the fimple plan of diftinguifhing not his horfes only, but his bulls and rams
by *letters*, inftead of lefs elegant *names*.

tively small proportion of food, observable
in some individuals, be in its nature, hereditary; be obtainable with any tolerable degree of certainty, by management in breeding; as those who have experience assert it
is—not in this only, but in every other species of livestock;—it is a most interesting circumstance in the nature of domestic animals.

BREEDING. To gain a comprehensive idea
of this subject, it will be proper to examine
the male and female separately.

STALLIONS. Viewing the district at large,
stallions are bred and managed in different
ways. Some are bred by *farmers*, who draw
them, and cover with them in the season.
Others by *breeders*, who either cover with them
themselves, or let them out to others for the
season, or sell them, altogether, to farmers or
stallionmen, who travel them about the country, as in the practice of other districts.

The *letting* is done either at the breeder's
private shows, previously to the season of
covering; or at a public show, where they
are sold as well as let; as will appear in
MIN. 37.

The

The *prices* given for ftallions,—*by purchafe,* are fifty to two hundred guineas,—*by the feafon,* forty to eighty or a hundred, *by the mare,* half a guinea to two guineas. The celebrated horfe K. that has been defcribed, covered many years at five guineas, and the horfe, mentioned as having been fhown in London, is rated at the fame price.

The MARES are moftly kept by arable farmers, who work them in their teams, until near their times of foaling; and, moderately, afterward, while they fuckle; fhutting up the foals during working hours; giving the mares not more, perhaps, than a month's refpite from work.

The beft *time of foaling* is thought to be March and April: the *time of weaning,* October or November.

DISPOSAL. In the ordinary practice of the country, the breeders of thefe horfes fell them while *yearlings* (provincially " colts"), or perhaps when *foals:* namely, at fix or eighteen months old; but moft generally the latter.

The *firft places of fale,* for *yearlings* *, are

X 4 the

* The *places of fale* for *foals* are the autumnal fairs of Afhby (de la Zouch) and Loughborough (in Leicefter-fhire), where they are taken with the dams, previoufly to their weaning.

the autumnal fairs of Burton (on Trent), Rugby (in Warwickſhire), and Aſhburn (in Derbyſhire), where they are moſtly bought up by graziers of Leiceſterſhire, and the other grazing parts of the Midland Diſtrict; where they are *grown*, among the grazing ſtock, until the autumn following; when the graziers take them to

The *ſecond places of ſale*—Stafford and Rugby; where, at two years and a half old, they are bought up by the arable farmers (or dealers) of Buckinghamſhire, Berkſhire, Wiltſhire, and other weſtern counties; where they are broken into harneſs, and worked until they be five, or, more generally, ſix years old; when theſe farmers, or dealers, who buy them up in the country, take them to

The *third place of ſale*—London! where they are finally purchaſed for drays, carts, waggons, coaches, the army, or any other purpoſe they turn out to be fit for.

The *prices*, for the laſt ten years, have been, for foals, five to ten pounds or guineas; for yearlings, ten to fifteen or twenty; for two-yearolds, fifteen to twentyfive or thirty; for ſixyearolds, twentyfive to forty guineas.

GENERAL

GENERAL OBSERVATIONS. This breed of horfes, viewed abftractedly in the light in which they here appear, are evidently a profitable fpecies of liveftock *. The *breeder* has the foals to help to maintain the mares, and to ftand, in fome degree, againft their firft coft, their lofs of work, and their decline in value after a certain age. The *grazier* is well paid for his year's keep. And the *arable farmer* has not their improvement in price only, but their work, to make up, in fome meafure, for their extraordinary keep. While the *brewer*, the *carman*, the *carrier*, the *coachman*, and the *army contractor*, are fupplied with animals which they want, and which they cannot breed and rear, with the fame conveniency as the farmer.

Therefore,

---

* It muft not, however, be underftood that all the horfes bred in the Midland Diftrict, pafs thro' the ftages, and fetch the prices, abovementioned. The breeder keeps them on, perhaps to the fecond ftage; perhaps to the third; befides what he keeps for his own ufe and brings to a lefs profitable market. While fome going blind, others lame, and others dying of the various difeafes to which this *fpecies* of animal is liable, are never marketable. What I mean to convey is a general idea of the moft prevalent practice of the diftrict.

Therefore, *so far as there is a market* for six-yearold horses of this breed, *so far*, the breed is profitable to agriculture.

But viewing the business of agriculture in general, throughout the island, not one occupier in ten can partake of the profit; and being kept in agriculture, after they have reached that profitable age, they become indisputably one of its heaviest burdens. For, beside a cessation of *improvement* of four or five guineas a year, a *decline* in value of as much, yearly, takes place. Even the brood mares, after they have passed that age, may, unless they are of a very superior quality, be deemed unprofitable to the farmer. Nevertheless, we see the majority of farmers, throughout the kingdom, working even barren mares and geldings down the stage of decline; though they know it will terminate in a ditch or a dog kennel. But, with the same unconcern, some men go to the gallows; though they know inevitable destruction will meet them there.

REFERENCES to the MINUTES on HORSES.

For an instance of their *affecting*, and thriving on, *clover*, see MIN. 17.

For a description of Ashby *stallion show*, 37.
                                                    For

For an inftance of horfes requiring *water* at grafs, 58.

For inftances of the *ftaggers* in horfes, 70.

For further inftances of the *ftaggers*, 104.

For ftill more inftances, fee MIN. 116.

35.

CATTLE.

THE BREED of this diftrict is the LONGHORNED : a breed which appears to have occupied, a length of time, the central parts of the ifland. See GLO. ECON.

In a general view, the old ftock of the country, notwithftanding the fingular efforts that have been made toward improvement, remains with little alteration. Each divifion of the diftrict has ftill its own breed, diftin-guifhable from that of the other divifions. There is a fimilar diftinction between the breeds of Staffordfhire and Derbyfhire, for inftance, as there is between thofe of Here-fordfhire

fordſhire and Glouceſterſhire (ſee GLO. ECON.).
The breeds of other diviſions of the diſtrict
have characteriſtics ſufficiently ſtrong to ſhow,
that the longhorned breed of cattle have,
during ſome length of time, been the prevailing ſtock of the country; and that, viewing
the diſtrict at large, Leiceſterſhire excepted,
no *radical* change, nor any *obvious* improvement or alteration, has yet taken place. A
ſtriking inſtance, this, of the ſlow progreſs
with which improvements in this department
of rural economy are made, even when carried on with every advantage.

But notwithſtanding the old ſtock may ſtill
be ſaid to be in poſſeſſion of the country,
every diviſion of it wears, at preſent, ſtrong
marks of improvement. WARWICKSHIRE,
STAFFORDSHIRE, and DERBYSHIRE, may
contend for ſome ſhare of this beneficial
change; and in LEICESTERSHIRE, the improved breed may be ſaid to have gained,
already, a degree of eſtabliſhment.

The HISTORY of this extraordinary improvement would be intereſting and uſeful;
as it might furniſh uſeful ideas to the improvers of other breeds. All I am able to
give is a ſketch.

CRAVEN

CRAVEN in YORKSHIRE has long been celebrated for a superior variety of the long-horned breed of cattle. From this source, it is well known, the LANCASHIRE cows have been, and, I believe, still are drawn;—the flower of these celebrated cows originating in CRAVEN HEIFERS.

Formerly, the Craven breed seems to have extended, in a similar way, into WESTMORELAND, also an adjoining county. From Westmoreland, bulls and heifers of this breed found their way into the MIDLAND COUNTIES. The present improved breed is traceable, by the indisputable evidence of many persons still living, to what was here called the "true old Westmoreland sort. *"

It

---

* The district of WESTMORELAND, from whence these cattle were drawn, is its southernmost extremity; about Kirby-Lonsdale, on the borders of Lancashire, and in the immediate neighbourhood of Craven.

It is an interesting fact, that while this breed has been under the most anxious cultivation, in the Midland Counties, it has been declining in Westmoreland; where it is now, I understand, giving way to the TEESWATER BREED. See YORK. ECON.

How is this to be reconciled? Is the Teeswater breed, for the soil and situation of Westmoreland, evidently superior to the Craven breed? or has the change been wrought, *solely*, by the Craven breed's being debased, in West-

It is generally underſtood, here, that
through this breed, and ſome fortuitous circumſtances, rather than from any fixed principles of improvement, Mr. WEBSTER of
Warwickſhire (of Canley near Coventry) became, ſome forty or fifty years ago, poſſeſſed
of a ſuperior breed of cattle ; and continued,
during many years, the leading breeder of the
Midland Counties *.   I have, indeed, heard
                                                         it

Weſtmoreland, through the circumſtances of the beſt of
its bulls and heifers being drawn off by the Midland
breeders ; while the beſt of thoſe of the Teeſwater breed
have been brought into it ?

This, among other changes of a ſimilar kind, that
have taken place in different parts of the iſland, form an
intereſting ſubject of enquiry.

* Prior to Mr. WEBSTER's day (or rather perhaps
to the time Mr. W.'s ſtock became popular) a ſuperior
breed of cattle made its appearance in _this_ neighbourhood ; at Linton ; where one WELBY, a blackſmith and
farmer, is ſaid, by thoſe who remember his day, to have
been in poſſeſſion of a very valuable breed of cows ;
which were ſaid to have been originally from DRAKE-
LOW on the banks of the Trent.   Whatever might have
been the quality of this breed, it was unfortunately
cut off by the diſtemper ; or ſo far reduced by it as to
loſe its eſtabliſhment as a ſeparate breed.

Since this article and the above note were written, I
have learnt from the beſt authority (Mr. PALFREY, a near
neighbour and intimate acquaintance of Mr. Webſter),
                                                         that

it faid, by a man who has himfelf been a
breeder of fome eminence, "that Mr. Webfter
had the beft ftock, efpecially of *beace*, that
ever were, or (he believed) ever will be, bred
in the kingdom."

To this bold affertion, however, I am not
ready to give full credit. I regifter it merely
as an evidence of the high degree of excellency which Mr. Webfter acquired. It is *im-
probable* that, after twenty or thirty years
anxious attention, not of *one* man only, but
of feveral, the breed, though excellent then,
fhould not, fince, have received fome degree
of improvement *.

Be this as it may, Mr. BAKEWELL is well
known to have got the lead, as a breeder
of cattle, through the means of the CANLEY
ftock.

that Mr. W.'s breed owes its original bafis to the
fame fource : having brought with him, from the banks
of the Trent, into Warwickfhire, when he firft fettled
there, fome fixty or feventy years ago, fix cows of SIR
THOMAS GRESLEY's breed : from which cows, and bulls
from Weftmoreland and "Lancafhire," he raifed his
celebrated flock.

* Another eminent breeder, on whofe judgement I
can better rely, is of opinion, that in beauty or utility of
form they have received little, if any, improvement fince
Mr. Webfter's day ; but thinks that in *flefh*, the more
valuable quality, they have been improved.

ftock. · His celebrated bull TWOPENNY,
that may be faid to have firft given the lead to
Mr. B. was out of a cow, purchafed, when a
heifer, of Mr. Webfter, and was got by a
bull from Weftmoreland ; a bull purchafed
in Weftmoreland.

Mr. FOWLER of Oxfordfhire (of Rollright on the borders of Warwickfhire),
whofe ftock is at prefent in the firft eftimation,
owes the fuperiority of his breed to the fame
fource. His cows are of the Canley blood ;
and his bull SHAKESPEAR, the beft ftock-
getter, I believe, the Midland Diftrict ever
knew, was got by a grandfon of Twopenny
(out of a daughter of Twopenny), and a cow
of the CANLEY blood.

Mr. PRINCEP of Derbyfhire (of Croxall in
this diftrict) acknowledges to have raifed his
prefent noble herd of cows—the firft dairy of
longhorned cows in the kingdom, I believe,
for form and fize taken jointly—from a cow
by the name of BRIGHT ; purchafed of the late
Mr. Chadwick of Caftle Bromwich : which
cow was got by Mr. Webfter's BLOXEDGE
bull, that is fpoken of here, as being the pureft
fountain of the Canley blood *.

The

* The BLOXEDGE bull was out of a threeyearold
heifer of Mr. Webfter's beft blood ; but was got by a
** Lar ...

The PRESENT STATE of the IMPROVED BREED of the MIDLAND COUNTIES, which might be well diftinguiſhed by the CANLEY BREED, is the following.

Mr. BAKEWELL is in poſſeſſion of many valuable individuals, males and females. His bull D. generally known by the name of the " mad bull," is a fine animal ; and is a ſtriking proof of the vulgar error, that breeding inandin, *weakens* the breed. He was got by a ſon of Twopenny, out of a daughter *and* ſiſter of the ſame celebrated bull ; ſhe being the produce of his own dam. Nevertheleſs, D. is the ſire of Shakeſpear, by another daughter of the ſame bull, and is probably the moſt *robuſt* individual of the longhorned breed; while D. himſelf, at the age of twelve or thirteen years, is more active, and higher mettled, than bulls in general are, at three or four years old.

This

" Lancaſhire" bull, belonging to a neighbour of Mr. Webſter. When a yearling, being unpromiſing, he was fold to a perfon by the name of BLOXDGE. But turning out a remarkably good flockgetter, Mr. W. repurchafed him; and ufed him feveral feaſons. He was afterwards fold to Mr. Harriſon of Drakenedge (War. wickſhire), and Mr. Flavel of Hogſhill (in this diſtrict), where he died.

This has long been esteemed Mr. Bakewell's best bull; and has been kept, principally, for his own use. He was never let,
except part of a season to Mr. Fowler; but
has had individual cows brought to him, at
five guineas a cow.

Mr. Bakewell's cows are of the finest
mould, and the highest quality: and his
HEIFERS beautiful as taste could well conceive them: clean and active as does. Mr.
B.'s exhibition of cattle would gratify the
most indifferent spectator, and could not fail
of being highly satisfactory to every lover of
the rural science.

Mr. FOWLER's cattle are, at present, in the
highest repute. His cows have long been
considered as of the first quality:—of the best
Canley blood. And his bull SHAKESPEAR,
already mentioned, has raised them to a degree of perfection, which, in the opinion of
the first judges, the breed of cattle under notice never before attained.

This bull is a striking specimen of what
naturalists term ACCIDENTAL VARIETIES.
Tho' bred in the manner that has been mentioned, he scarcely inherits a single point of
the longhorned breed; his horns excepted.
                                    When

When I faw him in 1784, then fix years
old, and fomewhat below his ufual condition,
though by no means low in flefh, he was of
this defcription.

, His head chap and neck, remarkably fine
and clean. His cheft extraordinarily deep; his
brifket down to his knees. His chine thin;
and rifing above the fhoulder points; leaving
a hollow on each fide, behind them. His loin,
of courfe, narrow at the chine; but remarkably wide at the hips; which protuberate in
a fingular manner. His quarters long, in
reality; but, in appearance, fhort; occafioned
by a fingular formation of the rump. At firft
fight, it appears as if the tail, which ftands
forward, had been fevered from the vertebræ,
by the chop of a cleaver, one of the vertebræ
extracted, and the tail forced up to make
good the joint: an appearance, which, on
examining, is occafioned by fome remarkable
wreaths of fat, formed round the fetting on
of the tail: a circumftance, which, in a *picture*,
would be deemed a deformity; but, as a *point*,
is in the higheft eftimation. The roundbones
fnug; but the thighs rather full, and remarkably let down. The legs fhort and their
bone fine. The carcafe, throughout (the

chine excepted), large—roomy—deep and well fpread.

His horns apart, he had every point of a Holdernefs or a Teefwater bull. Could his horns have been changed, he would have paffed, in Yorkfhire, as an ordinary bull of either of thefe breeds. His two ends would have been thought tolerably good ; but his middle very deficient. And I am of opinion, that had he been put to cows of thefe breeds, his ftock would have been of a moderate quality. But being put to cows, deficient where he was full (the lower part of the thigh excepted), and full where he was deficient, he has raifed the longhorned breed to a degree of perfection which, without fo extraordinary a prodigy, they never might have reached.

No wonder that a form fo uncommon fhould ftrike the improvers of this breed of ftock ; or that a carcafe they had been fo long ftriving in vain to produce, fhould be rated at a high price. His owner, however, happened to be among the firft of his admirers, and could never be induced to part from him, even for a feafon ; except to Mr. PRINCEP ; who had him two feafons, at the

extra-

extraordinary price of eighty guineas a feafon. A price at which no other bull has yet
been let.

This extraordinary animal is now (1789)
eleven years old, and firm in his conftitution;
but fo lame, in his hind quarters, as to render
him at prefent, and during the laft feafon,
entirely ufelefs.

His owner, however, has lefs to regret, as
he is in poffeffion of many valuable females
of his produce; and of one male, now three
years old, by the name of GARRICK *.

This bull was out of a cow got by a bull of
Mr. Bakewell, called the HAMPSHIRE BULL.

Thus, though we find Mr. Fowler, at prefent, in poffeffion of the lead, he has evidently obtained it through the affiftance of
Mr. Bakewell's ftock. But whether he has
gained the afcendancy by accident, merely,
or whether he had the better bafis to build
upon, may be a moot point difficult to determine.

Y 3

Mr.

* Mr. PAGET of Leicefterfhire (Ibftock in this
diftrict) is likewife in poffeffion of a promifing young
bull of the pureft of the Rollright blood; got by
Shakefpear, out of one of Mr. Fowler's beft-bred cows.
He is now a yearling; and leaps at five guineas a
cow.

Mr. Fowler's cows (about five and twenty in number) are many of them of an extraordinary mould; especially in the fineness of the forend, and the width and fatness of the hind quarters. A daughter and sister of Shakespear, being got on his own dam, is among the first of his herd: another evidence of the good effect of breeding from the same family .*.

Mr. Princep's cows, of his own breed, have been mentioned as being of a very fine quality: nevertheless, his present herd wears evident marks of improvement. Every cow and heifer of the Shakespear blood is distinguishable at sight;—by the extreme fineness of the forend,—the width of the hips,—and the formation of the rump; an

im-

* Mr. Fowler conducts his business on the old principle of *selling*, not on the modern way of *letting*, his bulls. Such heifers, too, as his own dairy does not require, he sells, and at high prices. Mr. Coaz of Norfolk has had all the cow calves he could spare, during the last three or four years, at, I understand, ten guineas each; taking them while young. Mr. F. has now (October 1789) ten bull calves (all, I believe, by Garrick), for which, *it is said*, he has refused five hundred guineas.

empreſſion which they have received with ſingular exactneſs.

Mr. Princep has two valuable bulls, by Shakeſpear: one of them out of the celebrated Bright.

Beſide the three herds that are here particularized, there are many others, in the Midland Diſtrict, that are entitled to great attention; but which, for various reaſons, I think may, with propriety, be omitted in this regiſter. Therefore, what remains to be added to the foregoing account of the preſent ſtate of the breed, is a GENERAL DESCRIPTION of its higher claſs of INDIVIDUALS.

The *forend* long; but light, to a degree of elegance. The neck *thin*; the chap clean; the head fine, but long and tapering*.

The *eye* large, bright, and prominent.

The *borns* vary with the ſex, &c. Thoſe of bulls are comparatively ſhort—from fifteen inches to two feet:—thoſe of the few oxen that have been reared of this breed are extremely large:—two and a half to three and

Y 4   a half

---

* A thick ſhort head, with a ſnub noſe, and a hollow face—provincially a "Dutch head"—is condemned, here, as a moſt hateful point.

a half feet long :—thofe of the cows, nearly
as long, but much finer; tapering to deli-
cately fine points. Moft of them hang downward, by the fide of the cheeks, and, if
well turned, as many of the cows are, fhoot
forward at the points *.

The *fhoulders* remarkably thin and fine,
as to bone, but thickly covered with flefh ;
not the fmalleft protuberance of bone dif-
cernible +.

The *girt* fmall, comparatively with the
fhorthorned and middlehorned breeds ‡.

                              The

---

* Too frequently, however, the double bend does
not take place ; the horns continuing to fhoot downward, until they would reach the ground, or point inward until they would gag the mouth which fupports
them, were not the points from time to time removed :
and, in fome individuals, while one horn is pointing to
the ground, or winding under the jaw fo as to prevent
its opening, the other is fhooting away from the head,
or taking fome other aukward direction : thus tending
to disfigure, and deftroy, the animal which nature or-
dained them to ornament and defend.

    + The Difhley breed, I think, excels in this point :
fome of the heifers have fhoulders fine as race horfes.

    ‡ Neverthelefs there are fome individuals, more par-
ticularly, perhaps, of Mr. Fowler's breed, that are
tolerably well let down in the girt.

The *chine* remarkably full, when fat; but hollow, when low in condition *.

The *loin* broad, and the *hips* remarkably wide, and protuberant †.

The *quarters* long and level; the *nache* of a middle width; with the *tail* set on variously, even in individuals of the highest repute ‡.

The

* This is confidered, by accurate judges, as a criterion of good flesh; as the large, hard, ligatures, which in fome individuals, when low in condition, we fee tightly ftretched along the chine, from the fetting on of the neck to the fore part of the loins, is a mark of the flesh being of a bad quality.

† The protuberance of the *bones* of the hips, is a point at prefent in the firft fafhion; but is always, I obferve, mentioned in the language of enthufiafm, not of reafon. A wide loin, with the hips protuberating in *fat*, is indifputably a moft defirable thing. But what ufe, or even ornament, two *knobs of bone* can produce, is not to me evident. In fome individuals they have to me an *artificial* appearance; as if the loin were a lid, and the hips handles to remove it. I can admire a *full* hip, and conceive its utility; but I am clearly of opinion, that there are many points of a bullock better entitled to the breeder's attention, than a *protuberant* one; yet, it is more than, probable, that, in the improvement both of this and the fhorthorned breed, points of fome confequence have been facrificed to this idol.

‡ The quarters of Shakefpear have been defcribed; thofe of the bull D. are not lefs remarkable: his tail appearing

The *roundbones* small; but the *thighs* in general fleshy; tapering however, when in the best form, toward the gambrels.

The *legs* small and clean, but comparatively long *. The *feet* in general neat, and of the middle size.

The *carcase* as nearly a cylinder as the natural form of this animal will allow. The *ribs* standing out full from the spine; receiving the *entrails* within them. The *belly* of course appears small †.

The

---

appearing to grow out of the top of his spine, rather than to be a continuation of the vertebræ; the upper part of the tail forming an *arch* which rises some inches above the general level of the back. This, viewing him as a picture, has a good effect; but, as a point, has a very bad one to the grazier; as tending to *hide* the fatness of the rump. It is remarkable, that in this, and many other points, the son and the sire are as dissimilar as if they had no consanguinity.

* More owing, however, to the gauntness of the carcase, than the positive length of the legs.

† The smallness of the belly is held out as a superior excellency. The viscera being lodged within the ribs is certainly such. But I cannot believe that a paucity of intestines is a valuable property of cattle: intestines are to them what roots are to trees. The ideas of *offal*, and largeness of *bone*, have, *perhaps*, in more points than one, led the improvers away from perfection. This, however, by the way.

The *flesh*, of the superior class I am describing, seldom fails of being of the first quality.

The *bide* of a middle thickness.

The *colour* is various: the brindle, the finchback, and the pye, are common: the *lighter* they are, the better they seem to be in esteem *.

The *fatting quality* of this improved breed, in a state of maturity, is indisputably good.

As GRAZIERS' STOCK, they undoubtedly rank high.

As DAIRY STOCK, however, their merit is less evident: dairywomen here, and elsewhere, bear witness against them: nevertheless,

---

* This colour, however, appears to be merely a matter of fashion. Nevertheless, it strikes me that a *light* colour of cattle is advantageous to the *grazier*.——It is a fact, in the nature of vision, that *white* objects appear to the eye larger, than *black* ones of the same size; and a light-coloured bullock, no doubt, appears larger in a market, than a darker-coloured one, of the same weight.

It may be remarked, in this place, that the six cows which formed the basis of Mr. Webster's breed, were *red*, and it is observable that some of Mr. Fowler's best cows are of that colour.

lcfs, the advocates for the breed aſſert their
eligibility in this character: ſome, indeed,
go ſo far as to ſay, that a cow which is profitable to the graziers is ſo to the dairyman: a
poſition that might be contradicted by a
thouſand evidences.

Nevertheleſs, it appears to me probable,.
that a cow may be ſo conſtitutioned, as to
convert her aliment into milk, while milk is
continued to be drawn from her, and, when
the draught is ſtopt, *but not till then*, to convert the ſame current of chyle into fat: a
verſatility of conſtitution, however, which,
I believe, does not belong to the breed under notice ; whoſe propenſity to fatneſs appears to be too great, to permit their lacteſ-
cent powers to preſerve the aſcendancy *long
enough* for the purpoſes of the dairyman.

As BEASTS OF DRAFT, the carcaſe of the
longhorned breed, viewed generally, renders them unfit : nevertheleſs, the carcaſe of
ſome of the beſt of the variety under notice,
is ſufficiently powerful for the purpoſe of
draft ; while their natural activity, and clean-
neſs of limbs, are very favourable to this
purpoſe.

But

But the enormous fize of the horns, of the oxen of this variety, would invalidate all their qualifications, were they greater than they really are. If they happen to take a convenient form, they may be difpenfed with ; but ftanding out aukwardly, as they frequently do, they become an infuperable objection.

A method of preventing their growth, or even of checking their exuberance, would be a moft valuable difcovery; to thofe, efpecially, who are in poffeffion of the breed, and wifh to make them ufeful as beafts of draft.

From this defcription of the improved breed of cattle of the Midland Counties, it appears very evidently, that the PRINCIPLES OF IMPROVEMENT, laid down aforegoing, have, to this fpecies of liveftock, been judicioufly applied. The UTILITY OF FORM has been ftrictly attended to : the bone and other offal fmall; and the forend light; while the chine, the loin, the rump, and the ribs are heavily loaded ; and with flefh of the fineft quality.

BREEDING.

BREEDING. The males and females require to be treated of separately.

BULLS. Viewing the district at large, its economy, with regard to bulls, is the same as that of other places. Dairymen, in general, use their own bulls, generally of their own rearing; and smaller cowkeepers employ those of their neighbours. But dairymen who pay a closer attention to their stock, purchase their bulls, or hire them by the season, of bullbreeders; who rear, perhaps, five to ten bulls yearly; the superior breeders, for letting; the inferior, for sale.

The practice of *letting* this species of male stock, probably, originated in this district; and in the practice of Mr. Bakewell; about twentyfive years ago.

In the spring, previously to the season of business, the breeders have their private *shows*; and beside these, as has been intimated aforegoing, there are public shows; more, however, for the purpose of sale, than of letting.

The *prices* given for bulls, *by purchase*, run from five to a hundred pounds; *by the season*, from ten to fifty or sixty; *by the cow*, from half a crown to five guineas.

The

The let bulls are *fent out* in April or beginning of May; being generally led in halters; or driven fingly; and are *returned* at the end of the feafon—generally in Auguſt, in the fame manner.

With refpect to the *age* at which bulls "do bufinefs," as it is technically termed here—the practice of this diſtrict differs from that of moſt others; where from two to four years old, namely three feafons, is the ordinary period of employment. But, here, they are pretty commonly allowed to leap while yearlings; and, if good ſtockgetters, are kept on fo long as they will do bufinefs; perhaps till they are ten or twelve years old. If they grow vicious, they are kept wholly in the houfe; if they throw gates or break paſture, they are humbled by a " bull chain," faſtened ingeniouſly to the noſtrils.

It is obfervable, in this place, that the bulls of this improved breed are not unfrequently, even while youthful, deficient in vigour :— the hired bulls being fometimes returned prematurely on this account.

This might be laid hold of as an argument againſt the practice of breeding inandin. It is, however, more probably owing to a different caufe.

A hand-

A handfome bull,—a bull nearly perfect in all his points,—is moft difficult to breed : yet the breeder's object is to render him, to the eye at leaft, as near perfection as may be. He is, therefore, made up for the fhow, by high keep; as well to evince his propenfity to fatnefs, as to hide his defects ; thereby fhowing him off to the beft advantage : the confequence of which is, being taken from this high keep, and lowered, at once, to a common cow pafture, he flags.

Hence, it is become a practice of judicious breeders, when their bulls are let early enough, to lower them down, by degrees, to ordinary keep, previous to the feafon of employment.

BREEDING COWS. There is only *one* inftance, I believe, of cows being kept folely for the purpofe of *breeding* : the dairy being here, as every where elfe, a joint intepion.

Such as are not employed in the rearing of calves, ought certainly, in common good management, to be made to pay for their maintenance by *milking* or *working* : the laft a ufe to which Mr. Bakewell alone, perhaps, has put them.

ORE

One circumſtance in the management of breeding cows, practiſed by leading breeders at leaſt, is noticeable. In the practice of leſs ſpirited and leſs judicious breeders, a cow or heifer, if ſhe happen to miſs the bull, is proſcribed, let her form and blood be what they may; and, as ſoon as her milk is obtained, is condemned, even for the firſt offence.

This, when dairying alone is the object of cowkeeping, is undoubtedly judicious; but, when breeding is a principal or even a joint object, as it is in the practice of moſt dairymen, ſuch a conduct may be highly blameable. For though it may be eaſier to breed handſome good cows, than bulls of that deſcription; yet, when we conſider how much of the ſucceſs of breeding depends on the female, it is evidently a want of common policy, to cut off a valuable cow, for one miſcarriage.

If ſhe do not breed this ſeaſon, let her maintain herſelf by working, until the next. Mares are kept, year after year, without breeding. And if mares. are found nearly equal to geldings, in work; why ſhould not cows be nearly equal to oxen, in the ſame intention?

REARING CATTLE. The rearing of cattle is here confined to BULLS and HEIFERS, for breeding and the dairy : there is not, in ordinary practice, a STEER reared in the district ; excepting some few of late years, for the purpose of draft.

The METHOD of rearing, here, differs little from that of other districts; except in the rearing of BULL CALVES, and sometimes high-bred heifers, by suffering them to remain at the teat, until they be six, nine, or perhaps twelve months old ; letting them run, either with their dams; or, more frequently, especially where the dairy is an object, with less valuable cows or heifers, bought in for the purpose ; and, when the intention is fulfilled, sold, or fatted : each cow being generally allowed one male calf, or two females.

The effect of this practice is a quick growth ; and, perhaps, like rearing vegetables in a rich soil, the practice may assist in meliorating the constitution, and enlarging the frame. Be this as it may, the growth of calves, reared in this way, is strikingly rapid.

The best method of the dairymen is this : —The calves suck a week or a fortnight, *according*

cording to their strength (a good rule): new milk in the pail, a few meals :—next, new milk and skim milk mixt, a few meals more : then, skim milk alone ; or porridge, made with milk, water, ground oats, &c. and sometimes oilcake,—until cheesemaking commence : after which, whey porridge, or sweet whey, in the field ; being careful to house them, in the night, until warm weather be confirmed.

Turneps are not thought of as a food of calves; nor, in the ordinary practice of the district, is either corn, cake, or linseed in use ; milk, whey, hay, and grass, being the sole food of rearing calves *.

The *time of rearing* extends, in this district, through the winter months; but is confined, in a great degree, between the beginning of December and the latter end of March.

In the treatment of YOUNG STOCK, I find little in the practice of this district, that requires particular notice.

The bulls, in the common practice of dairymen, are suffered to ride while yearlings;

Z 2 namely,

* Until autumn, when turneps are usually given.

namely, at fifteen to eighteen months old;
and the heifers to take them, while two years
old; bringing them into the dairy at three years
old : generally keeping them from the bull
until late in the summer,—as the latter end of
July, or the beginning of August ;—it being
a pretty general opinion, that heifers should
come in at grafs : beside, by this practice,.
one bull ferves both the dairy cows and the
heifers. I have known a dairy of twenty or
thirty cows, and ten or twelve heifers, ferved
by a "calf ;"—a yearling bull.

In the practice of fuperior breeders, heifers
are fometimes kept from the bull until they
be three years old ; bringing them in at four :.
efpecially in that of their enterprizing leader ;
in whofe fuperior practice, maiden heifers, as
well as dry and barren cows, are occafionally
enured to harnefs : a laudable example, that
might be profitably followed by every other
breeder of cattle.

DAIRY COWS. Under this head, I fhall
confider cows, abftractedly, as they relate to
the DAIRY.

In the CHOICE OF COWS, *dairy farmers* are
guided by criterions different from thofe
which

which have been enumerated as the favourite points of *graziers* and *modern breeders.*

The DERBYSHIRE cow remains the favorite of the old "dairiers." They argue, that the grazier and the dairyman, diſtinctly conſidered, require different animals, to ſuit their reſpective purpoſes. The dairier's object is *milk* ; the grazier's *beef*; and it is a trite remark, among dairymen in different diſtricts, that a cow which "runs to beef" is unprofitable to the dairy : for notwithſtanding the excellency of her bag, and the plentifulneſs of her milk, preſently after calving, her natural inclination to *fleſhineſs* draws off her *milk :* while a cow that is by breed, or natural conſtitution, prone to *milk*, will ſupply this, at the expence of her *carcaſe*, let her paſture be ever ſo plentiful.

Theſe popular opinions, however, though they contain much truth, are not altogether well founded. They hinge on a falſe principle. Cows are uſeful, and in a great degree neceſſary, in a twofold capacity : as dairy-cows, and as grazing ſtock : the dairyman and the grazier *cannot* have diſtinct animals : one and the ſame individual *muſt* ſerve both their purpoſes. And a breed of cows fit for ·

the

the grazier only, is, in a general light, not lefs eligible, than a breed which is fit only for the dairyman.

The Derbyſhire cows are unprofitable as grazing ſtock. They have neither beauty nor utility of form ; being loaded with offal of every kind. The head thick, the chap and neck foul ; the bone proportionably large, the hide heavy, and the hair long : even the bag is not unfrequently ſo overgrown, as to be almoſt hid in hair ; a point of milking cows to which dairymen, of moſt diſtricts, have an objection : this however only ſerves -to ſhow that popular criterions are ſeldom to be depended upon. Were the fleſh and fatting quality of the Derbyſhire cows equal to their quality as dairy cows, the hairineſs of their bags might well be difpenſed with.

The STAFFORDSHIRE cows bear a different characteriſtic. Taking them together, they are rather adapted to grazing, than the dairy ; moſt of them being tolerably clean. But, in general, they are too gaunt in their carcaſes to be eligible, either as dairy or grazing ſtock.

Nevertheleſs, there are individuals of this breed ; or rather, perhaps, of a breed between this and the Derbyſhire ; that may be ſaid to be be at once eligible as dairy cows and grazing ftock. At leaſt, they come nearer my idea of what a cow ought to be, than any other breed or variety of the *longhorned* breed, I have yet had an opportunity of obſerving.

Whether the individuals, now under notice, have or have not been produced by a mixture of the Staffordſhire and Derbyſhire blood, they are the moſt prevalent on the banks of the Trent, which divides the two counties : it is, indeed, the breed which is there found, more particularly on the Derbyſhire ſide, from Walton towards Stanton, which falls under this deſcription.

The following are accurate dimenſions of a middleaged cow of this kind ; ſomewhat low in fleſh, and young in calf.

Height at the withers, four feet two inches and a quarter.

——— of the briſket, nineteen inches.

Smalleſt girt, ſix feet, five inches,

Largeſt girt, ſeven feet eight inches and a half.

Length from forehead to nache, ſeven feet three inches.

——— from ſhoulder-knob to the center of the hip, three feet eight inches.

——— from the center of the hip to the out of the nache, twentyone inches.

Width

Width at the fhoulders, twenty inches.

――― at the hips, twentytwo inches.

―――― the nache, thirteen inches.

Length of the horns, twentyfour inches; their width from point to point, three feet four inches.

The forend fine, long, and ftanding low.

The head fmall, and the neck thin, but deep, according with the depth of her bofom,

The fhoulders fine; the ribs full; and the loin broad,

The thighs remarkably thin below, as if to give room to her bag, large, clean, and bladder-like; with long teats, and remarkably large elaftic milk veins; furnifhing an ample fupply of milk.

The legs fhort, with the bone fine (7½ inches girt).

The flefh good, and the hide of a middle thicknefs. .

The colour a " brinded mottle," with a " finch back," and white legs.

In temper remarkably cadifh, " gentle ;" a quality of confiderable value, in a cow in-tended for the pail.

The principal diftinction obfervable, be-tween the form of what is here fpoken of as a *dairy* cow, and that of a cow of the mo-dern

dern breed, or what is more generally understood by a "good grazier's cow," is, the
former is more roomy and better let down in
the cheft; the latter, better topped; fuller.
on the chine and loin; and, generally, fuller
in the thigh. Both of them are clean in the
forend, and shoulder; the bone in both is
fine; the flesh of both good (but that of the
modern breed indifputably better); and their
hides of a middle thicknefs.

But the moft material difference, and that
which determines the *dairyman* in his choice,
is, the one lofes her milk a few months after
calving; the other, if required, will milk the
year round.

The PLACES OF PURCHASE of dairy cows
are the fairs of the diftrict, and, during the
fpring months, a weekly market at Derby;
to which cows, frefh in milk, are brought,
chiefly by drovers, and moftly *without their
calves.*

At the fairs, and in the ordinary practice
of this diftrict, cows are almoft invariably fold
as *incalvers*; frequently at the point of calving; fometimes dropping their calves by the
road. I recollect few if any inftances of feeing
cows at market, with *calves at their feet*; agreeably

ably to the ordinary practice of most other districts.

The *price* of an incalver of the description last recited, has been, on a par of the last ten years, about ten pounds, or guineas.

The MANAGEMENT of DAIRY COWS. In their *summer* management, I have met with nothing of superior excellence in this district. They are turned to grass, about Mayday; allowing from an acre and half to two acres to a cow: kept generally in one and the same pasture, until aftergrass be ready to receive them; and have turneps thrown to them (by those who grow turneps) on grassland, in autumn.

In this district, however, one instance of practice occurred to me which requires to be registered; namely, that of a dairy of fourteen or fifteen cows being principally *dried off together*, on one day (the middle of December); preserving two or three, only, in milk, for the family, during the winter months; keeping these at hay; putting the dried cows to straw; for which purpose, only, they were dried off in this remarkable manner.

It

It is obfervable, however, that this practice can be eligible only, when " cows come well in together:" to effect which they are " bulled as faft," that is to fay as near together, " as poffible."

Unnatural as this expedient will no doubt be deemed by many, it may, neverthelefs, in fome cafes, be eligible : all I fhall fay farther of it is, that had I not obferved it in the practice of one of the oldeft and beft managers in the diftrict, I fhould not have regiftered it *.

In the *winter* management of dairy cows, one circumftance may be noticed : that of their being frequently kept (in conformity to a modern practice adopted by fome leading men) in fheds, which have been defcribed under the head BUILDINGS, continually throughout winter, from the time of their being taken up in autumn, to that of their being turned to grafs in the fpring, generally four months,—*without any exercife!*

Some difcerning individuals, however, have already difcovered the inconveniencies of this practice, efpecially that of their hoofs cracking,

* Mr, LAKING, of Hall End, Warwickfhire.

cracking, let them loofe in a yard, a few hours every day, to moiften their feet, as well as to exercife their legs, and clean their coats.

The DISPOSAL OF COWS. In what might be called the natural practice of the diftrict, dairy farmers not only *rear* but *fat* their own cows. One of the largeft farmers in the dif- trict told me that " he never bought a cow in his life!" he rears fifteen, eighteen, or twenty calves yearly, and fats his own ftock ; or, for want of room, fells them to graziers.

This forms a beautifully fimple plan of ma- nagement; well adapted to a middlefoil farm ; and efpecially eligible for gentlemen, and others, who are deficient in judgement, and unacquainted with markets. The pro- portion of grafs and arable being determined upon, and the quantity of ftock afcertained, the machine is regulated, and nothing but a due attention to the number of heifers, an- nually reared, is wanted to keep it in con- tinual and uniform motion. A certain num- ber of dairy cows, with a lot of fatting cattle, and another of young ftock to follow them, in fummer, and to eat ftraw, in winter. No going to market, but with corn, dairy pio-
duce,

duce, and cullen cows. A plan of general management, beautiful in theory; and, if one may judge from the comfortable independency which the perfon above alluded to is poffeffed of, through a perfeverance, by his father and himfelf, in this courfe of management, it is eligible in practice.

DAIRY MANAGEMENT. WARWICK-SHIRE, almoft throughout, comes under the defcription of a dairy country; and, in the DISTRICT of the STATION, the dairy forms a confiderable branch of the bufinefs of almoft every farm. The outlines of practice are, therefore, requifite to be traced.

The SIZES of dairies, here, are feldom large: fifty cows form the largeft in the diftrict: thirty are confidered as a large-fized dairy: twenty a middling fize.

In taking a view of the dairy of this diftrict, it will be neceffary to feparate the three principal branches:

> Calves;
> Butter;
> Cheefe.

FATTING CALVES. The male calves, except fuch as are reared for breeding, are, as, has been intimated, almost Invariably fatted.

Calves are, here, fatted at the *teat* ; and, in the early part of the season, are kept to a good age.   But cheesemaking once begun, they are butchered as they drop : at not more, perhaps, than three or four days old ; nor at more, perhaps, than three or four shillings price.   The market, the manufacturing towns, and the collieries, of Staffordshire.

The only circumstance relative to the *management* of *fatting calves*, which requires notice, is an expedient used by some individuals, but not, I believe, in universal practice, to make them lie quiet ; more especially during a temporary scarcity of milk ; which will sometimes take place.   In this case, balls, made of wheat flour, and a sufficient quantity of gin to form it into a paste, are given them ; three balls, about the size of walnuts, being given about a quarter of an hour after each meal.   The effect is, that instead of wasting themselves by incessant " bawling," they lie quiet ; sleeping a principal part of their time.   By a little custom, the calves get fond of these PASTE BALLS ; eating them
freely

freely out of the hand ; a proof of their being acceptable to their ftomachs. As an *expedient*, they are evidently eligible; and may be of fervice to a reftlefs calf ; even when milk is plentiful. This, however, by way of intimation.

BUTTER. The only idea which I met with refpecting *milk* butter, and which is entitled to a place, here, is that of doing away the *rancidnefs* of *turnep* butter, and the *bitternefs* of *barley ftraw* butter, by a moft fimple and very *rational* means. Inftead of putting the cream, immediately as it is fkimmed off the milk, into the jar or other retaining veffel, it is firft poured upon *hot water*, and, having ftood till cool, is fkimmed off the water ! a new idea : but, I will venture to repeat, a moft rational one ; though I have not myfelf had an opportunity of proving it.

In the fame dairy in which the above expedient is ufed, a method of improving the quality of *whey* butter is practifed. This improvement is effected by *fcalding* each meal of cream, as it is taken off the whey ; by hanging it over the fire until " fcalding hot ;" being careful not to let it boil. This too, I regifter as a fimple and rational procefs,

cefs, and not as one whofe efficacy I have
proved by my own experience. I regifter
them, however, on an authority which I have
no reafon to doubt.

CHEESE. This is the grand object of the
Midland dairy. Very confiderable quantities are annually made; particularly, as has
been obferved, in Warwickfhire, and in this
neighbourhood,—where cheefe of a very
fine quality is not unfrequently produced.

It will, therefore, be proper to take a general
view of the fubject : for although, after the
recital of the practices of Glocefterfhire and
Wiltfhire, much important information cannot be expected; yet it is more than probable, fome interefting circumftances will
arife.

The particulars which, in this cafe, require
to be noticed, are

Soil,	Rennet,
Herbage,	Running,
Managers,	Curd,
Species of cheefe,	Cheefe,
Time of making,	Markets,
Quality of milk,	Produce.
Colouring,	

Soil.

Soil. For an account of the foils of the beſt dairy parts of *this* diſtrict, ſee **min.** 55, in which it appears that a *cool* ſoil is favourable to cheeſe.

Nevertheleſs, I received an idea, here, from a moſt experienced and intelligent manager, that a very cold " weak" ſoil is improper for the dairy : that is to ſay, a ſoil may be *too cool* for the purpoſe. The cheeſe it affords, though good in quality, is found deficient in quantity. His own farm being principally of that deſcription of land, he has, during the latter part of his life, made *rearing* his principal object ; conſidering his *dairy* merely as being ſubordinate to that end.

Herbage. An account of the herbage of the cheeſe farms of this diſtrict will likewiſe appear in **min.** 55.

What remains to be regiſtered, here, is the circumſtance of cheeſe being, not unfrequently, made from *new keys* ; even of the firſt or ſecond year ; while they conſiſt chiefly of *red clover*, with, perhaps, a mixture of *raygraſs* ; yet, from theſe cultivated graſſes, provided *trefoil* make no part of them, good

Vol. I. . A a cheeſe

cheefe is made. A fact which dairy farmers, in fome diftricts, would not readily credit.

MANAGERS. A ftriking inftance of the folly of dairymen being inattentive to the bufinefs of cheefemaking occurs in this diftrict ; where a dairy farmer declares, that, one year, he loft forty pounds, by the mifmanagement of his dairywoman. This led him to an inveftigation of the bufinefs, himfelf, and this to a fufficient degree of fuperintendance, to prevent, in future, a fimilar lofs. See GLO. ECON. on this fubject.

SPECIES OF CHEESE. The only " *factor's cheefe*," made in this diftrict, is *thin cheefe* of *new milk*. The fize, that of fingle Glocefterfhire, or fomewhat thicker *.

For

---

* The CHEESE VATS of this diftrict are merely " hoops" of afh, with a boarden bottom. I do not recollect to have feen one inftance of " turned vats" being in ufe. The diameter about fifteen inches. The depth two inches, more or lefs.

The " FILLET" of this diftrict is of wood : a long fhaving or fplint of afh ; an inch or more wide, and an eighth of an inch or more thick ; not formed into a hoop, but left open, with the ends tapering thin, and overlapping feveral inches. The part of the cheefe which rifes above the vat being gathered up

For "*family cheese*," more or less *skim milk* is used; and sometimes, I understand, *all* skim milk. But *this* not being conformable to the prevailing custom of the country, the practice is looked upon as sordid, and waste becomes the necessary consequence.

LEICESTERSHIRE is, at present, celebrated for its "*cream cheese*,"—known by the name of STILTON CHEESE.

This species of cheese may be said to be a modern produce of the Midland District. Mrs. Paulet of Wimondham, in the Melton quarter of Leicestershire, the first maker of Stilton cheese, is still living.

Mrs. P. being a relation, or an acquaintance, of the well known Cooper Thornhill, who formerly kept the Bell at Stilton (in Huntingdonshire, on the great north road from London to Edinburgh) furnished his house with cream cheese; which, being of

A a 2   a fin-

---

up and pinched in this fillet, its lower edge is entered within the vat, and, a broad cheese board being put upon it, sinks down with the upper part of the cheese into the vat.

1789. *The fillets* are now become prevalent: an admirable improvement. Some care, however, is requisite, it seems, to prevent their rusting.

a singularly fine quality, was coveted by his
customers; and, through the assistance of
Mrs. P. his customers were gratified, at the
expence of half a crown a pound, with
cream cheese of a superior quality; but of
what country was not publicly known : hence
it obtained, of course, the name of Stilton
cheese.

At length, however, the place of produce was discovered, and the art of producing
it learnt, by other dairywomen of the neighbourhood. Dalby first took the lead; but
it is now made in almost every village,
in that quarter of Leicestershire, as well as
in the neighbouring villages of Rutlandshire.
Many tons are made every year: Dalby
is said to pay its rent with this produce,
only.

Thus, from a mere circumstance, the produce of an extent of country is changed;
and, in this case, very profitably.

The sale is no longer confined to Stilton;
every innkeeper, within fifteen or twenty miles
of the district of manufacture, is a dealer
in Stilton cheese. The price, at present, ten-
pence a pound, to the maker; and a shilling

to

to the confumer; who takes it at the maker's weight.

Cream cheefe being an article of luxury merely, and a fpecies of produce which cannot become of general utility to agriculture, the art of making it does not come within the plan of this work; I therefore proceed to the manufacturing of milk cheefe, agreeably to the practice of the diftrict of the ftation.

TIME OF MAKING. Where the family is large, it is cuftomary to begin as foon as the cows afford milk enough for a cheefe; continuing to make " family cheefe," until the cows go out to grafs. From the beginning of May to the beginning of Auguft, is the time of making what is termed " year's cheefe:" continuing from that time, to the latter end of October, to make what is called the " latter weigh ;" likewife for the factor: and from that time, until the cows go off their milk, make " family cheefe."

QUALITY OF THE MILK. It is not fo cuftomary, here, as in the other cheefe countries, to fkim a part of the milk from which factor's cheefe is made : neverthelefs, in fome dairies

A a 3   it

it is practised; the proportion skimmed varying in different dairies.

COLOURING. In the ordinary practice of
the district, cheese is *not* coloured. Nevertheless, some few individuals use colouring;
and find their advantage in doing it. The
produce of one passes, at market, for WAR-
WICKSHIRE, that of the other for GLOCESTER-
SHIRE cheese: the factors of course will give
more for the latter than the former. To the
consumers, therefore, this filthy practice owes
its prevalency.

CORRECTING. In this district, an instance
is mentioned in which a large lump of *alum*
being kept in the cowl, during the time of
coagulation, was *believed* to be efficacious in
preventing the cheese from heaving. This,
however, by way of hint.

RENNET. No established mode of preparation.

RUNNING. The ordinary *heat of the milk*
85° to 90°. The *time in coagulating*, held out
as proper, is about an hour; but, in practice,
I have seldom or ever found so slow a coagulation.

In a considerable dairy, where tolerable
cheese was made, the practice was to *bring*
the curd in about a quarter of an hour! but

not

not to *break it up* in lefs than three quarters!
I mention this to fhew how many different
ways there are of producing cheefe of a moderate quality.

CURD. In fome large dairies, more particularly, perhaps, under the practice laft mentioned, the *breaking* is done, not with a knife
or the hand, but with the " churn dafh !" an
admirable thought, fo far as expedition is
thereby promoted. But, in a cowl of delicate
curd, this coarfe tool would no doubt be improper.

The *gathering* is done, in the ufual manner,
with the hands and the difh, the whey poured
off thro' a fieve, and the curd rebroken.

Scalding. In the prefent eftablifhed practice, the *curd* is not fcalded; except in the
practice of a few individuals; but generally
the *cheefe*. It is obfervable, however, and to
me is very interefting, that the fineft dairy of
cheefes I faw in this diftrict, was *not fcalded*,
either in the curd, or in the cheefe.

CHEESE, *in the prefs*. Having been vatted
hard with the *hands* (or in fome few inftances,
previoufly fqueezed in the *prefs*), and having
ftood about an hour, it is taken out of the
prefs and *fcalded*; by immerging it in *water*,

heated

heated to about 150°, letting the evening's cheeses remain in the scalding liquor all night; and the morning's cheeses, until the water be cold; when they are placed again in the prefs; in which having remained a few hours, they are (in common practice) taken out; the cloth finally taken off; the cheeslings *salted*; replaced in the prefs; and, having flood another meal (in the whole two meals) are finally taken out of the prefs.

On the shelves. Cheeses, here, remain only a few days, with no peculiarity of treatment.

On the floor, the year's cheese, or first weigh, is seldom or ever cleaned. The edges of the latter weigh are sometimes scraped; and sometimes only rubbed with a HAIR CLOTH; an admirable utensil in a cheese chamber.

MARKETS FOR CHEESE. *London*, the *manufacturing towns*, and the *north of England*, to which great quantities of cheese are sent from this district.

PRODUCE. I met with a well authenticated inflance, in this district, of the produce of cheese being materially influenced by the *season*.

One year twentyone cows produced four tons of factor's cheese, befide the expenditure
of

of the family ; together, upwards of four hundredweight a cow ; yet, next year, the same cows, with the addition of four or five more to the dairy, did not produce so much cheese.

The first summer was warm and moderately wet ; neither too wet nor too dry ; a happy mixture of warmth and moisture ; the pastures were eaten level, even to a degree of bareness, yet they always wore a freshness, and the cows, throughout the summer, looked sleek and healthy. The next was a wet summer.

The medium *produce of a cow* is three hundredweight, and upward.

The *produce of the district* would be difficult to ascertain ; as it has not, with respect to the dairy, any determinate bounds. WARWICKSHIRE, and the DISTRICT of the STATION send a quantity of cheese to market, nearly equal, perhaps, to NORTHWILTSHIRE and the VALES of GLOCESTERSHIRE.

GRAZING. The Midland District, viewed collectively, is a GRAZING COUNTRY. South and East LEICESTERSHIRE, and much of NORTHAMPTONSHIRE, fall entirely under this description. WARWICKSHIRE, as has been said, inclines more to the dairy.

The

The DISTRICT of the STATION contains a mixture of the two. There is one man, in this neighbourhood, fats not lefs than two hundred head annually. Moft large farmers, befide the cullings of their own dairies, purchafe folely for the purpofe of " feeding :"—feveral of them grazing fifty head.

The SPECIES of grazing, which is here practifed, is, in a manner folely, SUMMER FATTING on GRASS. Some may, every year, be finifhed with HAY and KEPT PASTURE : and a few individuals practife STALLFAT-TING, on HAY and what is called "CUTMEAT;" namely, oats in ftraw, cut in a chaff machine ; and fome, but very few, on OILCAKE *.

The

* FATTING CATTLE ON GRAINS. At Burton, in this diftrict, feveral hundred head of cattle, moftly cows, are annually fatted with HAY and GRAINS ; the pro-duce of the breweries of BURTON ALE ; which being brewed of fingular ftrength, and, in the ordinary prac-tice, little fmall-beer being made after it, the grains are of a very fuperior quality. They are moftly ufed frefh from the vats—fometimes warm—but never hot. When a redundancy happens, the overflewings are laid up in cafks and bins, covered up with mould. With thefe ftale grains melt duft is generally mixed. The ufual quan-tity of frefh grains, a bufhel a day ; with about half a hundredweight of hay a week. From five to fix months

The practice of SUMMER GRAZING is, alone, entitled to particular notice : and this requires to be registered in detail.

The SITUATION and SOIL have been described, as forming a rich middleland district : a description of country common to every quarter of the kingdom.

The HERBAGE, too, appears aforegoing : mostly a kind of temporary sward, which has been described ; with a small proportion of old rough grassland.

The description of CATTLE,—*cows* old or barren, and *heifers* which have missed the bull ; all of the longhorned breed of the district, or from the more northern counties of Cheshire, Lancashire, &c.   There is not, in the practice of *this* district, a single *ox* fatted ; except some few *Welch runts* ; and except, of late years, some *Irish bullocks* ; and these, only by a few individuals.

PLACES

is reckoned a moderate time for lean cows to get good meat, with this keep.   The price of grains threepence to fourpence a bushel.

In the winter of 1785-6, when hay, at Burton, was 5s. a cwt.! a principal part of the produce of these breweries was bought up, by cowkeepers and others in the neighbourhood, at fourpence a bushel.

PLACES OF PURCHASE. In *this* diſtrict, the ſpring fairs of the neighbourhood ; to which they are brought by dairymen, who do not " graze ;" or by drovers, who pick them up in the diſtrict ; thereby robbing the dairymen or the graziers of part of their profit ;—or bring them from a diſtance, performing, in this caſe, the office of uſeful men.

In South *Leiceſterſhire*, and the more grazing parts of the diſtrict, where a ſufficient ſupply of cows cannot be had to ſtock their " feeding pieces," the graziers draw cattle from almoſt all quarters of the kingdom, ſometimes going, in a ſcarce time, as 1786, to the very ſeacoaſt of Wales to buy them ; poſting from fair to fair, for a week or a fortnight, without returning home ; riding many hundred miles, perhaps, at a journey : a toil which nothing but the hope of " buying bargains" could enable them to go through. In general, however, they are brought, by drovers, into the markets of the diſtrict *.

The

---

* At preſent (1789) the markets, and the grounds of the more *grazing* parts of the diſtrict, are filled chiefly with IRISH CATTLE, of all ſizes ; from thin-
fleſhed

The POINTS moſt obſervable by the Midland graziers, would be difficult to define, in detail. Thoſe already held out as the deſirable points of a modern breeder, may be taken as thoſe deſirable to a modern grazier; the modern breed being, indiſputably, eligible in a ſuperior degree, as grazing ſtock. Nevertheleſs, there ſtill remain ſome few oldfaſhioned graziers, who prefer, or obſtinately affect to prefer, *bone* to *blood.*

In general, however, we may ſay of the graziers of this diſtrict, as of thoſe of every other, that they are led to their choice, not by any fixed principles or defined points, but by intuitive impreſſions, received from general appearances.

An experienced grazier knows, at ſight, (and by merely putting his hand upon her), whether a cow or a heifer will ſuit him. Her general form and "looks" pleaſe him. She is everywhere clean; has little offal about her. Her eye is full and vivid; her countenance

fleſhed lathy ſteers, of forty to fifty ſtone, to large heavy-fleſhed oxen, of ſeventy or eighty.

For further obſervations on Iriſh cattle, ſee MIN. 122. in the ſecond volume.

nance brisk; her skin alive; and her flesh mellow. All together, she resembles many which he has grazed with success. While he rejects another; because he recollects no instance of her likeness having done well; but, on the contrary, many which she resembles, having turned out unprofitably.

The art of purchasing is principally acquired by practice. The judgement is formed, not altogether by a scientific analysis, in detail; but extempore; being assisted in great part by the memory. And we may venture to say that no man can acquire an accurate and quick judgement, such as is requisite in purchasing cattle in a market, without some considerable share of practice.

Nevertheless, I may repeat, here, what I have said in another place, on the same subject *,—that the groundwork of this art, like that of every other, is reducible to science; and that the principles being ascertained, the student will be enabled to acquire the requisite judgement much *sooner* than he could without such assistance.

The MANAGEMENT of grazing stock is the same, or nearly the same, here, as in other districts.

* GLO. ECON. vol. i. p. 245.

diftricts. Each ground,—provincially "feeding piece,"—has fuch a number of *cattle and
sheep* turned into it, as, from experience, it is
known it will carry; allowing about one cow
and two fheep to two acres; more or fewer
according to the quality of the land, or its
ftate of productivenefs *.

The *fhifting* of ftock does not enter into the
practice of this diftrict : confequently, the
practice of grazing by headftock and followers is not here in ufe.   The ftock is turned
in at Mayday, or the individuals as they are
purchafed, and remain, probably in the fame
piece, until difpofed of : the only attention
beftowed upon this clafs of ftock being, to
give an eye to the fences, the pafture, and
the water, to have a bull in the piece among
cows †, and to attend to the health of the
individuals.

One

* From ten to fifteen cows, and fifteen to twenty
fheep to twenty acres.

† For the purpofe of making them lie quiet: not
under the generally received idea that cows feed better
—fat fafter—for being in calf.   Mr. Princep's cow
(fee MIN. 119.), though fhe fatted extremely fat, and
to an extreme degree of fatnefs, was not with calf.

One circumſtance in the treatment of grazing ſtock, in the Midland Diſtrict, requires to
be noticed. This is a want of RUBBING
POSTS; eſpecially in the more grazing parts
of the diſtrict; where, to ſpeak with little
latitude, there are townſhips without a tree
in them, or a poſt of any kind for the cattle
to rub againſt. In *this* diſtrict, hawthorns, and
other ſingle trees, are common in moſt large
pieces *.

Another circumſtance, however, common,
I believe, to the diſtrict, reflects credit on the
Midland graziers. This is the number of
PENS obſervable in the grazing grounds of
the diſtrict. Almoſt every conſiderable piece
has a pen belonging to it; either ſeparately
or jointly with adjoining pieces; the ſame
pen ſometimes ſerving three or four pieces.
Theſe pens, which are made high and ſtout
enough for cattle, and cloſe enough at the bottom for ſheep, are not only uſeful on many
occaſions as receptacles of ſtock, but likewiſe
are

* RUBBING POSTS. In Northamptonſhire they are
pretty common; but there, as in moſt other places, they
are merely a ſtraight naked poſt. Whereas a rubbing
poſt cannot be too rugged: a large bough, with the
branches left two or three feet long, is more natural,
and affords the cattle more *amuſement*, than a ſmooth
hewn poſt. See NORF. ECON. MIN. 66.

are convenient as places of communication, between piece and piece *.

MARKETS

* GRAZING IN A WET SEASON. I cannot with propriety omit mentioning, in this place, an incident of practice which has occurred to me, this autumn, 1789, a very wet year.

The general complaint is, that grazing flock, though they have this year rolled in grass, have not done well; Mr. HINTON of Hoby (in Leicestershire) being singular in saying, that his feeders have done tolerably. Indeed, his stock corroborate his assertion. He had a lot of cows at Loughborough, the 18th of August, the fattest in the show.

But his management is more remarkable than his success. He " foddered them with hay all the wet weather:" that is, HE MOWED THE BROKEN GRASS FOR THEM! beginning under the hedges, and continuing to mow the coarsest patches, throughout the piece.

The first day (the day it was mown) the cattle seldom touched it; but the second or third day, they fell to it freely; eating it " between whiles," in preference to grass. " In the morning it was always the first thing they filled their bellies with !"

The cattle having eaten up the more palatable parts of the herbage, the thistles and other offal were raked up, and carried off the ground: most excellent management !

His stock consisted of about sixty head. At first, one man, only, was employed in mowing, &c. But, before the rainy weather ceased, he set on another man.

What an admirable thought ! that which other men suffered to stand waste in itself, an encumbrance to the

· MARKETS FOR FAT CATTLE. On the subject MARKETS, it has been said, that the southern parts of the district send their fat to *Smithfield*; the northern to *Rotherham*; *this* quarter of it to *Birmingham*, and the other *manufacturing towns*. Of the last I shall principally speak.

It is observable, that the grazed cattle of this district are sold, much underfat; unfinished: mostly in that state, in which cattle, in Norfolk and Herefordshire, are put to fatting.

This, however, is not intended as an argument against the Midland practice of grazing: the practices may be said to originate in the markets, for which the stock is intended. In Smithfield, cattle sell at prices proportioned to their degrees of fatness. While in the markets of this district, even in that of Birmingham, where the manufacturers live in a style of extravagance, scarcely any difference is made, between beef that has been highly finished, and that which is in a state of forwardness—fleshy—" meaty." — This being the case, the butcher will give as much, or

nearly

ground, and a nursery of weeds, was converted to a food, more nutritious, in a wet season, than the best of the standing herbage.

nearly as much, by the pound or any other weight, for what are called "meaty things," as for thofe which are fat.

The *places of fale* are the grazing grounds, and the fairs of the neighbourhood; where they are bought, chiefly, by butchers from Birmingham, with a proportion from Wolverhampton, Walfal, &c. and fometimes from Manchefter; and fome few are driven out of this diftrict to London. Birmingham may, however, be confidered as the grand mart of the diftrict *.

B b 2   In

* Yet, extraordinary as it really is, the fairs of BIRMINGHAM are among the worft in the country, for fat flock! the butchers giving the graziers no encouragement to drive their ftock to them : preferring the toil of riding twenty, thirty, or perhaps forty miles from home, to pick up their "fat"! fpending a principal part of their time, and their profits, in an employment, truly ridiculous.

How convenient it would be to the grazier, as well as to the butcher, to have a WEEKLY MARKET—a *Smithfield*, at or near Birmingham! to the grazier, in thereby having a conftant and certain market, whenever he wanted either keep or money; and to the butcher, in faving time and travelling expences. Yet the few which are taken there, at prefent, are frequently drove out unfold!

But, at prefent, the day, Thurfday, the ordinary market day, is improper : Monday or Tuefday would be a more fuitable day : and SUTTON, perhaps, the moft fuitable place.

In regard to the art of SELLING fat cattle,
though it is not, perhaps, equally difficult as
that of buying, neverthelefs it requires great
judgement, and of courfe great or long practice, to conduct it with propriety. Not the
weight of the quarters only, but the quantity of tallow, ought to be accurately eftimated.

In judging this, the grazier has one advantage over the butcher : he knows the time
his cattle have had, and how they have done,
during the time they have been at high keep;
and another, he fees them from time to time,
and perhaps has the opinion of others upon
them. The butcher, however, muft, in the
nature of his employment, acquire a kind
of judgement, which the grazier cannot readily
arrive at. Neverthelefs, there are graziers
will judge with great accuracy, both as to
weight and tallow ; while, incredible as it
may appear, there are few butchers who are
accurate judges.

On the whole, we may venture to fay,
that THE ART OF GRAZING refts principally
on judgement in *buying* and *felling* ; not in
this diftrict only, but in the other diftricts I
have yet vifited. The myfteries of *manage-*
ment

ment are few. Nevertheless, it is the moſt dangerous department of rural affairs, the INEXPERIENCED can embark in. Jobbers and butchers are equally hackneyed in the ways of dealing; and it requires ſome practice to be a match for them. Nevertheleſs, by attention and perſeverance, a ſufficient judgement may, in no great length of time, be acquired, to riſe to a par with the generality of graziers. For, although there are ſome few who are deeply verſed in the profeſſion, the bulk of graziers are by no means proficient in the art.

PRODUCE. There are, not unfrequently, inſtances of *heifers* doubling their firſt coſt, by the ſummer's graſs. I have known an inſtance of two heifers doing this. But they were bought under particular circumſtances: namely, of a grazier, who, through want of judgement, thought them " weak conſtitutioned :" he, therefore, ſold them to another grazier, better verſed in the art of purchaſe, for eleven pounds; and, the ſame day, bought four cows, at ten pounds each. The former were ſold, in October, for twentytwo pounds; the latter, at the ſame time, for

thirteen

thirteen pounds each. I mention this circumstance (of a thousand others that might be adduced), to show how much of the profits of grazing depends on judgement in buying-in stock.

To speak generally of the ordinary produce of the district,—five to eight pounds is the par price of lean barren cows, in the spring; and nine to twelve pounds, a good price for a fat cow, in autumn: thus leaving four or five pounds for the summer's grass, interest of money, hazard, market-expences, and attention. This, however, is reckoned great profit. Fifty shillings, or three pounds, is a more ordinary profit of " common graziers:" that is, of men whose practice is confined, and whose judgement is secondary: THE PROFITS OF GRAZING RESTING PRINCIPALLY ON JUDGEMENT IN BUYING AND SELLING.

REFERENCES to MINUTES on CATTLE.

For an instance of the high price of *lean cattle*, with reflections, see MIN. 1.

For an instance of a *bad year* for graziers, 53.

For opinion on the present *scarcity* of stock, 110.

For

For an inſtance of practice in grazing *Scotch runts*, 121.

For an account of an extraordinarily *fat cow*, 119.

For obſervations on bullocks at turneps, 118.

For further obſervations on the *ſcarcity* of ſtock, and on *Iriſh cattle*, ſee MIN. 122.

36.

S H E E P.

THE MIDLAND DISTRICT abounds with SHEEP,—notwithſtanding the nature of the ſoil; which, in general, may be ſaid to be better adapted to cattle, than to ſheep.

The ſituation and the nature of the ſoil, however, are ſuch as render it, in general, a diſtrict in which ſheep *may* be kept, with a degree of ſafety.

The INCLOSURES, that are properly freed from ſurface waters, and are underdrained

where

where requisite, may be deemed *found* sheep pasture.

On the contrary, the COMMONS and COMMON FIELDS are most of them dangerous to this species of stock. In 1783, a memorable year for the *rot*, the stock of some of the fields were swept away, entirely, by this fatal disease.

The breeds of this neighbourhood are various. They may, however, be reduced to two classes:

Shortwooled sheep—inhabitants of the commons and fields—provincially "field sheep;" and

Longwooled sheep—principally confined to the inclosures—provincially "pasture sheep."

FIELD SHEEP are, in some part, reared in the district. But the principal part of the sheep, seen on the commons, and in the common fields, are ewes, brought from the hills of Shropshire, Staffordshire, and Derbyshire; but chiefly from the first; and, having *reared* their lambs, are either fatted in autumn, in the inclosures, or sold fleshy out of the fields, to the Walsal and colliery butchers, or are kept over winter, for another flock of lambs; which, in autumn, are driven into Worcester-

shire,

shire, and the lower lands of Shropshire; where they are fatted, either on the autumnal grafs, or are kept over winter, and finished in early spring;—the dealers bringing back a supply of ewes from the Shropshire fairs.

This machine has been going round,—this circulation has been kept up,—time immemorial; and, on reflection, appears to be a traffic founded on rational principles.

Befide the dangerous quality of the commons and fields, to a perennial flock, the keep they afford is not good enough for the " pasture sheep" of this country; but is sufficient for the maintainance of the small hardy mountaineers. It is not, however, sufficiently good to fat the lambs, even of this breed; but is equal to the purpose of *rearing* them; though produced by a crofs with a longwooled ram. On the other hand, the Shropshire hills are able to maintain their own breed, as breeding stock; but not to fat them: the old ewes are therefore sent, lean, to the open fields of this diftrict; by which means the Worcestershire farmers are supplied with strong lambs, suited to the rich lands of that country.

This

This is a ftriking fpecimen of the IN-
TERCOURSE OF DISTRICTS; which, while
much of the kingdom lay in an open ftate,
was probably more obfervable, and much
more confiderable, than at prefent.

PASTURE SHEEP. Formerly, there appears
to have been only one breed of longwooled
fheep, in the MIDLAND DISTRICT: a
ftrong largeboned fort; which is ftill common to WARWICKSHIRE, and to much of
the counties of LEICESTER and RUTLAND;
and may, indeed, be ftill found, in every
quarter of the diftrict.

In Warwickfhire and Staffordfhire, this
old breed of the country is diftinguifhed by
the name of the "WARWICKSHIRE" breed;
in Leicefterfhire, Rutlandfhire, Northamptonfhire, and Nottinghamfhire, by that of the
"OLD LEICESTERSHIRE" breed.

Of this breed, or rather of thefe two varieties, for they have their diftinguifhing
characteriftics, there may, no doubt, be
many valuable individuals; and a few flocks,
that have been attended to, are of a tolerable quality.

In general, however, they may, without
rifque, be faid to be an unprofitable fpecies

of

of ſtock; and, in many inſtances, intolerably bad. I was led to the ſight of a "true old Warwickſhire" ram, the moſt completely ugly, and altogether, I think, the worſt ſheep I ever ſaw *. His frame large, and remarkably looſe. His bone, throughout, heavy. His legs long and thick, terminating in large ſplaw feet. His chine, as well as his rump, as ſharp as a hatchet. As to fat, he had none; nor fleſh enough to aſcertain its quality; though his paſture was good: his ſkin might be ſaid to rattle upon his ribs, and his handle be conceived to reſemble that of a ſkeleton wrapped in parchment. Yet the proprietor of this creature rode all his ewes with him ſeveral ſeaſons; —giving for reaſon, that "he always finds his ſheep fat enough at the time he wants to ſell them:" a time, however, which, I underſtand, does not arrive until they be ſome three or four years old..

It

---

* Excepting one of the "true old Leiceſterſhire ſort," which was ſhown, *to be let by the ſeaſon*, at Leiceſter ram ſhow, in 1789. This creature might be ſaid to be in the loweſt ſtate of degeneracy. A naturaliſt would have found ſome difficulty in claſſing him; and, ſeeing him on a mountain, might have deemed him a nondeſcript; a ſomething between a ſheep and a goat,

It muſt not, however, be conceived that
all the rams of the " old ſorts" bear the
above deſcription; or that all the oldfaſhioned breeders are equally inattentive to their
ſtock : nevertheleſs, we may ſafely ſay, that,
upon the whole, the breeders are unpardon-
ably remiſs, and their ſtock, in general, in a
ſtate of ſhameful neglect.

All that is required to be ſaid farther of
the old ſtock of the country is, that it ſtill has
its warm advocates, and its leading breeders.

Mr. PALFREY of Fenham, near Coventry,
takes the lead in the Warwickſhire breed *;
and

Mr. FRIZBY of Waltham, near Melton
Mowbray, in the old Leiceſterſhire.

During the laſt thirty or forty years, the
old ſtock has been giving way to a MODERN
BREED—a NEW VARIETY—which may be
ſaid to be a *creation* of the Midland Counties;
in

---

* In juſtice, however, to the good ſenſe and diſcern-
ment of MR. PALFREY, he appears to have perſevered
the longer in the old breed, not under the dictates of his
own judgement, but in compliance with the prejudices
of his cuſtomers.

Mr. BARNARD, near Warwick, may perhaps be ſaid
to be, at preſent, the moſt zealous ſupporter of the
Warwickſhire breed.

in some parts of which it has already obtained
a degree of establishment, under the name of
the "NEW LEICESTERSHIRE" BREED.

This being, at present, the most *fashionable*
breed of the island, and, to the GRAZIER, one
of the most *profitable*, its history is an interesting subject, and its merits an object of enquiry *.

The ORIGIN of this breed appears to have
taken place in *this* neighbourhood. JOSEPH
ALLOM of Clifton, who had raised himself,
by dint of industry, from a plowboy, seems to
be acknowledged, on all hands, as the first
who *distinguished* himself, in the Midland
District, for a superior breed of sheep.

He was known to buy his ewes at a distant
market; and was, in his neighbourhood,
supposed to buy them in LINCOLNSHIRE; but,
on better information, it appears, that he had
them, principally, of Mr. STONE of Godeby,
in the Melton quarter of LEICESTERSHIRE.

In

---

* The TEESWATER BREED has been already noticed (see YORK. ECON.) : the NEW VARIETY OF
LINCOLNSHIRE *I have not yet seen*. Nothing, therefore, contained in these remarks, must be considered as
having any allusion to that variety; which, I believe,
is the only distinguishable variety of the island, that
has not already fallen under my observation.

In whatever manner he raised his breed, it
is certain, that, in his day, it was the fashion,
among superior farmers, to go to Clifton, in
the summer season, to choose and *purchase*
ram lambs; giving, as I have been informed,
by cotemporaries of Allom, from two to three
guineas apiece.

This seems to be the only man who became
distinguishable as a breeder of sheep, in this
part of the island, previously to Mr. BAKE-
WELL: and, it may be reasonably supposed,
the breed, through the means of Allom's
stock, had passed the first stage of improvement, before Mr. Bakewell's day.

We may nevertheless advance, and without
risque I think, that to the ability and perseverance of Mr. BAKEWELL, the Leicestershire breed of sheep owes the present high
state of improvement.

The manner in which Mr. Bakewell raised
his sheep to the degree of celebrity in which
they deservedly stand, is, notwithstanding the
recentness of the improvement, and its being
done in the day of thousands now living, a
thing in dispute; even among men high in
the profession, and living in the very district,
in which the improvement has been carried
on !

Some

Some are of opinion, that he effected it by
a *cross* with the *Wiltshire* breed; an impro-
bable idea; as their form altogether contra-
dicts it: others, that the *Ryeland* breed (see
GLO. ECON.) were used in this purpose; and
with some show of probability. If any *cross*,
whatever, was used, the Ryeland breed, whether we view the form, the size, the wool, the
flesh, or the fatting quality, is the most *probable* instrument of improvement.

. These ideas, however, are registered,
merely, as matters of *opinion*. It is more
than probable, that Mr. Bakewell, alone, is
in possession of the several MINUTIÆ of improvement; and the public can only hope,
that he will, at a proper time, communicate
the *facts*, for the government of future improvers.

Whenever this shall take place, it will
most probably come out, that no cross, with
any *alien* breed whatever, has been used; but
that the improvement has been effected, by
selecting individuals from *kindred* breeds;—
from the several breeds or varieties of longwooled sheep, with which Mr. B. was surrounded, on almost every side;—and by
breeding, INANDIN, with this selection: soli-
citously

citoufly feizing the fuperior accidental varieties produced; affociating thefe varieties;
and ftill continuing to felect, with judgement,
the fuperior individuals.

The practicablenefs of this method of improvement will appear in MIN. 60; where we
find an individual of a very inferior kind of
fheep, nearly approaching the beft of the improved breed. Had this individual been preferved, by good fortune, or fuperior judgement,
for the purpofe of breeding from him alone,
a variety much fuperior to the breed that
produced him, might without doubt have
been raifed.

Let the means of improvement have been
what they may, the improvement itfelf, viewed in its proper light, is evident and great;
evincing, in a ftriking manner, the genius
and perfeverance of its promoter. In the
improvement of HORSES and CATTLE, Mr.
BAKEWELL appears to have acted in compe-
tition with other enterprizing breeders: but
the improvement which has been effected in
the Midland breed of SHEEP, may be faid to
be ALL HIS OWN.

Mr. BAKEWELL, however (as other great
men have had), has his DISCIPLES, who have
affifted

affifted him, very effentially, in eftablifhing
and diffeminating the " new Leicefterfhire"
breed of fheep; or, as it might well be
named, from the place of its origin, the
DISHLEY BREED.

To enumerate the whole of Mr. Bakewell's
followers would be difficult and fuperfluous:
neverthelefs, it appears to me neceffary, to
the due execution of this work, to regifter
fuch individuals as come within the limita-
tion of PRINCIPAL RAMBREEDERS, of the
MIDLAND DISTRICT: a tafk whofe only
difficulty will be that of avoiding offence, by
a mifclaffification. The beft title to prece-
dency appears to be, the length of time,
which each has been in what is termed the
" Difhley blood."

Mr. Stubbins of Holm, near Nottingham.
Mr. Paget of Ibftock, in this diftrict.
Mr. Breedon of Ruddington, Nottingham-
fhire.
Mr. Stone, Quarndon, near Loughborough.
Mr. Buckley, Normanton, Nottinghamfhire.
Mr. Walker, Wolfsthorp, on the borders of
Lincolnfhire.
Mr. Bettifon, Holm, near Nottingham.
Mr. White, Hoton, Nottinghamfhire.

VOL. I. C c Mr.

Mr. Knowles, Nailfton, in this diftrict.

Mr. Deverel, Clapton, Nottinghamfhire.

Mr. Princep, Croxall, in this diftrict.

Mr. Burgefs, Hucklefcot, ————.

Mr. Green, Normanton, ————.

Mr. Robinfon, near Welford, Northamptonfhire.

Mr. Moor, Thorp, in this diftrict.

Mr. Aftley, Odfton, ————.

Mr. Henton, Hoby, Leicefterfhire.

Befide thefe leading men, there are many
of lefs repute, in the Midland Diftrict, and
many others, fcattered over almoft every part
of the ifland, particularly in Lincolnfhire,
Yorkfhire, and fo far north as Northumber-
land; alfo in Worcefterfhire, and Gloucefterfhire.

It is obfervable, however, and appears to
me an extraordinary circumftance, evincing,
in a remarkable manner, the weaknefs of men's
judgements, or the ftrength of their prejudices, that, notwithftanding the rapid progrefs this breed of fheep are making in diftant parts of the kingdom, and notwithftanding the decided preference given to them,
by thofe who have had experience of them
in this diftrict, the majority of the breeders

and

and graziers, not of Warwickſhire only, but of Northamptonſhire, Rutlandſhire, and Leiceſterſhire, even within ſight of Diſhley, are inveterately againſt the breed! and this notwithſtanding many of their charming grounds, at preſent, are ſtocked with creatures that would diſgrace the meaneſt lands in the kingdom *.

This ſeeming paradox can be explained in no other way, perhaps, than in the improper manner in which the improved breed have been promulgated.

Had the Diſhley ſheep, twenty years ago, been judiciouſly diſtributed over the diſtrict, and had been, on all occaſions, *permitted to ſpeak for themſelves*, it appears to me probable, that there would ſcarcely have been a ſheep, of any other breed, now left in the Midland diſtrict.

No profeſſional man, whoſe judgement were not biaſſed, or entirely carried away, by the ſpirit of oppoſition, could heſitate a moment
C c 2   in

* Nottinghamshire takes the lead in this improvement. In the country between Nottingham and Diſhley, the modern breed may be ſaid to have gained, already, a degree of eſtabliſhment.

in his choice. But so long as the fire is fanned, and the cauldron is kept boiling, so long the advocates of the breed must expect to be in hot water; and, in the nature of men's passions, so long the new Leicestershire breed of sheep must have its powerful opponents.

It now remains to give a DESCRIPTION of the superior class of individuals of this breed; especially EWES and WEDDERS; in full condition, but not immoderately fat. The RAMS will require to be distinguished in the next section.

The *head* long, small, and hornless, with ears somewhat long, and standing backward, and with the nose shooting forward.

The *neck* thin, and clean toward the head; but taking a conical form; standing low, and enlarging every way at the base; the *forend*, altogether, short.

The *bosom* broad, with the *shoulders, ribs,* and *chine* extraordinarily full.

The *loin* broad, and the *back* level.

The *haunches* comparatively full toward the hips, but light downward; being altogether small, in proportion to the fore parts.

The *legs*, at present, of a moderate length; with the bone extremely fine.

The

The *bone*, throughout, remarkably light.

The *carcafe*, when fully fat, takes a re-markable form : much wider than it is deep ; and almoft as broad as it is long. Full on the fhoulder, wideft on the ribs, narrowing with a regular curve towards the tail ; ap-proaching the form of the TURTLE, *nearer* than any other animal I can call to mind.

The *pelt* thin ; and the *tail* fmall.

The *wool*, fhorter than long wools in ge-neral ; but much longer than the middle wools ; the ordinary length of ftaple, five to feven inches ; varying much in finenefs and weight.

The COMPARATIVE MERIT of this breed will beft appear, by placing it, in its prefent ftate, in the feveral lights in which it may be viewed, comparatively with other breeds : thereby, at the famé time, afcertaining how far the PRINCIPLES OF IMPROVEMENT have, in this cafe, been judicioufly applied.

In BEAUTY OF FORM, the breed under notice furpaffes every other breed I have feen. I fpeak not of *picturefque*, but of *pofitive* beauty. Viewed as diftinct objects, the in-dividuals of it are peculiarly pleafing to the eye.

I do not, however, mention this as an evidence of their fuperiority. There are men of the firft abilities, and of great knowledge and experience in fheep, who, as has been before mentioned, prefer what is called a *ufeful* to a *handfome* fort; a rife in the back, or a fall in the fhoulders, to a want of flefh and fatting quality. If, however, beauty and utility can be united, which they evidently ' are in fome inftances, perfection may be faid to be more nearly approached.

UTILITY OF FORM. The moft diftinguifhing characteriftics of this breed,—that which might be confidered as its fpecific character,—is the fulnefs, and comparative weight, of its fore quarters.

This, however, feems to be contrary to the general principle of improvement, and affords matter of argument to the advocates of the old ftock ; who contend, that this form throws the meat upon the leaft valuable parts ; legs and faddles, not fhoulders and breafts, being the favorite joints.

The advocates for the new breed *argue*, in return, that the majority of the eaters of mutton are of the poorer clafs, and that the grand object of the improvement is their
fupply ;

supply ; *arguing* farther, that upon a given
set of bones, and with a given quantity of
other offal, a greater weight of meat may be
laid on the fore quarters, than on the hind
ones.

OFFAL. Another diftinguifhing character
of the modern breed is the fmallnefs of their
bone, comparatively with that of the old
ftock, and moft other breeds ; not of the legs
only, but of the ribs and other parts. I
have feen a rib of a fheep of this breed con-
trafted with one of a Norfolk fheep : the difparity was ftriking ; the latter nearly twice
the fize ; while the meat which covered the
former was three times the thicknefs : confequently *the proportion of meat to bone* was,
in the one, incomparably greater than in the
other.

Therefore, in this point of view, the improved breed has a decided preference. For,
furely, while mankind continue to eat flefh,
and throw away bone, the former muft
be, to the *confumer* at leaft, the more valuable.

The *other offal* is alfo light. The pelt thin,
and the head fmall ; and, *it is faid*, the inteftines,

teſtines, and even the blood, are ſmall in a
ſimilar proportion.

That the laſt two are comparatively ſmall,
in proportion to the carcaſe, when this is loaded with fat, in a manner that the carcaſe of
no other breed of ſheep, probably, is capable
of laying on, will be readily granted. But
that they bear a ſmaller proportion to the
carcaſe in this breed, than they do in others
of the ſame natural ſize, in the ſame condition, and going in the ſame paſture, remains, I believe, among a thouſand other
things relating to liveſtock, to be proved by
a ſeries of accurate experiments.

FLESH. The *criterions* of good and bad fleſh,
while the animal is alive, differ in different ſpecies of animals; and to aſcertain them with
ſufficient accuracy, to render them ſafe guides
in every ſtage of poverty and fatneſs, and to
render definitions of them, in the ſeveral ſtages,
intelligible, would require a courſe of experiments and obſervations on a variety of individuals of each ſpecies; attending them through
every ſtage of fleſhineſs to that of finiſhed fatneſs; following them from the grazing ground
to the ſlaughter houſe, and from thence to the
table; and this with an accuracy of attention
that has probably never been given; nor will,
in

in all probability, ever take place, fo as to become of PUBLIC UTILITY, without the patronage of a PUBLIC INSTITUTION.

Neverthelefs, in this diftrict, there are men, who, from a long courfe of attentive practice, though not, perhaps, fcientifically purfued, have acquired a fufficient degree of knowledge of this fubject, to enable them to judge, by the touch, while the animal is alive, and low in condition, what the quality of the meat will be, when fat, and the animal is flaughtered; and this with fome degree of accuracy: adequate, at leaft, to our prefent purpofe; which is that of giving the ftudent a general idea of the fubject; as well as that of regiftering, for the ufe of future improvers, the ideas at prefent known refpecting it.

The quality of the FLESH of CATTLE is beft afcertained when the animal is in a ftate of flefhinefs,—full of condition, but not fat. In this ftate, if the flefh be bad, it handles *hard*, with a degree of *harfhnefs*; if good, it is *foft* and *mellow*, with a degree of " *loofenefs*," or rather *fupplenefs*, or *flexibility*; which, as the animal acquires a ftate of fatnefs, gives place to a degree of *firmnefs—faftnefs*;—a quality

quality fo nearly · allied to hardnefs, that,
without attending to the general ftate and
condition of the animal, they might, by the
inexperienced at leaft, be miftaken for each
other.

But the FLESH of SHEEP is to be judged
by fomewhat different criterions. Thefe
criterions, however, are not yet fixed. Profeffional men — breeders even of the firft
clafs—differ in their ideas of the fubject : a
proof that it has not yet been fufficiently
ftudied.

It is, neverthelefs, allowed, by all fuperior breeders, that *loofenefs* is a *bad* quality of
the flefh of *fheep*, when living ; as being
the criterions of coarfe-grained, fpungy
mutton.

But the criterions of *good* flefh are not yet
fettled. One fuperior breeder is of opinion,
that if the flefh is not loofe, it is of courfe
good ; holding, that the flefh of fheep is
never found in a ftate of hardnefs, like that
of ill flefhed cattle :—while others make a
fourfold diftinction of the flefh of fheep ;
as *loofenefs, mellownefs, firmnefs, hardnefs :* confidering the firft and the laft equally excep-
tionable, and the fecond and third equally
defirable ;

defirable; a happy mixture of the two being deemed the point of perfection.

The flesh of sheep, *when slaughtered*, is well known to be of various qualities. Some is composed of large coarfe grains, interfperfed with wide empty pores, like a fpunge: others, of large grains, with wide pores filled with fat: others, of fine clofe grains, with fmaller pores filled with fat: and a fourth, of clofe grains, without any intermixture of fatnefs.

The flesh of sheep, *when dressed*, is equally well known to poffefs a variety of qualities: fome mutton is coarfe, dry, and infipid; a dry fpunge; affording little or no gravy of any colour. Another fort is fomewhat firmer; imparting a light-coloured gravy only. A third plump, *short*, and palatable; affording a mixture of white and red gravy. A fourth likewife plump and well flavored; but difcharging red gravy only; and this in various quantities.

It is likewife obfervable that fome mutton, when dreffed, appears covered with a thick, tough, parchmentlike integument; other, with a membrane comparatively fine and flexible.

But

But these, and some of the other qualities of mutton, may not be wholly owing to
breed ; but, in part, to the *age*, and the *state
of fatness*, at the time of slaughter ; and I
wish to have it underſtood, that what is here
offered, is intended to agitate, rather than to
define with ſufficient accuracy, a ſubject
which may be ſaid to be, at preſent, in a
ſtate of obſcurity ; but which is well entitled
to a ſcientific diſcuſſion.

FAT. Examined in this light, whether
we conſider the *degree* of fatneſs, or their
natural propenſity to a ſtate of fatneſs, even at
an *early age*, the improved breed of Leicef-
terſhire ſheep appear with many ſuperior
advantages.

I have known an inſtance, in the ordinary
practice of a minor breeder, of " lamb-hogs"
(yearling wedders,—barely a year old),
being ſold in April (1786, a dear time) for
27s. to 28s. a head ; while the common run
of ill bred things were not worth more than
18s. each. There has, I am told, and by
indiſputable authority, been an inſtance of
yearlings of the beſt blood being ſold, in
Auguſt (about a year and a half old), at 35s.
a head !

a head! and other inftances of their profit-
ablenefs, to the *grazier*, will appear in the
MINUTES.

The GRAZIER's object, undoubtedly, is to
get fheep that will fat *quickly:* for even fuppofing them to eat more food than fheep
which fat more flowly, there is a material advantage accruing from their reaching market
a fortnight or three weeks fooner than other
fheep: grafs mutton, for inftance, bears a
better price, at its firft coming in, than it
does a few weeks afterward; when a glut
feldom fails of being poured into market.
So far, however, from thefe fheep confuming
more food than others, it feems *probable* at
leaft, that fheep which are, in their nature,
difpofed to a ftate of fatnefs, become marketable at a fmaller expence of food, than
fheep which are, naturally, of a leaner conftitution.

This is among the firft of the many things
defirable that remain to be *proved.* Some
attempts have been made, in this diftrict.
But experiments, of a complex nature, require a degree of leifure, a minutenefs of
attention, a fund of patience and perfeverance, and, above all, a habit of expe-
rimenting,

rimenting, that few men of bufinefs
poffefs.

The *degree of fatnefs* to which the individuals of this breed are capable of being
raifed, will, I am afraid, appear incredible, to thofe who have not had an opportunity of being convinced by their own
obfervation. I have feen wedders, of
only two fhear (two to three years old)
fo loaded with fat, as to be fcarcely able
to make a run; and whofe fat lay fo
much without the bone, it feemed ready
to be fhook from the ribs, on the fmalleft
agitation.

It is common for the fheep of this breed
to have fuch a projection of fat upon the
ribs, immediately behind the fhoulder, that
it may be eafily gathered up in the hand,
as the flank of a fat bullock. Hence it has
gained, in technical language, the name
of the FOREFLANK ; a *point* which a modern
breeder never fails to touch, in judging of the
quality of this breed of fheep.

What is, perhaps, ftill more extraordinary,
it is not rare for the rams, at leaft, of this
breed to be "CRACKED ON THE BACK;" that
is, to be cloven along the top of the chine,

in

in the manner fat sheep generally are upon the rump. This mark is considered as an evidence of the best blood.

Extraordinary, however, as are these appearances, while the animals are living, the facts are still more striking after they are *slaughtered*. At Litchfield, in February 1785, I saw a fore quarter of mutton, fatted by Mr. Princep of Croxall, and which *measured* upon the ribs *four* inches of *fat !*

But this I saw far exceeded in the mutton whose bone has been mentioned, and which, notwithstanding its extreme fineness, was covered with about an inch of muscular flesh, interlarded, and *five* inches of fat !

Since then (1786) several sheep of this breed have laid six inches of meat on their ribs.

It is observable, that in sheep of this extreme degree of fatness, the muscular parts decrease in thickness as the fatness increases, and are so intermingled with fat as to give the whole a fatty appearance; and this most especially in aged sheep; which, as aged cattle, have more fat in proportion to lean, than younger carcases. A loin of mutton of a sheep (ten shear) of twentysix pounds a quarter,

quarter, weighed, when the fat was taken off, only two pounds and a half!

Thefe are certainly interefting facts. But reflection aptly fuggefts the queftion, to what ftomach can mutton like this be grateful?

The anfwer held out is, "fat mutton is the poor man's mutton: it goes farther than lean; and has, of courfe, a fmaller proportion of bone than lean mutton. A poor man gives eightpence a pound for bacon, but only fivepence for fat mutton."

This femblance, between fat mutton and bacon, is not altogether imaginary. When falted, and kept fome time in pickle, even the palate perceives a ftrong refemblance. The advocates for growing bacon on fheep's bones, inftead of producing it, as heretofore, upon thofe of fwine, will fay, that the art of preparing it has already been carried fo far, as to deceive the palates, even of connoiffeurs in eating. If they can really fupply the markets with good bacon, at fourpence or fivepence a pound, their country will certainly have fome reafon to thank them. But this by the way.

It

It is alfo obfervable, in this place, that
the breed of fheep under confideration,
though they lay fo great a quantity of fat
upon the bones, feldom, in the butcher's
phrafe, " *die well :*" while the Norfolk fheep,
for inftance, as feldom " deceive the butcher."
This accounts, in fome meafure, for the preference given to the latter, by the butchers in
Smithfield. Tallow is a kind of boon which,
if not forthcoming, incurs a difappointment
the butcher cannot brook *.

The Leicefterfhire fheep, however, appear
to me to poffefs a quality, which more than
counterbalances that deficiency. They weigh
above their appearance. They have, likewife, lefs offal (head feet and pelt), and, when
fully fat, *proportionably* lefs " infide," than
fheep in general. When highly finifhed,
they appear as a folid lump of flefh. Though
fmall to the eye, they will weigh thirty, or
perhaps, forty pounds a quarter. Their flefh

is,

* With refpeft to TALLOW, however, much depends
on the AGE at which the animal is butchered; much,
alfo, on BREED. Thus, were the new Leicefterfhire
fheep to be kept on to three years old, their produce of
tallow would be encreafed : and the Norfolk breed,
though moftly butchered at two years old, are remarkable
for their produce of tallow.

is, in reality, firmer than that of sheep which collect or lay up their fat within, while their muscles and their adipose membranes are left porous and spungy.

On the whole, we may venture to say, that, in respect to CARCASE, the NEW LEICESTER-SHIRE sheep have a decided preference to most, if not all, other breeds; and that the PRINCIPLE OF IMPROVEMENT is, *this far*, well founded.

WOOL. Viewing the coat, abstractedly from the carcase, the Leicestershire sheep, compared with most other longwooled sheep, appear to disadvantage; and the Leicestershire breeders, perhaps, may seem liable to a degree of censure. Indeed, the coat, throughout the improvement, appears to have been set at nought; the carcase, alone, having engrossed the whole attention of the improvers.

But this is conformable with the general principle of improvement. Flesh—*human food*—is the object the improvers have had in view; and it is highly probable that the more sustenance there is expended on the wool, the less there will remain for the carcase; beside a heavy fleece being, at certain seasons, inconvenient,

convenient, and not unfrequently fatal, to the sheep.

Nevertheleſs, it appears, evidently, that a deficiency in the coat has, more than any other circumſtance, hurt this breed of ſheep in the eyes of the old graziers ; and has, beyond diſpute, greatly retarded their adoption.

It is a circumſtance ſomewhat extraordinary, however, and which, in juſtice to the breed, ought to be made public, that the deficiency of coat, which has done them ſo much injury, has ſcarcely any other exiſtence than in the *arguments* of their own advocates ! who abſurdly affect to prize them for a poverty of wool : holding out, in the *wildneſs of argument*, that a breed of ſheep *without wool* would be the moſt deſirable ! No wonder that *ſuch arguments* ſhould produce in the minds of men, who know the value of a fleece of wool, and who, perhaps, have only ſeen the ſheep *in argument*, ſhould conceive unfavourable ideas of them, and conſider the ſtir that has been made about them, as a viſionary flight, above their comprehenſion.

I mention theſe ridiculous arguments, the rather, and with greater freedom, as they not only retard the progreſs of this improvement,

but

but militate againſt its leading principle;
that of laying weight on the moſt valuable
parts : for ſuppoſing an increaſe of wool incurs, neceſſarily, a decreaſe of carcaſe ; yet,
ſurely, wool at eightpence a pound (the medium price it has now been at ſome years) is
more valuable, to the grazier, than mutton at
fourpence.

The *fact* is, this breed of ſheep, when *ſeen*
and *examined*, are *not greatly* deficient in wool.
The wedders generally run about four to the
tod (of 28 lb.) ; the ewes about four and a
half ; the fleeces of the former weighing ſix to
eight, of the latter five to ſeven pounds each.

Indeed, their cooler advocates *argue*, and
with ſome ſhow of *reaſon* on their ſide, that
they not only produce more mutton, but
more wool, *by the acre*, than any other breed
of ſheep.

This however remains, with the other de-
ſiderata relating to liveſtock, to be *proved*, by
a ſeries of accurate experiments.

GENERAL OBSERVATIONS.   From this
comparative view, it evidently appears, that
the modern breed, of Leiceſterſhire, are a
valuable variety of longwooled ſheep.

In

In CARCASE, they may be faid to be nearly perfect * : fuperior, at leaft, to any other breed of longwooled fheep I have feen.

In WOOL, however, they fall fhort, I believe, of every other longwooled breed : owing principally, it fhould feem, to a falfe principle of improvement.

Neverthelefs, taking them as they are at prefent, they are, to the *grazier*, profeffionally and diftinctly confidered, a very profitable breed of fheep.

It now remains to place them among the other breeds of fheep in the ifland, and confider the whole, collectively, as a fpecies of domeftic animal.

The ufe and value of the CARCASE, as a fpecies of animal food, being obvious, we proceed to examine the ufes and value of the WOOL.

In the warmer climates, favages go naked, and civilized focieties may difpenfe with vege-

D d 3   table

---

* Viewing this as a diftinct breed, the difproportionate weight of the forequarters appears to me an imperfection. But confidering the prefent form of thefe fheep, as being capable of correcting the imperfections of almoft every other breed of longwooled fheep, it might, in figurative language, be faid to be *more than perfect*.

table coverings. Flax and cotton may fcreen the body from the fun, and give it, occafion-ally, the requifite degree of warmth.

But in more frigid climes, the natural na-kednefs of the human body requires a warmer covering : animal productions are in a degree neceffary. In the favage ftate, the entire fkins of animals are transferred from brutes to the human body. But, in a ftate of civil fociety and cultivation, the native animals are no longer adequate to the fupply. It has, therefore, been found requifite to domefticate an animal, for the purpofe of furnifhing a fubftitute.

In the choice of this animal, there appears to have been no alternative. Indeed, when we confider the natural defencelefsnefs of the fheep, among other animals in a ftate of na-ture, human vanity is ready to fuggeft, that it was formed for the benign purpofe of fur-nifhing mankind, in a ftate of civil fociety, and in a fituation of inclemency, with co-vering, of which they are naturally deftitute. The quantity and quality of their fur, and the circumftance of its being eafily collected, year after year, renders it indifputably, in the
present

prefent ftate of fociety, and in the climature of this ifland, the moft valuable of animal produ&ions. There are many animals capable of affording us food, equally wholefome ; but no one, in nature, able to furnifh us with clothing, equally comfortable.

Hence, even as a fource of happinefs to individuals, the coat of the fheep is an object of attention. But when we view it, at the fame time, as the encourager of induftry, and the main fupport of commerce, it becomes, in this country, an object of ftill higher importance.

This nation, in particular, might be happy within itfelf, and refpectable among other nations, without the carcafe, but not without the coat ; which is well known to be the grand bafis of our commercial, if not of our political confequence. Befide, it is an indigenous produce of the ifland, which can always be had at will, and is not, like many other materials of manufacture, liable to the fate of conqueft, or dependant on thofe who fhall hold the empire of the fea.

Therefore, as an object of NATIONAL ATTENTION, the coat of the fheep is of the firft importance ; and every wilful attempt to fupplant or debafe it, is an act of treafon againft the ftate.

'Ex-

Extending this enlarged view of the useful purposes of sheep to the several branches of RURAL ECONOMY, a third valuable property appears. Sheep, viewed collectively, beside affording food and covering to the human body, are applicable to the use of MELIORATING THE SOIL. And a fourth is equally evident. Sheep, if properly chosen, render productive a class of country, which makes noinconsiderable part of the surface of this island, and which, without them, would, while it remains in its present state, lie entirely waste to the community. The description of country here meant is HEATHY MOUNTAIN.

In this general view of the INTENTIONS for which sheep are propagated in this island, the *form* and *disposition* become entitled to no inconsiderable share of attention.

To the mere GRAZIER, it is true, it matters not how short the legs, how compact the carcase, or how sluggish the disposition, of his sheep ; so they will travel to market : quietness is, to him, a desirable quality. It is immaterial, to him, whether the face be black or white, whether the head has horns or knots, whether the wool and the legs be short or
long,

long, or whether the bones lie in this or that
form,—any farther than as such points are
characteristic, or not, of a profitable animal,
to him. The shambles must determine the
value of his carcase, and the woolsorter's
warehouse the quality of his coat. The
butcher and woolstapler *jointly* are the men
whom the grazier has to look up to; and
that sheep which will fat the soonest on a
given quantity of food, and whose carcase
and wool *jointly* will fetch the most money
when the animal is fat, is the most profitable
sheep to the grazier; no matter as to size or
form, the length or lightness of wool, or
the colour or length of leg. These, to a
mere grazier, in a well soiled inclosed country, are not objects of attention ; provided a
disposition of wildness, and a desire for ram-
bling, do not thereby become a consequence *.

But

---

* It has been observed, aforegoing, that the legs of
the improved breed have been considerably lengthened,
since their first stage of improvement; and with a good
effect: they are now better nurses, and better able to
travel to market, than they were before. But it appears to me that the improvement, in this respect, has
reached the degree of perfection ; and, perhaps in some
individuals, has already overtopped it : I have seen
strong

But, to a MOUNTAIN SHEPHERD, activity
is an essential property of his stock. There
are many thousand acres of heathy mountains, on which the breed of sheep under
notice could not exist. The same beds of
heath, which afford the deerlike inhabitants
of those wilds a principal part of their sustenance, would *smother* a shortlegged longwooled sheep. A furze cover, or a thicket
of thorns and briars, would be, for this, as
eligible a pasture.

For the ARABLE FARMER, who keeps sheep
for the purpose of the FOLD, the longwooled
breeds are equally improper. He, likewise,
wants an active, cleanlimbed, longlegged,
shortwooled sheep, that can travel, in all seasons, without fatigue. In open barren countries, where sheep have half a mile, or perhaps
a mile, to go to fold; and, when they return
to their walk, have a great space of ground to
go over, before their hunger be satisfied, remaining upon their legs almost the day
through,

strong symptoms of *wildness* in this breed: a property
of sheep, adapted solely to the grazier, which is among
the first of bad properties to be avoided: and domestic
animals, in general, appear to be in a considerable degree wild, or cadish, according to their respective
powers of flight.

through, shortlegged longwooled sheep are uselefs in this intention. I tried them in Norfolk, on a clean sandy soil, with a good walk, and an easy drift. They sunk under what heath sheep would have got fat upon; and on which the larger breed of Norfolk throve, as store sheep.

It is, however, held out by the advocates of this breed, that they are, now, since their legs have been lengthened, calculated for the fold; having been proved in this purpose.

It is readily granted, that, for a few weeks, or a few months of fine weather, immediately after they have been shorn, they may be well enough adapted to folding. But, whoever has seen " *longwooled sheep*" (no matter as to any nice diftinction of forts) waddling to and from the fold, in any other season, with loads of mud and water hanging to them, equal perhaps to twice the weight of their natural coats, would never think of fpoiling a valuable species of *grafsland* sheep, under an idea fo truly visionary; while we have other breeds, I mean, which are, already, adapted to the purpose.

Nevertheless, it is much to be feared, that their legs have been lengthened, and their

coats

coats ſhortened, under the *extravagant* idea of
rendering them fit for *all* the purpoſes of rural
economy, thereby qualifying them to fill
every uſeful purpoſe of ſheep, in order that
they may become the *ſole* breed of the
iſland !!!

Viewing ſheep generally, and in their various capacities and intentions, as well NA-
TIONAL as ECONOMICAL, it appears demonſtrably, that, of the numerous breeds and varieties, at preſent in this iſland, ſome *three*,
four, or *five* diſtinct breeds are, indiſputably,
and indiſpenſably, neceſſary to its preſent
ſtate of proſperity.

A very longwooled ſheep, as the Lincolnſhire *, or the old Teeſwater, for the richeſt
of ſound graſslands; and for the fineſt worſted
manufactures.

A ſecond, as the new Leiceſterſhire, for
leſs fertile graſsland, as well as for rich incloſed
arable lands, on which the fold is not uſed;
and for the coarſer worſteds, ſtockings, bays,
coarſe cloths, blankets, carpets, &c.

A third,

---

* I ſpeak of the old Lincolnſhire: the new variety, I underſtand, are equally well, or ſtill better,
wooled.

A third, a middlewooled breed, as the Wiltshire, the Norfolk, or the Southdown (of Suſſex), or the three, for well ſoiled arable lands, on which folding is practiſed; and for cloths of the middle qualities *.

A fourth, a finewooled ſort, as the Rye-land, for the fineſt cloths †.

And a fifth; as the Shropſhire, or a ſtill more hardy race, for heathy mountain.

This general view, of the uſeful purpoſes to which ſheep are applicable in this iſland, has not been taken with the intention of depreciating the breed under conſideration; but with the deſign of placing them in their true light, and of aſſigning them their proper ſoil and ſituation.

Nor can it be publiſhed with a view to cen-ſure the ſpirited improvers of this breed, while the reſult of it reflects on them ſo much credit: they

---

* By cloths of the MIDDLE QUALITIES, I mean narrow cloths, of three or four, to broad cloths, of twelve or fourteen, ſhillings a yard : a latitude of qua-lity which no one of the three breeds, here particularited, can, I believe, fill up; the *three*, or other breeds, equally *various* in the qualities of their wool:, being requiſite to the preſent ſtate of the wooſlen manufactory of this iſland.

† See GLO. ECON.

they have evidently raifed into exiftence a
breed of fheep, which is peculiarly well adapted to their own foil and fituation ; and, in
doing this, have infinite merit ; as having
acted on the grand bafis of all rural improve-.
ments. And although I have already expref-
fed myfelf generally on this fubject, I think it
proper to repeat, in this place, that, for
grafslands of a middle quality, as well as for
arable lands where the fold is not in ufe,—a
defcription of country which includes a large
proportion of the valuable lands of the ifland,
—the modern breed of Leiceflerfhire fheep
may, without undue praife, be faid to be
near perfection ; and that *fo long as a full demand for the fpecies of wool they produce continues,*
fo long they, in their nature, muft be, *to the
grazier,* a very profitable breed of fheep : and
further, that, fo long as any other breed of
longwooled fheep remain with thin chines
and loofe mutton, fo long they muft be, *to the
breeder,* a ftill more profitable fpecies of liveftock.

BREEDING. To give a comprehenfive
idea of this fubject, the males and the females
muft pafs feparately in review.

RAMS.

RAMS. In the practice of the Midland District at large, the management respecting rams is similar to that of other parts of the island; the breeders *rearing* or *purchasing* them.

It is observable, however, that the advocates of the old breeds, though they will not adopt the modern stock, have fallen, in some degree, into the modern practice of *letting by the season.*

Mr. PALFREY (mentioned above) lets a considerable number of the Warwickshire *; and Mr. FRIZBY a still greater number of the old Leicestershire: both of them, however, at low prices, comparatively with those given for the MODERN BREED, of which chiefly I shall speak under this head †.

The

* Mostly, however, tinctured, at present, with the new Leicestershire blood.

† Mr. FRIZBY is said to let not less than " fourscore" rams, annually, at the price, one with another, of five guineas a ram. At Waltham fair, in September 1789, Mr. F. had a show—(a fair to himself)—consisting of about an hundred rams of different ages. And every year, it seems, the principal part of his rams are let on that day. Thus, for nine or ten months keep of a hundred rams, and keeping open house one day, he is making some hundreds a year.

The rams of the MODERN BREED are never *fold*; but are paffed from breeder to breeder, *by the feafon*, only.

For the purpofe of promoting this inter-courfe, each principal breeder has his SHOW OF RAMS; commencing, by common confent, the 8th of June; and lafting until Michaelmas, or until the whole are let.

During a few weeks after the fhows commence, every rambreeder may be faid to keep open houfe.—Breeders and others, from all quarters of the kingdom, as well as the promoters of the breed who refide in the neighbourhood, attend thefe fhows; going in parties from one to another : fome to take ; others to fee and pafs their judgements.

Thefe private exhibitions clofe with a PUBLIC SHOW, at Leicefter, the tenth of October; when rams of every defcription, but moftly an inferior fort of the improved breed, are collected; being brought in waggons; many of them a confiderable diftance ; fome to be *fold*; but chiefly to be *let*.

This fhow has been held, I believe, time immemorial; not, however, for the purpofe of *letting*; but for that of *fale*.

, The

The LETTING OF RAMS, BY THE SEASON, has long, I underſtand, been a practice in LINCOLNSHIRE *.

The ORIGIN, in the MIDLAND DISTRICT, may be traced—to a ram let, by Mr. BAKEWELL, at Leiceſter fair, about forty years ago, at the low price of ſixteen ſhillings †.

Humble, however, as was this beginning, it proved to be the firſt ſtone of the foundation of a department of rural buſineſs, that has already riſen to an aſtoniſhing height, and may, for ſome length of time, continue to bring in a copious ſource of wealth to the country.

The method of conducting this novel branch of rural buſineſs will require to be detailed.

In the MANAGEMENT OF RAMS, kept for the purpoſe of letting by the ſeaſon, the following particulars require attention.

The

---

* Whether the *letting* of rams is, or is not, an ancient practice, in England, the buſineſs of *dealer* in rams is, probably, of long ſtanding; or whence the *ſurname* of TUPMAN? a provincial appellation, at preſent, ſynonimous with RAMBREEDER.

† Mr. B. letting two more, the ſame day, at ſeventeen ſhillings and ſixpence each.

The choice, &c. of ram lambs.
Making up rams for showing.
Method of showing.
The points of rams.
Method of letting.
The conditions of letting.
The prices given.
Treatment after letting.
Sending them out.
Method of using them.
Expected treatment while out.
Treatment after their return.

The principal rambreeders save, annually,
twenty, thirty, or perhaps forty RAM LAMBS;
castration being seldom applied, in the first
instance, to the produce of a valuable ram.

For, in the CHOICE of these lambs, they
are led more by blood, or parentage, than
by form; on which, at an early age, little
dependence can be placed.

Their TREATMENT, from the time they
are weaned, in July or August, until the time
of shearing, the first week in June, consists in
giving them every indulgence of keep; in
order to push them forward for the show: it
being the common practice to let, such as are

fit

fit to be let, the firſt ſeaſon; while they are yet yearlings—provincially "ſharhogs."

Their firſt paſture, after weaning, is pretty generally, I believe, clover that has been mown early, and has got a ſecond time into head : the heads of clover being conſidered as a moſt forcing food of ſheep. After this goes off, turneps, cabbages, colewort, with hay, and, report ſays, with corn. But the uſe of *this* the breeders *ſeverally* deny; though *collectively* they may be liable to the charge.

Be this as it may, ſomething conſiderable depends on the ART OF MAKING UP; not lambs only, but rams of all ages. Fat, like charity, covers a multitude of faults; and, beſide, is the beſt evidence, their owners can produce, of their *fatting quality*,—their natural propenſity to a ſtate of fatneſs : while in the fatneſs of the ſharhogs is ſeen their degree of inclination to fat, at an *early age*.

Fatting quality being the one thing needful, in grazing ſtock, and being found, in ſome conſiderable degree at leaſt, to be hereditary,—the *fatteſt rams* are of courſe the *beſt* : though other attachments, well or ill placed, as to *form*, or *faſhionable points*, will perhaps

E e 2   have

have equal or greater weight, in the minds of some men : even in this enlightened age and diſtrict.

Such ſhearlings as will not make up ſufficiently, as to form and fatneſs, are either kept on to another year, to give them a fair chance, or are caſtrated, or butchered, while ſharhogs.

SHOWING. The ſhows of the principal breeders conſiſt, by common conſent, of forty rams each; moſtly from one to five ſhear; they being ſeldom found efficient after that age : ſome, however, will continue in vigour to the ſixth or ſeventh year *.

During the ſhow, they are moſtly kept in ſmall incloſures, of two, three, or four acres; with

---

* But, even at thſe ages, the decay of vigour is not *natural*; but is brought on prematurely, by the unnatural ſtate of fatneſs in which they are kept, and of which a variety of diſeaſes, as well as a general unwieldineſs of frame, are inevitable conſequences. Female ſheep are found to be prolific to a greater age.

It is obſervable, however, that the females, as well as the males, of the breed under notice, enter the ſtage of decay ſooner than thoſe of other breeds. This circumſtance is accounted for, in their entering the ſtage of fatneſs ſooner than other ſheep; and there may be ſome truth in the idea.

with three, four, or more rams in each ; according to their ages, and the advancement of the feafon.

In a corner, or other convenient part of each paddock, a fmall pen, made with hurdles, is placed ; for the purpofe of handling them. Into thefe pens they go, through cuftom, as tractably, as worked oxen to their ftalls. Indeed, the old rams, from the unwieldinefs of their frame, and the load of fat they have to carry at this feafon, as well as from habit, will fuffer themfelves to be handled abroad ; and even appear to take a pleafure in the refpect which they have fhown them.

Of late, *a new method of fhowing* has been ftruck out by the leading breeder, and adopted by *one*, at leaft,—his *faithful* follower. Inftead of fhowing them abroad, and driving three or four of them up together, into a pen, they are fhut up in hovels, and fhown feparately ; being *never feen together*.

Among accurate judges, this mode of fhowing may be well enough ; but, to thofe who have had lefs experience, it gives offence ; as it deprives them of their beft guide, comparifon;

son ; and I can see no fair advantage accruing
from it to the letter.

The desirable POINTS of a ram are those
which have been already enumerated.   But
the *choice of the hirer* is determined, in some
measure, by the intention for which he is
about to hire; as whether it be that of getting *wedders*, or mere grazing stock ; or *rams*,
for the purpose of letting.   Hence the grazier, and the rambreeder, choose different
sheep *.

The characteristic difference between what
is termed a " RAMGETTER," and a " WED-
DERGETTER" or a " good grazier's sheep,"
is that of the former being everywhere
cleaner, finer :   the head small, the bone and
offal light, the flesh good, and the form beautiful.   The mere grazier likes a ram no
worse for having a strength of frame, and is
less scrupulous about his form than the rambreeder; whose great object is fineness: his
ewes,

* There is, however, one general guide, common
to them both, and to which the judicious part of both
pay some attention ; namely, the imperfections of their
ewes.   In whatever quality or point they are most deficient, a ram possessing that particular quality or point,
ought certainly to be chosen.

ewes, and the natural tendency of the breed, ſerve to give his offspring ſize and ſubſtance *.

LETTING. A novel circumſtance has like-wiſe taken place, lately, in the buſineſs of letting. The long eſtabliſhed cuſtom of *ſetting a price* is exploded; at leaſt, by Mr. Bakewell and one of his diſciples; whoſe cuſtomers are now left to make their own valuations, and—bid what they pleaſe.

This, as well as ſhowing them ſeparately, gives great offence; eſpecially to ſtrangers; who cannot brook the idea of being " both buyers and ſellers."

The letter, however, has more than one advantage, in reſerving the price (provided he do not thereby drive away his cuſtomers): he is, in effect, letting to the beſt bidder. Beſide, he is, through this mean, enabled to *regulate his prices to his cuſtomers*, without giving any of them *pointed* offence.

The principal breeders are, in the nature of their buſineſs, competitors; and it is

no

---

* Some, however, ſet aſide this diſtinction; and, if there be no poſſibility of breeding grazing ſtock too fine, they are undiſputably right.

no more than common good policy, in the
leader at leaft, to advance himfelf, and keep
back thofe who prefs upon him clofeft. It
is therefore good management, in him, to let
a fuperior ram to an inferior breeder, whofe
ewes are yet of bafe blood, at a lower price,
than to one who is farther advanced, and
whófe ewes, perhaps, are nearly equal to his
own : for, if the hirer may not thereby be
able to get the lead from him, he may run
away with part of the beft prices; and the
only line, the leader has to tread, is, either
to refufe him, or to make him pay in the
firft inftance. And, again,—fometimes two
or three capital breeders will join, in the hiring of one fuperior ram; and, in this cafe,
the blood being more widely difperfed, tho
price ought to be, and always is advanced, in
proportion to the number of partners.

Hence, *in the leader*, a refervation of price
may be allowable; efpecially in the letting
of firftrate rams.

Conditions of letting. Notwithftanding the number of years the letting of rams has
now been in ufe, and the extraordinary height
to which the prices have rifen, the tranfac-
tion does not appear to have received, yet,
          any

any settled form; nor to have been rendered *legally* binding, by any written articles, or conditions of letting; much being still left to the *honor* of the parties.

It is, however, generally understood, that the price agreed upon shall not be paid, unless the ram in contract, " *or another as good,*" impregnate the stipulated number of ewes. If, through accident or inability, part only be impregnated, a proportional part of the price is abated. If he die while at ride, the loss falls on the letter, whether his death happen through accident or neglect: no *case*, I understand, having yet been otherwise determined.

It is likewise understood, that the hirer shall not suffer him to serve any other than his own ewes; and, of these, no more than a stipulated number, which is proportioned to the age or ability of the ram, and the mode of using him. And further, that if a grazier hire a valuable ram, at a *weddergetter's* price, (which is not unusual at the wane of a season, when valuable rams happen to be unlet) it is understood—or rather agreed—that he shall not rear *rams* from him: a condition which may frequently be advantageous to

both

both parties. The letter pockets five or ten guineas, which otherwise he might not have had; and the hirer, by suffering himself to be "tied down" as it is termed, gets a greater improvement in his stock, than otherwise he could have got, for the same money.

The time of paying the money is, I understand, unfixed: seldom, I believe, until after the ewes have brought proofs of the ram's efficiency.

THE PRICES FOR RAMS BY THE SEASON. From the first letting (see page 417.) to the year 1780, the prices kept gradually rising, from *fifteen shillings* to *a guinea*; and from one guinea to *ten*. In 1780, Mr. BAKEWELL let several at *ten guineas* each; and, what is *rather* inexplicable, Mr. PARKINSON of Quarndon, let one, the same year, for *twenty-five guineas*: a price which then astonished the whole country *.

From

* This ram was of the Dishley blood: but, though he was let at this superior price, and to a man of superior judgement, he did not long preserve the lead. Mr. Bakewell has been the greatest gainer by the circumstance; by which, in much probability, he has profited some thousand pounds.

From that time, to 1786, Mr. Bakewell's stock rose rapidly, from ten *to a hundred guineas*; and, that year, he let two thirds of one ram (reserving one third of the usual number of ewes to himself) to two principal breeders, for a hundred guineas each; the entire services of the ram being rated at *three hundred guineas!* Mr. Bakewell making that year, by letting twenty rams only, more than a thousand pounds!!

Since that time, the prices have been still rising. *Four hundred guineas* have been repeatedly given *. Mr. Bakewell, this year, (1789) makes, I understand, twelve hundred guineas, by three rams (brothers, I believe), two thousand of seven, and, of his whole letting, full three thousand guineas † !!!

Beside this extraordinary sum made by Mr. Bakewell, there are six or seven other breeders, who make from five hundred to a thousand guineas each. The whole amount of monies produced, this year, in the Midland

---

* Not, however, by individual breeders : three hundred have been given by an individual.

† Mr. B. now lets nothing under twenty guineas : a well judged regulation, which will probably be beneficial both to himself and his customers.

land Counties, by letting rams of the modern breed, for one feafon only, is eftimated, by thofe who are adequate to the fubject, at the almoft incredible fum of TEN THOUSAND POUNDS.

It is, I know, a popular idea; efpecially of thofe who, living at a diftance, have only heard of thefe extraordinary things, without having an opportunity of coming at facts; that the extravagant prices, which are talked of, are merely nominal; the principal part of the money being returned; the actual prices given, being fmall, in proportion to thofe held out.

This, however, is, I believe, and on the beft authority, an erroneous idea. At the firft fetting out of the high prices, there might be fome tranfactions of that nature; but, if they ever exifted, they have ceafed long ago. Mr. Bakewell, at prefent, has the name, at leaft, of being parfimonious, even to the fhepherds of the flocks on which his rams are employed. His higheft prefent, I underftand, is five fhillings; if the price be under fifty guineas, only half a crown.

The enormoufnefs of thefe prices may be explained on other grounds.

The

The *high* prices are not given by GRAZIERS, for the purpose of getting WEDDERS, as grazing stock; but by RAMBREEDERS, for the purpose of getting RAMS, to be let to graziers: the *highest* being given by the PRINCIPAL BREEDERS, only; not for the purpose of getting rams, to be let to graziers, as WEDDERGETTERS; but for that of getting rams, to be let out again, to inferior tupmen, as RAMGETTERS.

The *graziers' prices* run, even now, from one to ten guineas. I have not heard of more than ten guineas being given by a *mere* grazier for a ram, for the *sole* purpose of getting grazing stock: five or six guineas is the common price.

Supposing he give the highest price, ten guineas, and that the ram serves a hundred ewes, or even gets a hundred lambs (some single some double), the cost of getting amounts to no more than two shillings ahead; which is inconsiderable, compared with the difference between a well and an ill grazing sheep: between a sheep that will get as fat at two years old, as another will at three: or, in other words, which will, at two years and a half old, fetch ten or fifteen shillings more
than

than his comrades, of another breed, but of
the fame natural fize, and going in the fame
pafture *.

The *middle prices,*—as thofe from twenty to
fifty guineas,—are, *under prefent circumftances,*
equally reconcileable to common fenfe.   If
a breeder, who gives fifty guineas, rear ten
tolerable rams, fit for the grazier's ufe, and
let them at five guineas each, he brings himfelf home, even the firft feafon of letting;
befide having the rams for another and another feafon; and befide a general improvement of his ftock.

Thofe who give the *higher prices,*—as one
to two hundred guineas,—have, or ought to
have, proper bafes to build upon—fufficient
ftocks of well bred ewes : in which cafe, they
have a fair chance of producing ramgetters,
worth—while the prefent fpirit of improvement lafts—twenty to fifty guineas a feafon †.
                                                  With

---

* See MIN. 30.

† There are inftances, though they are not very common, of the more valuable rams being kept, as ftallions;
the owners taking in ewes to be ferved by them.   The
price by the ewes, ten to fixty guineas a fcore.

It is likewife in practice, efpecially on letting the more
valuable rams, for the letter to referve a ftipulated number of ewes to himfelf; either ufing the ram before he be
fent out, or fending the ewes to the hirer's grounds.

With refpect to the *very high prices*, they are given by a few firftrate breeders, who are playing a high game—running a hard race—for the pride and profit of being leader, when Mr. Bakewell *is not*. A contention which may laft as long as Mr. Bakewell; and be, at once, an honor to his genius, and a reward of his fervices.

TREATMENT OF RAMS AFTER LETTING. The breeders of rams, as well as of bulls, find it expedient to reduce them, from the cumbrous ftate in which they are fhown, previous to the feafon of bufinefs ; the old rams, in particular, being frequently returned upon their hands nonefficient. Hence, as they are let, they are transferred to *private* paftures, and moderate keep; it being a pretty general rule not to *fhow* a ram after he is *let*.

SENDING OUT LET RAMS. The ufual *time* of beginning to fend out is the middle of September. The *means* of conveyance, carriages of two wheels, with fprings, or hung in flings; fome of them being large enough to hold four rams. In thefe they travel from twenty to thirty miles a day : being fent in this way, fometimes, two or three hundred miles.

The

The METHOD OF USING thefe rams has lately received a very great improvement.

Inſtead of turning the ram loofe among the ewes, at large, as heretofore, and agreeably to the univerſal practice of the iſland,—he is kept apart, in a ſeparate paddock or ſmall incloſure, with a couple of ewes only, to make him reſt quietly; having the ewes of the flock brought to him ſingly; and ſerving each no more than once.'

By this judicious and accurate regulation, a ram is enabled to ſerve near twice the number of ewes he would do, if turned loofe among them; eſpecially a young ram.

In the old practice, ſixty or eighty ewes were eſteemed the full number for a ram : in the new, from a hundred to a hundred and twenty are allowed : ſeven ſcore have been ſerved by one ram, in a ſeaſon.

THE EXPECTED TREATMENT OF A RAM AT RIDE, is merely that of keeping him well, and free from diſorders, ſuffering him to ſerve no other than the hirer's own ewes, and of theſe the limited number only, and to return him ſafe when he has done; generally, the beginning of December; or, if the hirer has met him on the road (which is cuſtomary),
the

the latter, in return, meets him on his journey home.

The AFTER‚TREATMENT confifts in ftriving, by every devifable means, to reload his carcafe, and thereby make him look, as fat and handfome as may be, at the enfuing fhow.

EWES. The *fize of breeding flocks*, viewing the diftrict at large, is various. Some GRAZIERS, namely, men who breed for their own grazing, will keep five or fix hundred ewes. But the ewe flocks of the RAMBREEDERS of the modern breed (of which, only, I fhall fpeak) run generally from one to two hundred.

In the MANAGEMENT of thefe flocks, there is no myftery, I believe; nor have I met with any thing extraordinary in it, or ftrikingly different from that of other breeding flocks. The management of ewe flocks, however, being a fubject which has not yet entered fully into this regifter, it will be introduced with fingular propriety, in this place.

The fubject divides, analytically, into

The choice of ewes.
Their fummer treatment.
The time of admitting the ram.

Their winter treatment.
Their attendance at lambing time.
Their treatment after lambing.
Weaning the lambs.
Treatment of ewe lambs.
Culling the ewes.

In the CHOICE OF EWES, the breeder is led by the same criterions, as in the choice of rams. *Breed* is the first object of confideration. Excellency, in any species or variety of live-ftock, cannot be attained with any degree of *certainty*, let the male be ever fo excellent, unlefs the females employed, likewife inherit a large proportion of the genuine blood ; be the fpecies or variety what it may. Hence no prudent man ventures to give the higher prices for the Difhley rams, unlefs his ewes are deeply tinctured with the Difhley blood.

Next to breed is *flefh, fat, form,* and *wool.*

With ewes poffeffed of thefe qualities, in any tolerable degree, and with a ram of the fame defcription, good WEDDERGETTERS, at leaft, may be bred, with a degree of certainty : and with thofe, in a higher degree, accompanied with a fuperior degree of neat-nefs, cleannefs, finenefs, and with a ram of
this

this defcription, RAMGETTERS may be reafonably expected.

SUMMER TREATMENT OF EWES. After the lambs are weaned, the ewes are kept in common feeding pieces, at moderate keep; without any alteration of pafture, previous to their taking the ram. If, however, double lambs be defired, a flufh of keep, at that time, might be eligible. See YORK. ECON. v. ii. p. 223.

The ufual TIME OF ADMITTING THE RAM is, as has been intimated, about new Michaelmas; fooner or later, according to circumftances.

The WINTER TREATMENT confifts in keeping them well, on grafs, hay, turneps, and cabbages: no difference, I underftand, being made in their keep, previous to the time of lambing. But fee YORK. ECON. as above *.

With refpect to ATTENTION AT LAMBING TIME, it may be taken for granted, that, where the lofs of a fingle lamb may, poffibly, incur

F f 2   the

---

* The alterations of keep, that are here intimated, may, however, be lefs requifite, in the management of the flocks, now more immediately under notice, which are always at what may be called high keep, than in that of more ordinary and lower kept flocks.

the lofs of a thoufand guineas, no attendance
or attention is fpared.

The ewes of the modern breed, however,
lamb with lefs difficulty, I underftand, than
thofe of moft other breeds of longwooled
fheep *; the heads of the modern breed being
much finer. Their fhoulders, I underftand,
are the moft common caufe of obftruction.

TREATMENT AFTER LAMBING. From the
time of lambing, to the time of weaning the
lambs, the ewes are treated with every indulgence of keep : not more on account of a
general defire to pufh the lambs forward, than
on that of the ewes of this breed being, generally, bad nurfes ;—deficient in milk.

As the modern breed of Midland cattle
" run to beef"—its modern breed of fheep
" run to mutton ;" and from the fame caufe : a
natural propenfity, of extraordinary ftrength,
to a ftate of fatnefs.   I faw a ewe in the
flock of a principal breeder, which, though
fhe had reared two lambs, was, in the beginning of Auguft, in a high ftate of fatnefs.
The fact was, that, at weaning time, the latter
end of July, this ewe was entirely dry, and
                                                    how

* See NORT. ECON. MIN. 76.

how long she had been so, was not then to be ascertained.

This property of the modern breed is not held out as a charge against them: it is, on the contrary, a circumstance that appears, to my mind, much in their favor. The use of the milk of ewes (in England at least) is merely that of rearing their lambs; and is not, like that of cows, extended to the dairy. If a ewe can keep her lamb on milk, until it can keep itself on herbage, she has, to a store lamb at least, done her duty. More than will effect this is superfluous, and sometimes inconvenient or dangerous; and is, no doubt, a check to her thriving.

WEANING. The *time* of weaning is the latter end of July, or the beginning of August.

Previous to the separation, the lambs are, or ought to be, *identified*, by ear-marking, or otherwise *; to guard against accidents, and the imperfections of the memory.

It is true, an experienced and attentive shepherd requires no other distinguishment,

F f 3   than

---

* For the sire, the ear is generally marked: .for the dam, ochre, or pitch is used; marking the ewe and her lamb, previously to the weaning, in the same part, or with the same number, or letter.

than their natural forms and countenances;
which, from a continued attendance, become
as familiar to him, as the persons and faces
of his neighbours.   There are shepherds, not
in this district only but in others, who are
able to couple the ewes and lambs of their
respective flocks; drawing them from two se-
parate pens, one containing the ewes, the
other the lambs; scarcely mistaking a single
countenance.   But the overseer of a plantation knows every negro upon it, though they
are in a manner naked; and an officer, every
soldier of his regiment, though their dresses
are exactly the same.

TREATMENT OF THE EWE LAMBS.   The
female lambs, on being weaned, are put to
good keep, but have not such high indulgence
shewn them as the males : the prevailing practice being to keep them from the ram, the
first autumn.

CULLING THE EWES.   At weaning time,
or previously to the admission of the ram, the
ewes are culled, to make room for the "thaves,"
or shearlings, whose superior blood and fashion
entitle them to a place in the breeding flock.

In the work of culling, the RAMBREEDER
and the mere GRAZIER go by somewhat different

ferent guides. The grazier's guide is principally *age*; seldom giving his ewes the ram
after they are four shear. The rambreeder,
on the contrary, goes chiefly by *merit*: a ewe
that has brought him a good ram or two, is
continued in the flock, so long as she will
breed: there are instances of ewes having
been prolific to the tenth or twelfth year;
but, in general, the ewes of this breed go off
at six or seven shear.

In the practice of some of the principal
rambreeders, the "culling ewes" are never
suffered to go out of their hands, until after
they are slaughtered: the breeders not only
fatting them, but having them butchered, on
their premises.

There are others, however, who sell them;
and, sometimes, at extraordinary prices.
Three, four, and even so high as ten, guineas
each have been given for these outcasts.

There are in the flocks of several breeders,
ewes that would fetch, at auction, twenty
guineas each. Mr. Bakewell is in possession
of ewes, which, if they were now put up to be
sold to the best bidder, would, it is estimated,
fetch no less than fifty each; and, perhaps,

F f 4   through

through the prefent fpirit of contention, much higher prices.

It is now, I underftand, in agitation TO LET EWES BY THE SEASON, in the manner rams are let.

Where this fpirit of breeding will end, or what will be its effects, time only can determine.

GRAZING. The fatting of fheep is a fubject new to this work. The outline of the practice may, therefore, be fketched, with fingular propriety, in this place; immenfe numbers being fatted, every year, in the Midland Diftrict.

The fubject divides into the following branches :

> Situation and foil.
> Materials of fatting.
> Defcription of fheep.
> Mode of obtaining them.
> Management during poffeffion.
> Markets.
> Produce.

SITUATION. The MIDLAND DISTRICT has been defcribed as a well foiled middleland tract ; chiefly in a ftate of grafs ; but with an

inter-

intermixture of arable land; especially in the DISTRICT of the STATION.

But the more GRAZING part of the district, namely, South and East LEICESTERSHIRE, with the ADJOINING MARGINS of Rutlandshire, Northamptonshire, and Warwickshire, consist chiefly of large grass feeding pieces, which are most of them stocked with a large proportion of sheep.

The MATERIALS OF FATTING are principally *grass* and *hay*; with some few *turneps* and *cabbages*; but, even in the District of the Station, the two latter can scarcely be said to enter into the ordinary practice of the country.

The DESCRIPTION OF SHEEP varies with the system of management: in the DISTRICT of the STATION, the prevailing stock is *culling ewes*, partly of the *longwooled*, and in part of the *shortwooled* breed, as has been already mentioned at the head of this article.

But, in the more GRAZING parts of the district, the *longwooled* breed, and mostly *twoshear wedders*, with a proportion of *culling ewes*, are almost the only description of fatting sheep.

The MODES OF OBTAINING these several forts of sheep are various. The " graziers"

many

many of them *rear* a confiderable part of their
ftock; others *purchafe* wedder lambs of the
breeders who do not "graze." On the
contrary, the arable "farmers" moft of them
purchafe; excepting fome leading men, who,
having adopted the modern breed, *rear* their
own ftock of grazing fheep.

The places of purchafe of the fhortwooled
ewes have been mentioned to be, principally,
the fairs of Shropfhire and Staffordfhire:
Dudley is the moft noted place for thefe
fheep. The longwooled ewes which are fatted in *this* diftrict, are purchafed at the autumnal fairs of the neighbourhood; but more
particularly at the market of Tamworth; to
which, in autumn, they are brought weekly;
fome out of Gloucefterfhire; but moftly out
of Leicefterfhire, and chiefly by one dealer;
who brings fome thoufand fheep every year
into the diftrict.

It is obfervable that, in the lots of thefe
two defcriptions of fheep, individuals of all
fizes and all ages, from a thave to a crone, are
intermixed; no other feparation being made,
than that of keeping the two forts diftinct.
This circumftance, however, difgufting as it
may be to a ftranger, who has been ufed to fee

fheep

sheep sorted agreeably to their ages, is the cause of less inconveniency, as they are all of them equally intended to be fatted, the ensuing summer.

In the *choice* of grazing sheep, graziers differ, and in the most essential points. While one man is purchasing a lot for their neatness and cleanness from offal, another buys a pen of " rare strong boney sheep ;" of which description the markets of long-wooled sheep principally consist.

The MANAGEMENT OF FATTING SHEEP. The *ewes* have the *rem* about Michaelmas, or later: some before, some after they are purchased. Grass being the only dependence, here, for ewes and lambs, it is thought bad management to bring the lambs too early in the spring.

The *keep* varies with the stock. The wed-ders, the first year, while shearlings, and the ewes the first winter, are kept as store stock *;
but

* Little or no FOLDING is done in the Midland District : I do not recollect seeing one instance; except in a light sandy field (Queniborough's) between Lei-cester and Melton. In this case the hurdles were set leaning outward, and propped with forked props, as in Glocestershire : not set upright, in the ground, as in most districts.

but the ewes from the time of lambing, and
the wedders the second summer, are of course
at head keep; the prime wedders reaching
market about September. The culling ewes
are seldom ready until the ensuing spring.

The method of *stocking* has been mentioned to be, that of mixing them with fatting cattle, or dairy cows, in the proportion
of two to one : and, taking the district at
large, this may be the nearest proportion;
but, in some of its more grazing parts, I
have observed large tracts of ground appearing to be stocked chiefly with sheep; the
proportion of cattle being small *.

The only circumstance that requires particular notice, in the *management of ewes and
lambs*, is that of the lambs being, sometimes,
taken from the ewes, before they are fit for
the butcher; and fatted, without the ewes,
at clover or other high keep! a novel practice
in grazing.

The leading principle, at least, is good.
The ewes, of course, come sooner to market,
than they would if the lambs remained with
them

---

* These, however, are, I believe, chiefly store sheep on
the most ordinary land, too weak for grazing bullocks.

them a longer time : and thofe who practife
this method fay, that after the firft flufh of
milk is gone, the lambs thrive better on grafs
alone, away from the ewes, than they would
if kept with them; by reafon of their hanging after a little milk, in this cafe, which
prevents their feeding freely on herbage.

I regifter this, not as the prevailing practice of the diftrict, but as that of fome intelligent judicious managers, who would
not follow it, if they, themfelves, were not
convinced of its eligibility *.

In

* FATTING LAMBS ON GRASS. 'The keep of the
lambs, in this cafe, ought certainly to be extraordinary ;
as raygrafs and white clover, early ; and red clover in
head, later in the fummer.

An improvement of this method is evident. Ewes
vary, exceedingly, in the time of lofing their milk ;
and to take away thofe lambs, whofe dams are yet in
full milk, is felfevidently wrong ; as removing thofe,
whofe dams are deficient in milk, from the ordinary
pafture of the ewes, to higher keep, is more than probably right. Hence, examining the ewes, from time
to time, and removing the lambs from fuch as are
found deficient, appears evidently, to be the line of
right management.

Rambreeders, at leaft, might, it is more than
probable, profit by fuch a practice. Many of the ram
lambs, at weaning time, appear in very low condition.

In the *shepherding* of sheep, in this country, a few circumstances may be mentioned
with propriety.

Trimming the buttocks in the spring—
provincially " *belting*" in this district, and
" *dagging*" in the grazing country—is well
attended to ; and the produce turned to profit. There are graziers, keeping perhaps some
thousand sheep of different descriptions,
who will make up a pack or two of " dag-
locks" yearly ! The locks are washed, spread
on the ground to dry, and packed up like
fleece wool : a *new* species of marketable
produce ; used, I understand, chiefly in the
carpet manufactories.

As a *preventive of the fly*, the Midland
shepherds use various applications, especially
to the lambs.   Trainoil is found to be efficacious ; but it fouls the wool, and makes the
sheep disagreeable to touch.   An ointment
made of butter and the flowers of sulphur
seems to be in the best repute *.

Insects

* The butter being melted, a sufficiency of brim-
stone is stirred into it, to form an ointment of a pretty
firm consistency.   In application, a piece the size of a
small walnut is rubbed between the hands, and these
drawn along the backs of the sheep.

There

Insects certainly have their antipathies, and to find out those of the sheep fly is an interesting subject of enquiry.

The method of *destroying maggots*, here, is effectual, and, if applied in time, simple and easy. Instead of cutting the wool off the part affected, and scraping off the maggots, with the points of the shears, the wool is parted, and the maggots picked out with a knife, or otherwise dislodged, without breaking the coat; and a small quantity of white lead scraped, from a lump, among the wool; which being agitated, the powder is carried evenly down, to the wound. Too much discolours the wool; a little prevents any farther harm from the maggots, that may be left among the wool; driving them away from the wound; and, at the same time, is found to promote its healing. In well shepherded flocks, which are seen regularly twice a day, there is no such thing as a broken coat.

Artificial *wash pools* are here common. In some countries, sheep are driven, perhaps two

or

There are some nostrums, in the shops, sold for this purpose; but those whose effects I have had an opportunity of observing, discolour the wool.

or three miles, to the wash pool : a practice which is not only inconvenient to the shepherd, but dangerous to the sheep. Here, the smallest rill is rendered subservient to the purpose of washing sheep. In a convenient part, a wall is built across the rivulet, with an opening in the middle, to let the water pass, in ordinary ; and with a small floodgate fixed in the opening, to stop it occasionally. On one side is the pen, and on the other side a paved path, for the sheep to walk up, out of the pool.

With respect to *shearing*, I have met with nothing noticeable ; except the extreme neatness with which the sheep of this district are sometimes shorn ; especially the show rams.

MARKETS. The markets for *carcases* have been mentioned : *London*, for the wedders, &c. fatted in the southwestern quarter : *Birmingham*, &c. for the ewes and lambs fatted in the district of the station.

The markets for *wool* are various. Heretofore, most of it has been bought up by woolstaplers, living in different parts of the district. Some of it is sorted, and, what is not wanted

for

for the manufactures of the diftrict (namely, hofiery in Leicefterfhire, and coarfe worfteds in Northamptonfhire) is fent to the diftant manufactories for which it is fuitable.

But, of late years, the manufacturers, themfelves, from Yorkfhire and other diftricts, have bought up fome fhare of the wool, immediately of the growers.

The *price* of " pafture wool," namely, of the wool of the longwooled fheep of this country, has been, during the laft feven years, fixteen to twenty fhillings a tod, of twentyeight pounds. The price this year (1789) rofe from feventeen to nineteen fhillings;—with fcarcely any diftinction as to quality ! though, to the forter or the manufacturer, it may vary feveral fhillings a tod. But the " breaking" of wool is a myftery, which lies not within the province of the grazier.

PRODUCE. The wedders, in eighteen or twenty months, are expected to pay, on a par of years, ten to twelve fhillings a head, in *carcafe*, befides two coats of *wool*, worth

five or fix fhillings each; together, twenty
to twentyfive fhillings; or about fourpence
ahead a week *.

The ewes and lambs, of the longwooled
breed, pay more. Suppofe the improvement of the ewe five or fix fhillings, and
the produce of the lamb as much, with the
fleece of the ewe three or four fhillings,
together twenty fhillings; for twelve or
fourteen months keep of the ewes, and
two or three months of the lambs.

• The fhortwools are allowed to pay ftill
better, but they are wilder and more mifchievous; and are chiefly in the hands of
the fmaller farmers.—The Shropfhire wool,
however, though fine, is very light; the
ewes feldom yielding more than one to two
pounds each fleece; worth, perhaps, from
. a fhilling

* On the calculation of this country, where *four
fheep* are, as grazing flock, efteemed equal to *one cattle*,
this appears to be a low produce. If, however, we
eftimate the firft nine or ten months at threepence, and
calculate on the proportion of *fix to one*, the produce
of the laft us or eight months will be equivalent to that
of a half is at two and fixpence a week.

a fhilling to eighteen pence a pound; or about two fhillings a fleece.

REFERENCES TO MINUTES ON SHEEP.

For an inftance of the different *qualities* of fheep arifing from *breed*, 30.

For a ftriking *accidental variety* of fheep, 60.

For obfervations on the *fatting* of *young* fheep, 105.

37.

SWINE.

THE NUMBER of fwine kept, in this diftrict, is above par. The farms, of fome of the more modern farmers, are mere hog warrens. But in what may be called the eftablifhed practice of the diftrict, the number kept is few; but the fize extraordinarily large; thirty to forty ftones (of 14 lb.).

With refpect to the PROPORTION OF SWINE TO COWS, I found, in the practice of one fu-

Gg 2   perior

perior manager, only eight hogs to twenty
cows, though no calves were reared. And,
in that of another, in which calves are reared,
only four or five to twenty cows. (See
GLO. ECON. v. i. p. 317.)

The SPECIES of swine, in this diſtrict, are
various. The large black-and-white *Berkſhire*
breed is the favourite, among the orthodox
of this diſtrict. But in the yards of more
faſhionable farmers, the " tonkey," or half
bred *Chineſe*, are more commonly ſeen *.*

Of ſwine, as of every other ſpecies of
ſtock, Mr. BAKEWELL poſſeſſes a ſuperior
breed; a mixbred ſort; which I mention the
rather, as it furniſhes the only inſtance, I
have met with, of this ſpecies of ſtock being
improved by *breeding inandin;* a practice
which, though it is admitted as applicable to
the three ſuperior ſpecies of liveſtock, is
conſidered by intelligent men, even of
this diſtrict, as inimical to the ſpecies under
notice.

One

---

* There is, in this diſtrict, a very extraordinary
variety of the black breed of hogs: a " whole-footed
ſort." The hoof being entire, like that of the aſs;
not cloven, as that of hogs in general.

One superior breeder *believes* he pursued the practice, until all his pigs became "ricketty;" another until they were all "fools!" and even Mr. Bakewell had a want of success at the outset of improvement. He persevered, however. He continued to send his sows, year after year, to the same celebrated boar (belonging to a gentleman in his neighbourhood), which boar is the father of the entire family: his daughters, and his daughters' daughters, having been regularly sent to him! The consequence is, the breed, so far from being worn out or weakened, has been highly improved, by this incestuous intercourse.

The LETTING of MALE SWINE has not, I believe, yet been introduced into practice. But the price of the leap is properly raised with the quality of the boar; as from one to five shillings a sow.

In the MANAGEMENT of STORE SWINE, I met with only one idea that requires registering: namely, that of *oats*, being, in the opinion of professional men, preferable to *barley*, as a food, not of young pigs only, but of breeding sows.

Another

Another opinion, however, may be mentioned : namely, that young pigs require *warm* meat to make them *grow*. Corn and cold water will make them sleek and healthy ; but warm beverage is considered as requisite to a quick growth. This, however, is registered as matter of *opinion*.

The FOOD of FATTING SWINE is chiefly *barley meal*. Sometimes *potatoes* are mixed with it. Few *beans* or *peas* are now used in fatting swine.

In the MANAGEMENT of FATTING SWINE, I met in this district with a minutia of practice, which well deserves a place in this register : namely, that of keeping two or three little store pigs, in the fatting sty ; for a purpose which theory would not readily suggest.

While the fatting hogs are taking their repast, the little ones wait behind them ; and as soon as their betters are served, lick out the troughs !

Beside the advantage of having, by this expedient, no waste nor foul troughs, there is another. The large pigs rise alertly to their food, left the small ones should forestall them ; and fill themselves the fuller, knowing that they have it not again to go to !

The

The difadvantage of this practice is, I understand, the large ones are apt to lord it, too much, over the little ones; efpecially in a confined fty. If, however, they had a feparate apartment affigned them, with an entrance too fmall for the fatting fwine to follow them, this difadvantage would be in a great meafure remedied.

In this diftrict *, I faw a FATTING STY, in a moft admirable fituation: by the brink of a ftream; which runs, on the dog kennel plan, through the yard of the fty.

The fty is a feparate building, fubftantial and commodious; the entire fite fhelving, from the gangway behind the troughs, down to the brook; .in which the hogs, in warm weather, delight to bathe themfelves: cleanlinefs is a neceffary confequence. A difadvantage is that of fome part of the fulliage being carried away by the ftream †.

G g 4   GENERAL.

* At FISHERWICK, the feat of the EARL OF DONEGAL.

† In a fituation, however, like this, where the ftream empties into *fifh pools*, no eventual lofs may enfue.

38.

GENERAL OBSERVATIONS

ON THE

IMPROVEMENT

OF

LIVESTOCK.

VIEWING THE LIVESTOCK of the kingdom at large, every species, and almost every breed, is capable of very great improvement.

Except what has been done in this district, with respect to cart horses, longhorned cattle, and longwooled sheep; in Yorkshire, with respect to cattle and sheep; and in Lincolnshire,

shire, with respect to sheep and horses; the stock of the island may be said to lie in a state of neglect, and to call loudly for improvement.

Therefore, to attempt, while in the grand scene of improvement, and while the subject is fresh in the memory, to ascertain the most suitable MEANS, and to enumerate the more evident EFFECTS, cannot be foreign to the present undertaking.

In a STATE OF CULTIVATION, the produce of a given country is applied, as much as may be, to the uses or abuses of the human species *possessing* that country. The three kingdoms of nature, so far as they are controulable by human art, are rendered subservient to the species. The native animals and vegetables, not conducive to human purposes, are extirpated (or ought to be), as far as in their nature and human industry they are capable of being extirpated, and such, whether native or exotic, as are adapted to the various purposes of mankind, are propagated.

In the choice of these productions, there are general rules observable : they ought to be adapted to the CLIMATURE and SOIL, to the STATE OF SOCIETY, and to the esta-
                                                    blished

bliſhed CUSTOMS and MANNERS of the given country.

In this iſland, it is cuſtomary to eat both vegetable and animal food, to go clothed, to ride on horſeback and in carriages, and to carry on huſbandry, manufactures, trade, and commerce.

The ſpecies of ANIMALS propagated, at preſent, in this country, for the purpoſe of furniſhing the requiſite animal productions, are principally four :

> Horſes,
> Cattle,
> Sheep,
> Swine.

The purpoſes for which theſe four ſpecies of domeſtic animals are ſeverally propagated, in this country, are theſe :

HORSES for the ſaddle, for carriages, and for other purpoſes of draft, in manufactures and trade ; and, at preſent, in the works of huſbandry.

CATTLE for draft ; and for animal food, as beef, and dairy produce.

SHEEP for a material of clothing and manufacture ; and for animal food ; as well as for meliorating the ſoil, in a manner which,

perhaps,

perhaps, no other domeſtic animal, of this
country, is capable of effecting *.

SWINE (with rabbits, poultry, &c.), for the
purpoſe of food only.

The SPECIES of liveſtock, and the PUR-
POSES for which they are propagated, being
aſcertained, it will be proper to examine,
next, the MEANS OF IMPROVEMENT.

One GENERAL PRINCIPLE of IMPROVE-
MENT, common to the four ſpecies, is evident.

The iſland being limited in extent, the
quantity of vegetable produce, in the preſent
ſtate of cultivation, is given; and the greater
quantity of *profitable* animals the ſuperfluous
part of this produce, after the appetites of the
preſent inhabitants are ſufficed with vegetable
food, can be made to ſupport, and fit for their

ſeveral

---

* It is unneceſſary to ſay that MANURE, though
collected in different ways, is a produce common to the
four ſpecies: its quality, *perhaps*, depending *more* on the
food conſumed, than on the *ſpecies* of animal through
which it paſſes: nevertheleſs, it is probable, *ſomething*
depends on the animal. The effects of the viſcera of
different animals, on the vegetable ſubſtances which paſs
through them, is a ſubject on which the chemical art
might be well employed; but which, probably, will
never be profitably inveſtigated, without the aid of a
PUBLIC INSTITUTION.

feveral purpofes, the more plentiful thefe animals will become : confequently, the greater
number of inhabitants may be fupplied, at
home ; or the better opportunity will be afforded of furnifhing our neighbours, either
with animal or vegetable productions, as
their wants may require.

To come at the MINUTIÆ OF IMPROVE-
MENT, it will be proper to examine each
fpecies feparately.

The HORSE being refufed as an article of
human food (of European cuftoms the fecond
in abfurdity), his perfection confifts, folely,
in *ftrength* and *activity*; with fuch a conftitution as will enable him, agreeably to the general principle, to fupport his ftrength and
activity, with the fmalleft expenditure, poffible, of vegetable food.

Fafhion, indeed, requires *beauty of form* ;
and even the *utility of form* varies with the particular purpofe for which he is intended. For
though a hunter and a dray horfe both of them
require ftrength and activity ; yet they require
them in different proportions, and, perhaps,
in different parts.

Hence, in this fpecies of animal, the utility
of form depends, minutially, on the intention :

tion: ftrength and activity, with a good conftitution, being the effential properties.

SWINE being ufeful merely as an article of
food, their perfection confifts in the fmallnefs
of offal; in the goodnefs of flefh; in the quality of fatting, early and quickly; on their
affecting herbage, efpecially fuch fpecies as
other domeftic animals refufe *; and in having
fuch a conftitution as enables them to convert the vegetable produce, they confume, to
the beft advantage.

SHEEP. The grand purpofe of fheep,
viewed in this general light, is evidently that
of producing a material of clothing, and an
article of commerce, which no other fpecies
of animal can fupply.

It has been fhewn above, that, in the prefent ftate of fociety and commerce in Britain,
wools of various degrees of length and finenefs are requifite; and that they require various foils and fituations, and various breeds
of fheep, to produce them.

Thus,

* I fpeak of fwine, as a fpecies of liveftock in *hufbandry*, merely; and leave it to thofe, whom it may
concern, to make a proper choice of them, for the purpofes of *manufactures* in which green herbage makes
no part of their fuftenance.

Thus, long wool, fit for the Norwich manufactures, could not, I believe, be grown on
the Ryelands of Herefordſhire ; nor fine
wool, fit for the Wiltſhire cloths, on the
marſhes of Lincolnſhire. It is ſtill more evident, that wool a foot long, could not
be grown on the Ryeland breed of ſheep,
though they were paſtured on the marſhes
of Lincolnſhire ; nor wool an inch long, on
the Lincolnſhire breed, though they were
kept on the Ryeland hills *.

The fact appears to be, ſomething depends
on *climature* and *ſoil*, much on *breed*; for although the various breeds of ſheep, now in
propagation, may be, in nature, *the ſame ſpecies*;
being what naturaliſts term *varieties* †,—produced

* I wiſh to have it underſtood, that, by the RYELAND
HILLS (which are by no means well determined) I mean
a *light, dry, warm, upland* ſoil and ſituation.

† I confeſs, however, that I am here ſpeaking the
language of NATURALISTS, rather than the dictates of
my own experience : indeed, whether, in the ANIMAL
kingdom, VARIETIES are altogether *accidental* or *artificial*, or whether there are not, or have been originally,
natural ſubdiviſions of SPECIES, would, with reſpect to
DOMESTICATED ANIMALS, be now difficult to determine, and is not eſſential to the preſent diſcuſſion.

duced by climature, foil, accident, and art, under the guidance of reafon or fafhion, during a fucceffion of centuries; and although the three firft might, in a length of time, make a material *alteration* in the various forts; yet they never could, by the general law of *accident*, be able to *complete the reverfion* of the two forts abovementioned. Even with the affiftance of *art* it might take fome centuries to accomplifh it.

Hence, to attempt any material *change*, in the prefent breeds of fheep, would be imprudence in the extreme.

We have, at prefent, through time and the induftry of our anceftors, various breeds; fome of them adapted, though not perfectly, yet in a very confiderable degree, to the foils they are upon, and the purpofes for which they are wanted: and all we have to do, is, to felect fuch of them as are more particularly adapted to the purpofes required, and to the feveral foils and climatures of this ifland; and, having done this, to endeavour to COMPLETE THE IMPROVEMENT of thefe felect breeds: the general diftinguifhments of which have been already given.

In

In PRACTICE, the leading principle, on which every individual ought to conduct his improvement of this species of liveſtock is, evidently, that of adapting his *breed* to his *climature, ſoil,* and *ſyſtem of management.* .

His firſt buſineſs is to gain a general knowledge of the feveral ſuperior breeds of the iſland; and the next to examine whether, or not, the eſtabliſhed ſtock of the country, he is fixed in, is beſt adapted to his purpoſe: if not, and a decided preference appear in favour of ſome other breed, he has no more to do than to introduce it.

But if, on mature examination, he find, as he moſt probably will, that the eſtabliſhed breed of the country is, in its general nature, moſt ſuitable to his end, his next buſineſs is to obtain a general knowledge of the ſuperior flocks it contains, and from theſe to ſelect the ſuperior individuals: ſo far, I mean, as he can ſelect them fairly and prudently.

The firſt ſtep is to ſelect FEMALES ; and, in doing this, to be more anxious about the *quality,* than the *number.*

The ſelection of females being effected, their IMPERFECTIONS are to be aſcertained :
and

and this effected, the next step is to procure,
if poffible, wherever he may be found, the
MALE beft qualified to correct thefe imperfections; and, in the choice of him, to pay
more regard to his parentage, and the ftock he
has got, than to any other qualification.

The foundation being thus laid, the means
of carrying up the fuperftructure are evidently
thofe of breeding inandin, and felecting,
with judgement, the fuperior individuals produced; having ever in view the idea of perfection.

The PERFECTION of fheep, therefore, becomes a fit fubject of difcuffion. It varies, of
courfe, with the breed to be improved.

With refpect to *wool*, it confifts in its being
adapted, not to the given SOIL, and fyftem of
MANAGEMENT; only; but, *perhaps*, to the
given CLIMATURE: otherwife, if we may
reafon from analogy, the improver appears to
be fetting himfelf againft nature; a powerful
opponent.

The coats of furred animals, in general, are
fuller in winter than in fummer; and the
coat of a horfe, kept abroad during winter,
is *thicker*, and appears *longer*, than that of the
fame horfe would be, if kept in a warm ftable,

during

during the fame feafon. But whether the
coats of fheep are influenced by the fame law
of nature, as thofe of other furred animals,
may not yet be determined; but probably
remains an important fubject of inveftigation.

With refpect to *carcafe*, the perfection of
fheep has been already intimated. It varies
with the INTENTION; as whether it be food
merely, on a genial foil, or melioration of the
foil, as well as food; or food folely, in an
inclement fituation. But, for thefe different
purpofes, fome difference in ftature and difpofition is the only requifite difference of
carcafe.

In every fituation, a *lightnefs of offal*, a *firm-*
nefs of flefh, a *ftrength of conftitution*, and a *ufe-*
fulnefs of form, are requifite.

The laft, the UTILITY OF FORM, is the
only one which requires to be noticed in this
place.

The prevailing imperfection of the form of
fheep, in the kingdom at large, is a deficiency
of the fore quarters: a part which, in the
modern breed of this diftrict, is, in the light
of pofitive utility of form, evidently over-
loaded: but, confidering this breed as capable of correcting the other breeds of longwooled fheep in that part, its individuals may
be

be faid to be at prefent of a moft ufeful mold. Whenever they have accomplifhed the re-'quifite reform, it will, I am clearly of opinion, be right to lower the fize of their fore quarters.

The moft ufeful form of a fheep, for the SHAMBLES, appears to me to be this: the ends equal, with a middle fo proportioned to them, that, when the fheep is in full flefh, the entire carcafe may take, as nearly as the nature of a quadruped will allow, the cylinder form: with a property of laying on its fat as evenly over its back and fides as the nature of its frame will admit; taking, when in a ftate of fatnefs, the oval form: with a low fhort forend, growing out of the center of the carcafe; the neck and head, with the nofe fhooting forward, forming a cone: a form, which, in my mind, is not only the moft *ufeful*, but the moft *beautiful*, a fheep can take.

The moft likely means of PROMULGATING a fuperior breed of fheep, and of promoting their adoption, appears to me, evidently, to be that of DISPERSING THE WEDDERS: fending them, while young, into the diftricts for which the breed is calculated: fhewing them

H h 2   publicly,

publicly, there, in open market: putting
them to grazing, in the neighbourhood of
the place of fhowing; and, when moderately
fat, fhowing them, again, in the fame market:
having them flaughtered, in the place; and
fhowing their carcafes, on the fhambles, the
next market day: not fo fat as to turn men's
ftomachs, but fat enough to ftimulate their
appetites, and fhew them how foon the flefh
is brought to fo defirable a ftate: fending
joints to the leading men of the diftrict; to
let them judge of it when dreffed: doing all
this, not as with an intent of convincing men
by force; but, merely, by way of giving
them an opportunity of convincing themfelves.

If a breed of fheep will not bear this teft;
coolly and firmly tried, and repeated; they
are not, probably, fit to be propagated.

CATTLE. On all foils, and in every fituation, mountains and fens excepted; cattle are
requifite in their three capacities of

Dairy ftock,
Beafts of draft, and
Grazing ftock.

It may, however, be proper, before I proceed farther, to produce fome evidence that

they

they are, in the prefent ftate of agriculture and population, and under the prefent cuftoms of this country, *requifite*, as BEASTS OF DRAFT IN HUSBANDRY.

That they are not, under prefent circumftances, *neceffary*, in this capacity, at leaft not in any great degree, is pretty evident in the fmallnefs of the number worked at prefent, compared with the number of horfes now in ufe for that purpofe. It is probable that, in England, not more than one fixth of the work of hufbandry is, at prefent, done by cattle *.

But great and interefting as the fubject of beafts of draft in hufbandry undoubtedly is, it would be improper to enter largely into it, in this place. I have already touched upon it, repeatedly; and may, hereafter, have occafion to enter fully into its difcuffion : therefore, all I fhall offer, at prefent, will be a ftatement of the COMPARATIVE EFFECTS of horfes and cattle, as beafts of draft in hufbandry.

H h 3   This

* This eftimate muft be received as, in great meafure, conjectural. It would be difficult to adduce data fufficient for an accurate eftimate.

This kingdom contains (near enough, at least, for our prefent purpofe) thirty thoufand fquare miles of CULTIVATED SURFACE.

Suppofing the works of hufbandry to be carried on folely by HORSES; and fuppofing twenty horfes to be employed on each fquare mile (or about three to a hundred acres), the number of horfes, employed in hufbandry, would be fix hundred thoufand: from which deduct one fixth for the proportion of cattle worked at prefent, there are, on this ftate-ment, five hundred thoufand horfes now employed in agriculture.

Admitting that each horfe *works* ten years, the number of farm horfes which die annually, in this kingdom alone, is fifty thoufand: each of which requires four years keep before he be fit for full work *: for which confumption of vegetable produce he returns not to the community a fingle article

of

* It is true, that horfes are *broke in* at three, fome at two years old; but they are, or ought to be, *indulged*, in keep and work, until they be fix: fo that the coft of rearing, and fitting for full work, may be fafely laid at four years ordinary keep.

of food, clothing, or commerce *. Hence
it is evident, that, by the practice of working
horfes in hufbandry, the community is lofing,
annually, the amount of two hundred thoufand years keep of a growing horfe; which,
at the low eftimate of five pounds a year,
amount to a million of money annually.

On the contrary, fuppofing the bufinefs
of hufbandry to be done folely by CATTLE;
and admitting that oxen may be fatted with
the fame expenditure of vegetable produce,
as that which *old* horfes require to fit them
for full work; and that, inftead of fifty
thoufand horfes dying, fifty thoufand oxen,
of no more than fiftytwo ftone each, were
flaughtered, annually; it is evident, that a
quantity of beef, nearly equal to that which
the metropolis now confumes, would be, annually, thrown into the market; or, in other
words, a hundred thoufand additional inhabitants might be fupplied with one pound of
animal food a day each; and this without
confuming one additional blade of grafs.

H h 4   I am

---

* Even his fkin, for economical purpofes, is barely
worth the trouble of taking off.

I am far from expecting that cattle will, in a fhort fpace of time, become the univerfal beafts of draft in hufbandry; nor will I contend, that under the prefent circumftances of the ifland, they *ought*, in ftrict propriety, to become fuch : there *may be* fome few fituations in which horfes ought, in propriety, to be ufed. But *I know* that cattle, under proper management, and kept to a proper age, are equal to every work of hufbandry, in moft, if not all, fituations. And I am *certain* that a much greater proportion, than there is at prefent, might be worked with confiderable advantage, not to the community only, but to the owners and occupiers of lands.

If only one of the fifty thoufand carcafes, now loft annually to the community, could be reclaimed, the faving would be an object.

Impreffed with thefe ideas, I return to the general fubject.

On all foils, and in every fituation, MILK is a neceffary of life.

On all foils, and in every fituation, BEEF is an article of human food,

On all foils, and in every fituation, fens and mountains excepted, BEASTS OF DRAFT are neceffary.

In every *culturable* fituation, the three are requifite: and they are the *principal* requifites of cattle, in every fituation *.

Hence, the requifite qualifications of CATTLE are the fame, in every culturable fituation,

Thefe qualifications form an interefting fubject of enquiry.

DRAFT requires a cleannefs of limb; a depth of carcafe; a thriving conftitution; and a head unencumbered with horns †.

MILK

---

* MANURE, LEATHER, and TALLOW, are the infeparable productions of cattle. The quality of the firft may depend, as has been intimated, on the quality of the food confumed. But the quality of the fecond, a neceffary of life, and the quantity of the laft, one of its greateft conveniencies, depend altogether on breed; and, certainly, ought not to be loft fight of, in the improving of cattle.

† In the ruder ftages of fociety, HORN ranked among its firft conveniencies: at prefent, it is little in ufe: even the poftman has, at length, found a fubftitute in *tin*.

MILK the fame: carcafe is requifite; and horns not only ufelefs, but dangerous *.

BEEF the fame; except a depth of carcafe; and whether, in the prefent ftate of fociety in this country, a lightnefs of fore quarters is, or is not, eligible, appears to be a matter of doubt †.

Upon

* The horns of cattle are dangerous, not to horfes and the other fpecies of liveftock only, but to each other; more efpecially to cows in calf: many abortions, I apprehend, are caufed by them.

† The idea held out, by modern improvers, with refpect to CATTLE, is, that a grazier ought to endeavour, as much as may be, to manufacture his materials—whether grafs, turneps, or other material of fatting,—into "prime joints:" as rumps, ribs, and furloins, worth fourpence to fixpence a pound; rather than into fhoulder blades and neck pieces, worth not more, perhaps, than twopence or threepence.

Yet with refpect to SHEEP, a different language is held forth: in thefe, legs—the prime joints of a fheep— give place to fhoulders and breafts, which are ftyled "the poor man's mutton."

The fact appears to be, that thefe arguments have been contrived, and ingenioufly enough, to recommend the modern breeds of cattle and fheep of Leicefterfhire; and are not raifed on any general principle of utility, either to the grazier or the community; as they evidently militate againft each other.

While there remains a fcarcity of "prime joints," and a fufficient plenty of "poor man's meat" in the market,

Upon the whole, I think, we may ſafely conclude, that ALL CATTLE ought to have the SAME POINTS : the only poſſible diffe-rence,

market, it may be political in the grazier (merely as ſuch) whether of cattle or ſheep, to endeavour to throw in prime joints, and, by that means, to work up his materials to the beſt advantage.

But ſuppoſing cattle and ſheep, in general, to be got into ſuch a form, and into ſuch a ſtate of fleſh, as would greatly encreaſe the number or quantity of prime joints; and, in proportion, di-miniſh the quantity of poor man's meat, it appears to me, that neither the grazier, nor the community at large, would profit by ſuch an *improvement*. For the price of a commodity, at market, being in pro-portion to the demand, the price of palatable joints would be lowered, as the quantity were augmented : and as the quantity of inferior meat were leſſened, its proportionate price would of courſe be encreaſed, ſo that the moſt probable effect of the *alteration* would be, the opulent would be relieved, and the poor diſtreſſed.

The proportion of *bone*, and other *offal*, cannot be too much lowered ; provided the ſtrength and conſti-tution of the animal be not injured. But until an equa-lization of property take place, it might be wrong to attempt (were it poſſible) an equality in the price of meat.

This far, at leaſt, I am clearly of opinion, that, in the general light we are now viewing cattle and ſheep, preſerving ſo much of the fore quarters of cattle, or encreaſing them ſo far, where they are at preſent de-ficient, as to give them the requiſite ſtrength in draft, would be no detriment, either to the landed in-tereſt, or to the community: and farther I contend not, here.

rence, requifite, being that of SIZE: and this, foil and climature would give, in a great degree.

In a lightfoiled upland fituation, the SAME BREED of cattle, which, on a deep ftrong foil, and genial climature, were lufty and powerful in frame, would become comparatively light and active. But whether we confider cattle as beafts of draft, or as grazing or dairy ftock, this change would be moft defirable.

It is not my intention to recommend, to breeders in general, the adoption of one univerfal breed of cattle; but to fhow that no inconveniency, whatever, would arife to the community, were the various breeds of *this* kingdom, at leaft, reduced to one. Nor, after the change were effected, would there, I apprehend, any inconveniency accrue to individuals.

At prefent, however, we have feveral valuable breeds of cattle, in the ifland: and, in the diftricts in which thefe fuperior breeds are eftablifhed, it would, I am clearly of opinion, be more eligible to improve the eftablifhed breeds, than to introduce new ones,

Never-

Neverthelefs, there are other diftricts of the ifland, whofe prefent breeds of cattle are incapable of being rendered, in any moderate length of time, fit for the three grand purpofes of cattle.

In thefe diftricts, therefore, a frefh breed is requifite; and it certainly behoves the owners and occupiers of them to introduce the moft perfect breed the ifland at prefent affords, or to raife a FRESH VARIETY, and reach ftill nearer perfection.

To afcertain the PERFECTION of cattle, in their joint and feveral capacities of beafts of draft, dairy, and grazing ftock, is a matter of the firft importance in rural affairs. But the fubject having never, perhaps, been agitated, no man may, at prefent, be equal to it: it is, however, a fubject to which I have paid more than common attention; and I will here fet down what I conceive, *at prefent*, to be the moft defirable qualities of cattle, viewed generally, in their THREE CAPACITIES. The fketch may, at leaft, throw fome light upon the fubject; and may be ferviceable to thofe, who fhall have occafion to think upon it, in practice.

The

The head fmall and clean, to leffen the quantity of offal, and to give a livelinefs of difpofition; and hornlefs, for conveniency in draft, and for general fafety; with the noftrils wide, for eafe in work; and the eye bright and placid, to give the requifite quicknefs, and docility, in the fame intention.

The neck thin and clean, to give lightnefs to the forend, as well as to leffen the collar, and make it fit clofe and eafy to the animal in work *.

The carcafe large: the cheft deep, and the bofom broad, with the ribs ftanding out full from the fpine; to give ftrength of frame and conftitution, and to admit of the inteftines being lodged within the ribs; thereby giving freedom to activity, and beauty to the general form.

The

* The "SHIFT" is a point the grazier will not readily give up. I wifh that the fhoulder, as every other part, fhould be mellow, in moderate condition, and well covered in a ftate of fatnefs. But the large BUNDLES of fat, which fome individuals, of fome breeds, form between the fhoulder and the neck, are, when cattle are full of flefh, as working cattle ought to be, inconvenient in draft.

The fhoulders light of bone, and rounded off at the lower point, that the collar may lie eafy ; but broad, to give ftrength ; and well covered with flefh, for the greater eafe of draft; as well as to furnifh a defired point of fatting cattle.

The back, throughout, wide and level, as a receptacle of beef; the fpine being ftraight from the withers to the tail, to pleafe the eye, and *perhaps* to give a due proportion and arrangement of parts.

The quarters long, lying up high, and ftanding wide at the nache, to give fize to the prime joints, and fymmetry to the form.

The thighs thin, and ftanding narrow at the roundbone, to give fafety to the dam, and activity to her produce; and, *perhaps,* for various other reafons.

The udder large when full, but loofe and thin when empty, that it may contain the greater quantity of milk ; with large " dug veins" to fill it; and with long elaftic teats, for the greater eafe in drawing it off.

. The legs (below the knee and hock) ftraight, and of a middle length: their bone,.

in

in general, light and clean from flefhinefs,
to leffen the quantity of offal; but with the
joints and finews of a moderate fize, for the
purpofes of ftrength and activity.

The flefh mellow, in the ftate of flefhinefs,
and firm, in the ftate of fatnefs; thefe being,
I apprehend, the beft criterions of the flefh
of cattle : the back and fides being covered,
in either ftate, as evenly as the carcafe of this
fpecies of animal is capable of being covered,
to give as even a diftribution as poffible, of
flefh and fat ; with a proportional quantity
of the latter, on the infide, to enable men
to gratify their fight, while they are gratify-
ing their appetites, with that laid on without, and, *perhaps*, to endeavour to leffen
the prefent import of FOREIGN TALLOW,—
apparently, enormous and inordinate.

The hide mellow, and of a middle thicknefs; this appearing to be, on the whole,
the beft : but the proper thicknefs of the
hide is, perhaps, lefs underftood than any
other property belonging to cattle. Breeders,
dairymen, arable farmers, and graziers, differ much in their opinions refpecting it ;
and the leatherfeller, perhaps, has not yet
been confulted.

The

The colour,—any which can be joined with the foregoing qualifications; it being, perhaps, of little, if any essential import. If I had the choice of it, it should be white, or nearly approaching that colour.

The constitution free from hereditary disorders, and inheriting the property of *hardiness*, whether by this term be understood, a superior faculty of bearing hard weather, hard fare, or hard work; as well as that of milking well on good keep, while milk is drawn, and of fatting quickly, and at an early age, when milk is not required.

There are several breeds of cattle in the island, which come so near this description, that, with attention and perseverance, they might, in no great length of time, be brought perhaps sufficiently near perfection; except with respect to HORNS.

These are the breeds of Herefordshire, Gloucestershire, and South Wales, middlehorned breeds; the short and middlehorned breeds of Yorkshire; the Sussex, a middlehorned breed; with those of Devonshire and Somersetshire, of the middle cast of horn, but somewhat long.

In YOKE, in which the breeds here enumerated are still chiefly worked, horns are in a degree neceſſary.

But, in HARNESS, in which cattle in every quarter of the kingdom are now beginning to be worked, and in which, only, they are equal to every department of huſbandry, even the middle horns are extremely inconvenient, and in a degree dangerous (I ſpeak from ſufficient experience), and have, indiſputably, done more, than any other circumſtance, toward preventing cattle from being uſed, in common, as beaſts of draft in huſbandry.

Wherever the LONG HORN prevails, as it does on a very conſiderable part of the beſt lands of this kingdom, cattle may be ſaid to be incapacitated as beaſts of draft; and, *if no expedient can be hit upon to prevent, or check its growth*, it becomes indiſputably neceſſary, to the PERFECTION OF ENGLISH AGRICULTURE, to extirpate the longhorned breed of cattle.

Wherever the breed requires to be *changed*, whether from the longhorned, or any other imperfect breed, common prudence dictates, that the *moſt perfect* breed ought to be introduced:

duced : and, of courſe, in my idea, a HORN-
LESS BREED, of the foregoing deſcription.

Horns, it is true, are natural to cattle : the
buffalo, in a ſtate of nature, requires them ;
they are his only defence. But, in a ſtate of
cultivation, horns are as uſeleſs to cattle, as
they would be to horſes ; and who, of two
breeds of horſes, one with horns, the other
without ſuch an encumbrance, would chuſe
the horned breed ? What farmer, with his
wits about him, would work a longhorned
horſe ? a horſe with large heavy horns, a yard
or more long, hanging down below his mouth,
ſo as to prevent his coming either at the rack
or manger, or ſtanding out from his head, ſo
as to prevent his keeper's coming within reach
of it, with ſafety ? while there were others,
without this encumbrance, to be had at the
ſame coſt ?

Horns are natural to ſheep ; but, although
they are not materially injurious in a ſtate of
cultivation, our anceſtors have thought fit to
eſtabliſh breeds of ſheep without them : and
no inconveniency, whatever, appears to ariſe
from the change.

The practicableneſs of producing cattle
without horns is out of diſpute : there are

already,

already, in this island, three or four distinct breeds of hornless cattle ; or rather breeds of cattle, many individuals of which are horn-less, from which, properly chosen, a breed free from horns might, no doubt, be pro-duced.

These breeds are the old shorthorned breed of Yorkshire ; the Suffolk breed ; a breed in Nottinghamshire, propagated chiefly by the late Sir Charles Sedley, probably a variety of the Yorkshire breed ; and the breeds of Scotland ; all of which, I believe, produce occasionally hornless individuals. The gal-loways send out a breed, almost wholly with-out horns, and some of them of a good size.

For strong and middlesoiled districts, there are individuals of the YORKSHIRE breed, nearly perfect; especially for the purposes of *milk* and *draft* : as *grazing stock*, the quality of their flesh may require some improve-ment *.

For

---

* Some of the GALLOWAY cattle are not deficient in the quality of their flesh. That of the NOTTING-HAMSHIRE breed has not fallen sufficiently under my notice to speak of its quality. That of the SUFFOLK breed is well known to be of a good quality.

For lighter lands, there may be fuperior individuals of the SUFFOLK breed, in their prefent ftate, fufficiently perfect, for a bafis at leaft. This breed has lately been introduced, as beafts of draft, in Norfolk; and (I fpeak from fufficient authority) with fingularly good effect.

I have digefted my ideas, on this fubject, with greater folicitude, as I am clearly of opinion, that, fhould agriculture be carried on, for a length of time, with the fpirit, and on the principles, it is at prefent purfued, a breed of cattle, anfwering nearly, if not exactly, the foregoing defcription, will, in the nature of human affairs, become prevalent, if not common to the kingdom; and I am of opinion, equally devoid of doubt, that, wherever a *change* of breed is requifite, not a feafon fhould be let flip, before a change, which promifes fo much benefit to agriculture, and the community at large, be begun.

In *this* country, where the working of cattle may be faid to have gained a footing among leading men; where the inconveniencies of the longhorned breed is, of courfe, feverely experienced; and where the

art

art of breeding is well understood; there is
a fair opportunity for genius and enterprize
to exert themselves, with good effect; and,
it is needless to tell the breeders of this diftrict, that he who sets about it, first, with
judgement and spirit, has the fairest chance
of profiting by the change.

The means of improvement scarcely need
to be detailed. The first step, whether in
producing a fresh breed, or in improving one
in a state of neglect, is to select females; and,
their imperfections being duly ascertained, to
endeavour to correct them by a well chosen
male; continuing to breed, on the principles
already repeated, with this selection; which
cannot, therefore, be made with too great
circumspection.

The means of publishing and disseminating
a superior breed of cattle, appear to be those
of showing the oxen in harness, and the
cows in full milk, and both in a state of fatness, wherever there appears a prospect of introducing them; and letting the bulls by the
season, or as stallions by the leap.

The ADVANTAGES to be expected from a
GENERAL IMPROVEMENT, of the several species of livestock, in these kingdoms, will require

quire to be examined, in a threefold light,—
as it would affect

> The improver,
> The diftrict, and
> The community.

To the IMPROVER, provided he were to act
prudently on proper principles, the advantage
would be, in a degree, certain. The ordinary *hazard* incident to breeding, might be
fomewhat encreafed, at the outfet, by the
extra coft of the firft ftock; but fo it is in
buying valuable horfes for the purpofe of
making up, or prime bullocks for the purpofe of grazing.

Befide the inftances which this diftrict affords, almoft every other furnifhes evidences,
which tend to prove the advantages arifing
to individuals, from the improvement of liveftock: even a fingle male, purchafed perhaps
by accident, has been known to be highly
advantageous, in improving the value of a
man's ftock, and, of courfe, in encreafing the
amount of his profits *.

The

* This diftrict affords an inftance. Mr. LAKING
of Hall End, near the banks of the Anker, owed his fuperior breed of cattle to a bull which he bought inci-
dentally

The truth is (though men in general do not appear to be fufficiently aware of it)—in a ftate of property, every man's poffeffion is limited : each man occupies fo many acres, and no more : confequently, in the prefent ftate of agriculture, he can produce no more than a certain quantity of vegetable food for ftock ; or, in other words, his farm does, under his prefent management, produce only a certain quantity of herbage : and it is, of courfe, a thing of importance to him, whether this herbage be applied to a profitable or an unprofitable purpofe ; whether it be fent to a good or a bad market.

He is well aware of the advantage of felling his wheat at fix fhillings a bufhel, inftead of four; and the fame, or a greater proportional advantage, indifputably depends, on whether he expend his herbage on fuperior, or inferior, breeds of ftock.

This advantage, alone, is a fufficient motive to improvement : but when that of eftablifhing

dentally at an extraordinary price (at the time he purchafed him), but which he acknowledges was the cheapeft he ever purchafed. From a cow, his defcendant, and a bull of Mr. Bakewell, the celebrated fnow ox (fhown fome years ago in London) was bred,

blifhing a fuperior breed; and of profiting by letting out the males, and perhaps by felling inferior females at high prices, are added, the inducement becomes ftill ftronger: and it ought, in every cafe, to be remembered that he who fets out, firft, has the higheft chance of profiting by the improvement.

If the root be judicioufly chofen, and the leading branch be preferved, nothing but perfeverance is wanted, to bring home profit and honor to the improver *.

The advantages arifing to the DISTRICT of improvement are evident, in this diftrict. The fums of money, which are annually drawn into it, have been mentioned; and to this

* This diftrict furnifhes leffons to IMPROVERS: Mr. WEBSTER, tempted by high prices, parted with his leading ftock, and loft his breed. Mr. BAKEWELL, Mr. PRINCEP, and Mr. FOWLER (until lately), by keeping their beft ftock in their own hands, have, refpectively, improved their breeds.

Even DISTRICTS appear to be influenced by the fame principle. WESTMORELAND, "by felling any thing for money," has loft that breed which LEICESTERSHIRE, "by giving any money for a good thing," has raifed as high, perhaps, as, in its nature, it is capable of being improved. And, under the fame mifconduct, CRAVEN, it is to be feared, is now playing the lofing game.

this advantage muſt be added, that ariſing
from the improvement of ſtock within the
diſtrict.

Yorkſhire, too, affords inſtances of this
advantage. The introduction of even one
male horſe drew, perhaps, ſeveral thouſand
pounds into the Vale of Pickering, which,
otherwiſe, it would not have received:
and the improvement of the cattle of the
Vale, has been calculated at ſeveral ſhillings
an acre, on the lands it contains.

This, indeed, will ever be, eventually, the
reſult of improvement; and it certainly concerns men of landed property to promote, by
every prudent means, the improvement of
liveſtock, in the diſtricts in which their eſtates
are ſituated.

In Yorkſhire, there are BULL SHOWS: not
for the purpoſe of ſelling or letting; but for
obtaining a prize medal, or other reward, to
him who can *produce* the beſt.

Rewards of this kind are highly laudable;
but the prize ought not to be to him who
produces, but who *breeds*, the beſt. In the
former

former cafe it may be *bought*; but in the latter a degree of *merit* muft obtain it.

Another laudable example which I met with in the fame fcene of improvement, was that of a gentleman keeping a bull, of a fuperior breed, for the ufe of his tenants: an example which every landed gentleman, whofe eftate lies round his refidence, might well copy. For although, in the firft inftance, occupiers, as they ought, have the profits of improvement, they reft, eventually, with the owners of eftates.

The advantages expectant to the COMMUNITY, from a general improvement, in the feveral breeds of liveftock, is evidently that of general plenty. For, the ifland being limited in extent, the quantity of vegetable produce, in the prefent ftate of cultivation, is given; and the greater quantity of *profitable* animals, the fuperfluous part of this produce, after the appetites of the prefent inhabitants are fufficed with vegetable food, can be made to fupport and fit for their feveral purpofes, the more plentiful thefe animals will become :—confequently, the

greater

greater number of inhabitants may be supported at home, or the greater opportunity will be afforded of furnishing other nations, as their respective wants may require, with animal or vegetable productions.

END OF THE FIRST VOLUME.